PR403   Empson, William, 1906-
.E47   Using biography / William Empson. --
1984   Cambridge, Mass. : Harvard University
               Press, 1984.
               viii, 265 p. ; 23 cm.
               Includes index.
               ISBN 0-674-93160-2

         1. English literature--History and
criticism.   2. Authors, English--
Biography.   I. Title

   21 NOV 85   11371662   BYUHs2   84-22581

USING BIOGRAPHY

USING BIOGRAPHY

William Empson

HARVARD UNIVERSITY PRESS

Cambridge, Massachusetts

1984

This book is printed on acid-free paper, and its binding
materials have been chosen for strength and durability.

Library of Congress Cataloging in Publication Data

Empson, William, 1906–
Using biography.

Includes index.
1.   English literature — History and criticism — Addresses, essays, lectures.
2.   Authors, English — Biography — Addresses, essays, lectures.
I.   Title.
PR403.E47   1985   820'.9   84-22581
ISBN 0-674-93160-2

CONTENTS

ACKNOWLEDGEMENTS

Several of the essays in this book appeared in journals or books, in versions which have since been revised and expanded to varying degrees, and thanks are due to the editors and publishers concerned. Details are as follows:

'Natural Magic and Populism in Marvell's Poetry', given as the Ferens Fine Art Lecture at the University of Hull in February 1978, was published for the University by Oxford University Press in 1979.

'A Deist Tract by Dryden' was published in *Essays in Criticism*, Vol. xxv, January 1975, No. 1.

'Looking Back' was originally published under the title 'Dryden's Apparent Scepticism' in *Essays in Criticism*, Vol. xx, April 1970, No. 2.

'*Tom Jones*' appeared in *The Kenyon Review*, Vol. xx, Spring 1958.

'The Variants for the Byzantium Poems' originally appeared in *Essays presented to Amy G. Stock*, a volume published by the University of Rajasthan, Jaipur, in 1965, to mark the departure of Professor G. A. Stock.

'My God, man, there's bears on it', a review of *The Waste Land* by T. S. Eliot (a facsimile of the original drafts, edited by Valerie Eliot and published by Faber & Faber in 1971), was published in *Essays in Criticism*, Vol. xxii, October 1972, No. 4.

'Joyce's Intentions' first appeared in *Twentieth Century Studies*, University of Kent, November 1970. See the footnote on p. 203.

'The Ultimate Novel' was published in the *London Review of Books*, Vol. 4, Nos. 15 and 16, August and September 1982. I am grateful to Karl Miller for clearing up some of the argument, but I have since found that it needed some additions.

Publisher's Note

The Acknowledgements above have been compiled from information provided by the author, who was putting the finishing touches to the typescript when he died on 15 April 1984. He had intended to enlarge on the subject of irony, to which he refers in the Preface, with a view to including in this book the review of Wayne C. Booth's *A Rhetoric of Irony* which he wrote for the *Journal of General Education*, Vol. xxvi, No. 4, Winter 1975. Otherwise his work on *Using Biography* was complete.

PREFACE

I am reaching an age when I had better collect the essays which I hope to preserve, and a book made among others with that purpose cannot always have much unity. But it need not be a mere rag-bag, and these essays do contain more biography than most of my output. The 'use' is all for our better understanding of the work, and does not always succeed in giving that. One is not tied to the author's biography; Stephen Dedalus is practically the young Joyce but Bloom has a different biography from the elder Joyce. An actor or critic of Shakespeare ought to consider the backgrounds of the fictional characters, though I do not know of any striking result. That would be out of place, but the type is more clear-cut when the backgrounds are considered

Any such work is excluded by the Wimsatt Law (see p. 104 following) which says that no reader can ever grasp the intention of an author. This paradox results from a great failure to grasp the whole situation. Any speaker, when a baby, wanted to understand what people meant, why mum was cross for example, and had enough partial success to go on trying; the effort is usually carried on into adult life, though not always into old age. Success, it may be argued, is never complete. But it is nearer completeness in a successful piece of literature than in any other use of language.

The irony of Fielding in *Tom Jones*, for instance, is very impersonal, being a means of insinuating his beliefs. He seldom mentions his past life, and then is not at all shy about it. Biography is only needed here to show that his ethical system had gained a further point since his previous novel, and that he wrote *Tom Jones* to demonstrate that. The point seems an important one, as so much of the vigour of the book comes from it. But only a narrow kind of irony is illustrated. In an important book on the subject, *A Rhetoric of Irony* (Chicago, 1973), Wayne C. Booth includes practically nothing about biography, though there is a natural connection. When an author is admitting the source of his interest in a subject, and thereby asking his reader to share in it, he will often want to keep the surface of his argument unbroken; perhaps to reassure one type of reader without disturbing another type. This leads to irony at once, and it is practically the only means for an author to break the Wimsatt Law, to tell some of his readers what he is not telling. Of course they may all know, with an enjoyable connivance, that he is only pretending to keep it from some of them.

A student of literature ought to be trying all the time to empathize with the author (and of course the assumptions and conventions by which the author felt himself bound); to tell him that he cannot even partially succeed is about the most harmful thing you could do.

Or it may be objected that this subject is a very tricky and difficult one, and needs to be dealt with by a full-blown theory, not a heap of occasional pieces. I agree so well that I expect many future problems will arise, all classed under this head, each of them sufficient to outdate the theory. Meanwhile a collection of examples need not be useless.

Most of my examples are discoveries, not always my own but I thought they were new when I wrote them up. It seems best to begin with an example which has been well understood for some time, and not always accepted as in the poet's favour. This one can be recalled briefly and considered without distraction. Lord Rochester, a friend of Charles II, wrote some smart poems in favour of drunkenness and promiscuity; they are often exquisitely graceful, though one may reflect that his ladies were probably disagreeable.

> Then talk not of inconstancy,
> False hearts, or broken vows.
> If I by miracle can be
> One live-long minute true to thee,
> Tis all that Heaven allows.

But in his surviving letters, and a few late poems, it becomes clear that he remained deeply in love with his wife, with whom he had eloped, and hated his iron duties at court as a leader of fashion, which were plainly dragging him down to an early death. He had some conversations with Bishop Burnet shortly before he died, which were interpreted as a complete betrayal of his previous enlightened views, in the hope of escaping from Hell; but in fact they are reasonable, responsible and unafraid. He need not be claimed as a profound thinker, but his apparently careless verses undoubtedly proceeded from an inner conflict. Whether his life and work are tragic or ridiculous or positively good after all, only the individual reader can decide.

MARVELL

Natural Magic and Populism
in Marvell's Poetry

Three hundred years should be long enough to make up our minds; we now seem to have arrived at an orthodox opinion about Marvell, but at the cost of ignoring the old opinion altogether. He is now a very perfect or triple-distilled kind of poet, always seeing round a question; John Carey, in his Penguin Critical Anthology *Andrew Marvell* (1969), has written that he was like the painter Vermeer, who was working at about the same period and not thought at all special, but two centuries later was found to be glowing from within, holding some secret which made him unique. It is not a very recent opinion; at the tercentenary of his birth, not quite sixty years ago, practically all the things we say now were being said, and I would like to recall a fine sentence on that occasion by Edward Wright, a promising critic who died soon after. He said that Marvell 'expressed into poetry a philosophy as large as that which Coleridge could not render into prose. He was a singing Cambridge Platonist.' A lot of people since then have said something like that, but I think he did it first, and it was never said better. Otherwise the chief thing to recall about 1921 is that some of the trams of Hull were decorated for the occasion. How plain it is that one could not do that to a bus; it would seem very out of place. Those times of innocence are past.

The parallel with Vermeer breaks down because Vermeer when discovered was not already famous for something else. If Hull gave Marvell a centenary celebration in 1778, as may well have happened, he would have been praised as an untiringly useful MP, an incorruptible fighter for liberty, who also kept up the spirits of his faction, at a risk to himself, in dark times, by fierce but coarsely jovial lampoons. This picture of him is hard to reconcile with the exquisite retiring poet at his best when praising Nature in solitude. And one cannot quite escape from the Satires by saying that they were written as a painful duty, obviously against the grain, in the last ten years of his life; they are mixed confusingly with bad work by other hands, but some extremely good poetry, typical of Marvell, is tucked away there. Two sides of him need fitting together somehow, and the clumsy term 'populism' seems to give a line of connection.

The whole title of this lecture is rather clumsy; but it was meant to convey that I shall be discussing the great Nature poems and also the Satires, while looking for a point of contact between them. For this one must first consider the experiences and convictions of the poet. We are usually told that after leaving Cambridge without an MA, because his father died, he became tutor to a rich man's son who went on the Grand Tour all through the Civil War. But nobody has found who the pupil can have been; these special tours were much gossiped about – if Marvell went on a secret one he was unique. Besides, if he had wanted to go in for teaching he would surely have taken his MA. It would have cost very little; there was less than a year still to go, and he had dining rights in his college. The main fact about Marvell's situation, when his father got drowned, was that his two sisters had both married merchant princes of Hull. Such men would regard it as hardly more than a practical precaution to get the in-law decently started in life, especially as there were no younger sons growing up to demand help in their turn. We hear of Marvell running away to London to join some Jesuits, and being caught there by his father, who lugged him back to Cambridge to go on with his lessons. This implies strong religious feelings but also unsettled ones; he might well not have wanted to become an Anglican country parson, which would have been the probable result of taking his MA. But he was always fairly canny; the MA was a kind of passport, and he would not have given it up unless offered an equally lasting alternative. Surely it is obvious that Edmund Popple offered to take him into the family firm (I leave out the other brother-in-law, Blaydes, because he is never mentioned in the letters; maybe he was already near retirement). We are told of a tradition that the poet 'served his clerkship in Hull', and I do not see why it is neglected; Edmund would naturally make that a first condition. He would say: 'What do you want an MA for? You ought to be joining us. First you must spend about a year in the office in Hull, learning the ropes; then you can go abroad. I will see you don't starve.' It would have had to be expressed vaguely and roughly, because one could not tell how the boy would turn out; but actually Popple would have been needing someone like Marvell very much. This was in 1641, just before the Civil War began, and when Hull was still recovering from a severe epidemic of plague. During the Civil War it was twice besieged (refusing entry to the King), and it would be hard to find Hull men free to go and handle the shipping trade in the ports of western Europe. Whether Hull was open at all was a thing that Europe would need to be reassured about (it was always open to receive supplies). Marvell would have had to be prepared to do the actual deskwork, in the English factory at Bordeaux or elsewhere, till the replacement man arrived, but he was a relief-man only, not looking for a settled job, often reporting possibilities or taking letters from one port to another. He came back as soon as the war was over because he was then at last released from doing this emergency work. The emergency had clearly left him enough time to learn four languages and acquire a lot of information. When Cromwell died, about ten years later, Marvell was elected MP for Hull, and a first stage in the process was to make him a freeman of the city; his brother-in-law Popple sponsored him to the Board, saying that the Bench were pleased to grant him this freedom, taking into consideration 'the good service he hath already done for this Town' (*The Poems and letters of Andrew Marvell*, 3rd edn, rev. P. Legouis and E. E. Duncan Jones, Oxford, 1971, vol. 2, p. 344). But how could he possibly have done good service for Hull, if he had only translated from one language to another, mostly for his rich pupils and then briefly for Cromwell? How could he even know what they wanted him to do?

A reason for supposing he was a tutor from 1642 to 1647, I must recognize, is that he became one from 1650 to 1657. But his two known later appointments were political; they kept him within earshot of the sources of power. To tutor a prospective son-in-law of Cromwell, while in line for a post as Secretary for Foreign Languages, and doing various propaganda jobs, was very unlike the ordinary job of bearleader; and, earlier on, to have won the good opinion of General Fairfax, while nominally tutoring his daughter, was a thing that Milton could mention when recommending him to Bradshaw. Marvell had refused to sign up as a regular member of Popple's firm precisely because he wanted to be independent and free for higher things. But to talk about his ambition may give a false impression; it was of a very modest sort. He was a natural 'back-room boy'; he wanted to be the man on the committee who had stopped them from doing the fatal thing. And not even this degree of ambition could have occurred to him when he agreed to go north as tutor to Fairfax's daughter. Somebody must have planned it for him as a rescue operation, and sprung it upon him with a scolding when he felt low; he is so very committed before, and the change is quick. He had arrived back in

England firmly supporting the side which had already lost the war; he wrote elegies for dead Cavaliers. There is a phrase of grudging respect for the Yorkshireman, General Fairfax, who is only said to be deceived, but it is clear that Marvell thinks him hopelessly on the wrong side. Marvell had been shown the poems of Lovelace before they were printed, and asked to write one of the introductory poems, which shows that he was recognized by the Cavaliers, who were still glamorous. His best piece of writing at this time is on the death of Tom May, a poet who had recently written on the Parliament side, for money of course, and as a reward, when he died of being strangled by his muffler while drunk, had a burial in Westminster Abbey. The reason for insisting on the drink, I take it, is that propagandists have to drink when at work, in order to tell lies with the needed air of conviction.

> Poor Poet thou, and grateful Senate they,
> Who thy last Reckoning did so largely pay.
> And with the publick gravity would come,
> When thou hadst drunk thy last to lead thee home.

This style is what Dryden has been so rightly praised for; the opponent is totally ridiculed, but he is put in the distance, as another strange and pathetic example of the fates of men. Still, Dryden was not doing it till thirty years later. Tom May died in November 1650, and by early March 1651 Marvell was writing a Latin epigram to congratulate a Government official on an appointment to go and negotiate with the Dutch. It is agreed that Marvell had got to Appleton House by then, and presumably Fairfax had suggested this bit of politeness. He is thoroughly committed when he gets back to London, two years later, and shows it by an angry joke against the Dutch, in early 1653. Hull had came out strongly for Parliament in the Civil War, and Marvell's father had been a Calvinist, so he would be expected to be on that side. His generosity, and perhaps his contrariness, had been what made him join the losers, we may feel sure; but he would need to impute worse motives, before he agreed to abandon this wild piece of self-sacrifice. Alas, he would say (as in 'The Coronet'), 'I find the Serpent old'; he had been trying to flaunt himself as a romantic aristocrat. This idea would make him feel free to change, but a friend would have to give the push, by fixing up the almost magical cure of the isolation hospital at Appleton House. The Parliament side was short of good writers, and no wonder they thought Marvell worth saving. But the degree of success can hardly have been expected. He immediately stopped being in love with dead Cavalier heroes; he fell in love with Nature and mixed farming.

While actually on the coach from London, I think, he would have remembered a similar occasion about ten years before, when his father had extracted him from the den of Jesuits and returned him to Cambridge. Again he would feel ashamed of what he had done and yet indignant at being allowed practically no choice; he would perhaps be surly, but within he would feel a vast relief. He had got himself into an almost hopeless jam, and now the more distant prospects, at any rate, were clear again; he would not really mind working for the honest side. He was still not quite thirty. But perhaps one should not allow him much indulgence for that – his sisters did not; this (it seems likely) was when they decided that he would always be unreliable, always prone to be a drag. His whole career, one should remember, was based upon their successful marriages; but they are never once mentioned in any of his letters.

I turn now to 'The Garden' and 'Upon Appleton House', and will assume that he wrote them while with Fairfax. So far as we know, he never tried to print them, or even showed them about; but he would at least have shown them to Fairfax, as they are designed to please him, and appear to have succeeded in this. Fairfax was translating into English, among other things, to occupy his retirement, a commentary by de Foix upon *Hermes Trismegistus*, a very basic work of occultism, which says a great deal about the spirits which underlie the operations of Nature. Also he had the poet under observation; it would be like one of those house-parties which used to decide whether you were accepted for the Foreign Office. The situation of the poet was complex; but it was anyway a situation that made the first verse of 'The Garden' seem particularly impudent. An air of boyish pluck is one of the most attractive features of this poetry – as has, I think, been said, though not often. Nothing depresses a father more than a son in his twenties who says: 'I don't need to study for a profession, or earn money or anything like that. I can get all the experience I need by just sitting in this garden. And what's more, I don't want to be bothered with girls either.' The mystical renunciation had of course great claims, as Marvell fully realised; but he would also have realized something in between the conflicting ideals. Part of his mind would be saying: 'What a marvellous bit of luck. This place looks frightfully dull, but really it is a springboard. From here one could become somebody, a heeded voice in the secret councils of the Revolution.' This hope he keeps hidden: but he sees no reason to hide his recognition that it is socially a very smart garden, implying power behind the puritanical reserve. There is some paradox also behind his next line of joke: that the gods were only pretending to want to rape the nymphs, whereas really they were trying to make immortal art-works:

> Apollo hunted Daphne so,
> Only that She might Laurel grow.
> And Pan did after Syrinx speed,
> Not as a Nymph, but for a Reed.

Well then, the gods had not renounced all effort to win admiration – as they were advised to do in Verse One.

Immediately after this elegant bit of fun Marvell becomes captivated by the garden, and all worldly ideas become impossible to him; he is swept away into an entirely different style.

> What wond'rous Life in this I lead!
> Ripe Apples drop about my head;
> The Luscious Clusters of the Vine
> Upon my Mouth do crush their Wine;
> The Nectarene, and curious Peach,
> Into my hands themselves do reach;
> Stumbling on Melons, as I pass,
> Insnar'd with Flow'rs, I fall on Grass.

> Mean while the Mind, from pleasure less,
> Withdraws into its happiness:
> The Mind, that Ocean where each kind
> Does streight its own resemblance find;
> Yet it creates, transcending these,
> Far other Worlds, and other Seas,
> Annihilating all that's made
> To a green Thought in a green Shade.

> Here at the Fountains sliding foot,
> Or at some Fruit-trees mossy root,
> Casting the Bodies Vest aside,

> My Soul into the boughs does glide:
> There like a Bird it sits, and sings,
> Then whets, and combs its silver Wings;
> And, till prepar'd for longer flight,
> Waves in its Plumes the various Light.

He goes through three stages in these three verses, and I want mainly to look at the first one. Long ago I said that it refers to the Fall of Man, also that two verses in 'Upon Appleton House' refer to the Crucifixion, but Professor Legouis disagreed: and his pioneer biography of Marvell (*Andrew Marvell: Poet Puritan, Patriot*, Oxford, 1965) is still much read, still saying Empson is wrong. I think he was killing the poetry in the interests of decorum, and that many English critics, though not all, have followed him in it; so I can claim that the question is not out of date. A possible cause of misunderstanding should be removed first; I certainly do not think Marvell wanted to say anything here about the Fall, or the Crucifixion, because he is concentrated upon describing his experiences with Nature; but he uses these two comparisons, among others, as a way to describe the experiences more clearly.

The repeated ME can be slurred over in reading aloud but had surely better be allowed its natural weight, and when this is done it is clear that Marvell feels he is being got at: 'Why are you picking on *me*?' The lushness of it all has been making him feel uneasy, and now the fruits are begging him to eat them, as if they were girls, and he would not like girls to be as forward as that anyway. He has an obscure feeling of guilt, or at least of flustered outrage; other people can sit in the garden without being badgered. So he closes his eyes, and imagines other places, which he is somehow stimulated to do; heaven perhaps, but where the other seas are we cannot guess. Then he can look at the garden again, and his soul, which is a quite solid object, can fly out into the fruit-tree and be easy there. It is a gentle sequence, in a short poem, but it seems carefully observed. What he has described is a slight teasing by fairies, very like those in *A Midsummer Night's Dream*; he does not claim any more intimate aquaintance with them in his own person, though he makes the Mower speak of them with confidence. He and Fairfax evidently accepted Middle Spirits in principle; this becomes clear in his grossest poem of flattery to Fairfax, 'Bilborough Hill', where he says that the trees on this hill are proud of their legal owner because of his successes in the world of men. That seems to us beneath the dignity of a spirit, though I suppose a classical poet could say it. But the poem adds "'Tis credible', in brackets, as though nudging Fairfax, and saying 'Remember your Cornelius Agrippa, please'. It would ring very false if he only meant: 'poets under Augustus were allowed to use this belief for flattery, because their barbarous ancestors had really believed it'. Only a century before the poem, the belief had been accepted by many respectable philosophers. Also the actual doctrine of the Fall in *Hermes Trismegistus*, which would be familiar to Fairfax, might well occur to him in reading 'The Garden'. It says that soon after the creation Man fell in love with Nature, because of her beauty, and she naturally loved him back, but this was an unfortunate entanglement for Man, because Nature was low-class and he was booked for a grand connection in heaven: so they always need to be separated; but still, the affair does them both credit, in a way. The expensive fruits in 'The Garden' belong to the same world of graceful sentiment; they are inquisitive about Marvell, as young calves would be.

Professor Legouis gives a quotation from another critic:

'Stumbling', 'Insnar'd', and 'fall' would normally image sin to the Puritan in Marvell, but here it is only on *Melons* that he stumbles, only by *Flow'rs* that he is insnar'd, only on *Grass* that he falls. Thus by contrasting the normal sin associations of these words with his safe helplessness now, he presents the occasion as amiably ludicrous.

Legouis comments: 'This is making sense of Empson's sensing "the Fall" here.' But it makes the poem complacent and footling; we should not want to have Marvell rolling on his back like a spaniel, saying to Nature 'Oh mummy, please tickle my tummy'; if he is having a vision of Nature, even a small one, he needs to treat her with decent awe. My view does at least let him rise to the height of being disconcerted and irritated.

In the Latin version of the poem he goes much further, and expresses a positive fear as well as reverence. He expects an English garden to be fairly small, whereas his Latin one might be the park of a Roman Emperor, so the Latin poem 'Hortus' overlaps the woodland of 'Upon Appleton House'. Desire is admitted to be a source of pain, and even the gods rejoice at being free from its fevers when they discover that they can love vegetables; and yet Jupiter falls madly, suicidally in love with an aged oak-tree, and Juno has never been in such despair. No doubt this is meant to be funny, but 'Hortus' does not suggest that the poet is sexless, as 'The Garden' does; indeed, he yearns for a purer life. (Perhaps Lady Fairfax did not read Latin so freely as her husband.) There is just one sentence about the presence of Nature. He has described himself as wandering far away into the still darkness of the garden; he takes no delight, he says, in herds of men, the din of the circus, or the bellowing of the market place:

> *sed me Penetralia veris,*
> *Horroresque trahunt muti, et Consortia sola.*

A commentary on 'The Garden' translates this as: 'Spring's inner chambers and numinous silences draw me, and that solitary communion', which is literal but takes effect as hushing up. Here is our English word *horror*, only different because the idea of 'bristly' comes in. It would be fair to translate: 'They drag me to them, the secret places of the spring-time, and the hair-raising silences when alone with the Alone.' It may be objected that 'alone with the Alone' belongs to Christian mysticism, but the phrase itself is not specific, and whatever spirit Marvell met in this wood it was not a companionable one.

Apart from this one profound line the Latin poem cannot be called better than the English, as that has all the philosophical part about the relations of mind and matter. A feeling of wonder about this old question, and probably some recall of recent controversy about it (Pomponazzi and the Mortalist heresy, for instance) could be relied upon to make the presence of the spirits more credible. I had puzzled about the meaning of *less* in 'Meanwhile the mind, from pleasure less, Withdraws into its happiness', and Legouis said that this was merely the sentence of Aristotle, that the pleasures of the mind are greater than those of the senses. But he was thinking in French; in English an adjective is only put after its noun to make some point. (J. B. Leishman agreed with Legouis because he considered Marvell a slovenly poet who would do anything for a rhyme.) I think Kermode got the sensible answer, taking *from pleasure less* to mean 'because the mind takes less pleasure in the garden than the senses do'; but maybe the poet as a whole took less pleasure in it when the fruits became so pressing and forward. Then Legouis's note insists that *curious* means 'made with art', and I agree that heat was used in growing peaches ('Upon Appleton House', l. 341), but it may just as suitably mean 'desirous of knowing what one has no right to know' (5c in the *Oxford English Dictionary*). I was blamed for dragging in the idea that the mind is like a mirror, forming images of whatever comes before it; but this is just the commonplace view which we cannot escape, however much we prefer to regard the mind as like the sea, with its own sea-lions and sea-horses. Aristotle is thoroughly snubbed in the next verse, when the poet's soul becomes a solid object, playing in the tree. The question here is whether there can be anything in the mind which was not first in the senses; but it is not prominent in the poem as a whole.

Legouis has a splendid sentence about the major question:

In neo-Classical poetry nothing will remain of mythology but a *caput mortuum*, an inert phraseology, but with Marvell the fiery liquor that intoxicated the poets of the Renaissance has not yet entirely evaporated.

Excellent, but what can it mean, when translated out of High Mandarin, except that Marvell was still able to believe in fairies? Modern Eng. Lit. is extremely shy of making this admission about any serious author, but it was not considered so ludicrous then. From as early as 1590, at least ten of the Cambridge colleges, including Marvell's own, had the *De Occulta Philosophia* of Cornelius Agrippa in their libraries: and this tells you how to call up nymphs in water-meadows. Instead, Legouis produces a theory that Marvell had communion with real vegetables, not with 'allegories'; implying that all Middle Spirits are only allegories, and I suppose also that nobody ever really believed in Venus or Jupiter. But the phrase 'into my hands themselves do reach' labours to insist that these peaches are behaving in a very unvegetable manner. You cannot have much conversation with a creature while you are eating it, and when Marvell does report communion with Nature it is of a more remote eerie kind.

Having thus removed the interests from the poem, Legouis points out that it is dull; and he blames the dullness upon the flippancy and triviality of the poet, who ends it by going back to his first jokes. But it is part of the structure, as well as being realistic, for the poet to emerge from his ecstasy and confess that he will himself soon be wishing for a return to the world; still more to remind himself that this garden, in its pious way, is a highly artificial one, a luxury of the grandee who won the

Civil War. The floral imitation of a clock, for that matter, may be contrasting itself to a vista of historical time.

There is another case, even more impressive, I think, in 'Upon Appleton House'; and here again my view is denounced by Legouis, so I am not grubbing up a forgotten controversy. Marvell has been following the agricultural year and arrived at the autumn, when the meadows around the river are flooded, and he retires to the woods; he remains there for quite a number of verses, emerging when the floods go down. He has become a kind of magician there, covered with the falling leaves:

> Under this *antick Cope* I move
> Like some great *Prelate of the Grove.*

He becomes free from anxiety.

> How safe, methinks, and strong, behind
> These Trees have I incamp'd my Mind;
> Where Beauty, aiming at the Heart,
> Bends in some Tree its useless Dart;
> And where the World no certain Shot
> Can make, or me it toucheth not.
> But I on it securely play,
> And gaul its Horsemen all the Day.

All the more, he becomes overtaken by terror at the thought of returning to the world, as surely he will have to do; unless the wood itself holds him by force, and he tells it to use the instruments of the crucifixion:

> Blind me ye *Woodbines* in your 'twines,
> Curle me about ye gladding *Vines*,
> And Oh so close your Circles lace,
> That I may never leave this Place:
> But, lest your Fetters prove too weak,
> Ere I your Silken Bondage break,
> Do you, *O Brambles*, chain me too,
> And courteous *Briars* nail me through.

No one has denied that *binding, fettering,* and *nailing through* fit the crucifixion: and I never thought this his only parallel. In the next verse he suggests using the penalty devised for pirates, who were staked down on the foreshore to drown slowly as the tide came up:

Here in the Morning tye my Chain
Where the two Woods have made a Lane:
While, like a *Guard* on either side,
The Trees before their *Lord* divide;
This, like a long and equal Thread,
Betwixt two *Labyrinths* does lead.
But, where the Floods did lately drown,
There at the Ev'ning stake me down.

Legouis says that Marvell is not 'masochistic', but I had never supposed
any disease. He does call the briars *courteous*, but pleading with the
tormentor in this way was an extra source of pathos, familiar in the theatre.
There is evidently an emotional pressure behind the passage, and it
comes where the poem as a whole needs to reach a climax, before he
expresses his final reverence for his pupil Maria. Here again, after
removing the crisis from the poem, Legouis complains that it is formless
and trivial.

I grant that if the poet is just a professional tutor, looking forward to
more such jobs after this one is over, the emotional pressure seems
uncalled-for. But he had just been rescued from making a fool of himself
in London, and would soon have to go back and make a position there;
surely an attack of stage fright is only to his credit – not to have felt any
would make him almost too unpunctureable. And the poem is written for
the eye of Fairfax, who understood very well how *the world* might *shoot* at
him. The danger from *beauty, aiming at the heart* might be understood by
anyone; after refusing to settle in the firm he could not afford a marriage
good enough for his sisters to approve, and surely an employee of the
Puritan Government could not risk an illicit affair. To talk as if he had
nothing to worry about is merely blinkered.

There is nothing so far to excite a populist sentiment; indeed admiring
the country estate might put him in favour of the landed gentry. The wise
thoughts of the General would, of course, be heard with attention, but a
sudden and permanent conversion is likely to have a more emotional
cause. I think he fell in love with the Mower. The tutor at the great house
would be socially isolated; he would sometimes meet young ladies on their
visits but their mothers had told them never to look at a man owning less
than a thousand acres – you could see it in every eye. Many readers of his
love-poetry feel that he has an uneasy relation to the girls addressed; he is

intensely interested, readily fascinated, but he does not seem to like them much. And he could not have easy relations with his inferiors either. It does him credit, I think, to have raised himself above this dismal situation by regarding a mower with (necessarily distant) yearning. At the hay-making in 'Upon Appleton House', indeed, he says that

> every Mowers wholesome Heat
> Smells like an *Alexanders sweat,*

but this seems to be a loose generalization; only one of them gets the full treatment in 'Damon the Mower':

> I am the Mower *Damon,* known
> Through all the Meadows I have mown.
> On me the Morn her dew distills
> Before her darling Daffadils.
> And, if at Noon my toil me heat,
> The Sun himself licks off my Sweat.
> While, going home, the Ev'ning sweet
> In cowslip-water bathes my feet.

Damon keeps saying he is in despair for love of a woman, and this allows love to be talked about, but he would not have accepted the situation so passively. It is the poet who is in love with Damon; Freud calls the device 'displacement', when interpreting dreams. They are exquisite poems, and much better when this obvious point is admitted. The only classical use of the name Thestylis comes in the second eclogue of Virgil, which gives a straightforward treatment of the real situation, and it is recalled here for a woman who brings the haymakers their dinner; Marvell was not hiding his source with any care. So the theme was a convention, you may answer; but which parts of it are conventional? I do not know that any other poet has praised the smell of a farm hand.

This must have occurred to a number of people who kept tactfully silent about it, but it has a relevance; it fits his secret marriage to his house-keeper, in later life. An article by F. Tupper ('Mary Palmer, alias Mrs Marvell', PMLA, 53, 1938) is commonly thought to disprove the marriage, but this is an obvious hush-up and ought not to have succeeded for so long. According to the statement of his widow, which was never confuted, he married her in the Liberty of the Minories, where the records were kept specially guarded for an eventual announcement; probably he intended to announce it when he retired. He hid it because he was afraid of his sisters, who would be indignant at such a marriage and might make mischief; they succeeded in hushing it up after his death, which came entirely unexpectedly.

The literary styles of a Cavalier poet and a Puritan controversialist are so very different that it is not clear what Marvell would consider permitted. But we need not doubt that Mrs Palmer was his mistress before they married, because he (practically) told the Hull Corporation so. He hardly ever makes a personal remark to them, but there is one in a letter written soon after the Plague and the Fire (9 February, 1667). Marvell feels he has to warn them against fires in Hull:

We haue had so much of them here in the South that it makes me almost superstitious ... But Gods providence in such cases is well pleas'd to be frustrated by humane industry but much more his mercyes are always propitious to our repentance.

The superstitious view would be that God was punishing the wicked King and his debauched courtiers, and some hurried angel might mistake Marvell for a debauched courtier unless he married Mrs Palmer. He married about three months after writing this letter; and since there was a secret marriage every day at the Little Minories, presumably one would have had to book ahead. In *The Rehearsal Transpros'd*, when he was rebuking the Jesuitical laxity of Parker, he says that all kinds of evil, even war, come

most of all from the Corruption of Manners, and alwayes fatal Debauchery. It exhausts the Estates of private persons, and makes them fit for nothing but the High-way, or an Army. (*The Rehearsal Transpros'd*, ed. D. L B. Smith, Oxford, 1971, p. 56)

Clearly this comes from the heart, but it could hardly apply to his relations with his housekeeper, even before they were married, as she cost him nothing so far as we learn. Several times, in *The Rehearsal Transpros'd* and other prose writings, he remarks that a celibate clergy are patently either hypocrites or living unnaturally; since he was keeping his own marriage hidden, he must have expected his readers to think some such arrangement normal.

Six pamphlets attacked the First Part of *The Rehearsal Transpros'd* and most of them accused the author of both sodomy and impotence. Marvell laughs at them for a moment in the Second Part, but makes no reply; and yet he must have known he would be thought to be recalling these accusations when he made an apparent confession to Parker:

For mine own part I have, I confess, some reason, perhaps particular to my self, to be diffident of mine own *Moral Accomplishments*, & therefore may be the more inclinable to think I have a necessity of some extraordinary assistance to sway the weakness of my belief, and to strengthen me in good duties. If you be stronger I am glad of it; and let every man after he has read and consider'd what we have of it in the Scripture, and what even in our Common Prayer book, take what course and opinion he thinks the safest. (*The Rehearsal Transpros'd*, p. 288)

Because of the variety of men, their consciences need more liberty than the authoritarian Parker assumes – that is all he needs to say, but he gives it a great air of spiritual depth. Commentators who notice the accusations at all generally say that the accusers found they could not catch him out in casual relations with women, and felt that was sinister enough in itself. I thought the explanation likely till I found this 'confession'; as a rule, if a man says he is unique, even if only for a tease, he really does think he is a bit special. Marvell had now been five years married, and maybe the private joke is merely that his wife is the 'extraordinary assistance'; but probably he could have enlarged on that. It was a time when the claims of ladies were felt to be severe; compare the Cleopatra of Shakespeare with Dryden's lady in *All for Love*, who obviously could not have ruled Egypt because she could not leave her drawing-room. Even King Charles himself, who could put up with ladies better than anyone, sometimes needed the fresh air of Nell Gwyn. Probably Marvell had had some cause to suspect himself of impotence, and had been relieved to find that he was quite all right with Mrs Palmer – it was only *ladies* who froze him up. This at least would give the sentence as much point as it seems to demand.

I submit that he was putting on an act in Restoration London, pretending to be poor and low-class, because that was the best means of mobilizing votes on his side; not at all a martyrdom, because it also suited his feelings, but he is decidedly upper-class when writing to Yorkshire. His enemy Parker said at the time that Marvell was obviously bred up among boatswains and cabinboys (presumably he knew that Marvell had been in the shipping trade); and in later life, when he could

invent more freely, though subject to check by other old men, he said
there had been a whole set of poverty-struck MPs. like Marvell:

But these fellows could never carry one point in the House, for they were always
treated with the utmost scorn and contempt.... As soon as one of them opened
his mouth he was hissed, and as often as our poet spoke, he was cudgelled for it.
(Samuel Parker, *History of His Own Times*, 1728, p. 216)

Marvell does seem to have been a bad speaker in the House, unless the
few records are malignant, but anyhow his main work was done in
committee. Compare now what Sir Henry Thompson writes to Marvell,
in December, 1675. Sir Henry is a pattern of advancement through the
Hull wine trade. After being Lord Mayor of York, he bought a country
house and became the first Thompson of Escrick Park, a long line; also he
is, at the time of writing, the head of the Thompson family in Hull:

I pay you my sincere thanks for your protection & repeated favors & I humbly
beseech you to believe yt with the best understanding I have I will ever honour
you in the acknowledging of them. (Margoliouth, II, p, 392)

Almost at once he is teasing Marvell about a rich old Nonconformist
woman, recently become a widow, whom Marvell had better marry. They
are on easy terms; it seems that Marvell was trying, not very hard, to clear
up some obstacle against his becoming MP for York. I suggest that the
reason for this one extravagantly polite sentence is that the Thompson
family firm, still based on Hull, is among those clubbing together to
provide a salary for Marvell; he wants to show, briefly but firmly, that he
accepts Marvell as an equal not a hired man. At any rate it is startlingly
different from the picture of him in London.

We can name at least four firms who would be contributing to this
allowance, and we should realize that they thought it proper. The
Corporation only paid a small dole while Parliament was sitting, and
usually only a rich old spokesman would get the job, but if a skilled whole-
time expert were needed he must of course get a salary. It is not till 1726
that we hear of Marvell starving in a garret and daffing aside the foppish
lords from the Court who offer him a fortune. The big men of Hull, at the
time, really did think Marvell an honest man, but they would not usually
have taken the risk of putting a man's honesty under so heavy a strain. The
wicked Farrington, after Marvell was dead, said that he never had any

money except what he got by cadging; and well might Farrington mouth these words, if he had stolen the entire hoard. His remark serves to make clear that Marvell looks better as a salaried man than as a moral hero. And I think a decisive piece of evidence can be found in his housing arrangements. His letters north are headed or ended 'Westminster' or 'Convent Garden' or 'Highgate', taking for granted that his full address in each district is known to the correspondent. He uses all of them (except perhaps the cottage in Highgate) till the end of his life, while he is actually living at his secret hide-out for Hull bankrupts in the sanctuary of St Giles. Now, if a man lives and dresses in a very modest way, and has modest lodgings in London – but three or four modest lodgings, that means he is trying to hide his riches. Probably Marvell was saving to be able to retire, as he urges his nephew to do that, but there is no reason to doubt that he and his wife were living comfortably.

'Clarendon's House-Warming', the first of the satires, was written in July or late June 1667, about two months after the wedding. The public needed a scapegoat and the unreasonable clamour against Clarendon set him free to complete his history. The poem is not ascribed to Marvell before 1726, and the first question is: 'How could he possibly have written so badly?' It is more or less in anapaests, a rhythm used mainly for songs, and has verses, as a song does; a number of similar poems were written in the next ten years, one of which says on the title-page that it is a song ('To the tune *Which Nobody can Deny*'), so presumably they all were. I do not know of anyone who has discussed the scansion except Legouis, who positively likes it; one should acknowledge here, he says,

... the presence of the Old, or at least the Middle, English accentual verse. . . . Marvell . . . showed the promise it held. He thus fought the ankylosis that threatened the poetry of his age, his own included, owing to its excessive submission to syllabic rules. (Margoliouth, 2nd edn. Oxford, 1968, p. 188)

One need not deny that bad verse often uses the native rhythms of colloquial English, and thus makes good prose. This has happened, for instance, in the line:

> To buy a king is not so wise as to sell.

But surely it is not 'accentual'. One cannot even say where the accents go. It might be called 'syllabic'; the man has counted eleven syllables, so that the words could fit the notes. Legouis does quote a line with a lot of short syllables, but very few are like that; maybe the author would complain that he had been misreported, or 'hadn't quite finished'. Most of the time we hear a pathetic struggle to hammer out anapaests, as in these lines from 'The Statue at Charing Cross':

> The Trójan horse, thó' not of Bráss but of Wóod,
> Had within it an Army that burnt up the Town.

This galumphs, but is meant to scan. Surely it has nothing to do with Anglo-Saxon poetry. On the other hand there are some very good verses in 'Clarendon's House-Warming' which seem clearly by Marvell; this of course is why the poem was ascribed to him later. If you number the verses and mark the ones likely to be Marvell's, the solution leaps to the eye. We are confronted by communal authorship, which enthusiasts for the ballad have ascribed to the primeval dancing horde: the ultimate sacrifice of a poet to democracy. One of the merits of it was to make the contributors feel safe, though brave, because no one of them had written the poem.

There are ten badly scanned verses, then two good verses by Marvell, evidently prepared beforehand; he has five guests, and has put himself at the end of the line. Then there is one loose and jovial verse by Marvell; they have given him an encore. This verse is about two jackals of Clarendon who recently came into the House drunk together, which not many people would know about; probably the five guests are MPs. Then ten more bad verses, then two good ones by Marvell. These are rather too literary, though very like Marvell; he does not get an encore here. Probably the second time round was an unexpected mark of success, and he had had to invent his contribution while waiting his turn. Then come three final verses about what they hope to do to Clarendon when Parliament meets, on 25 July; the main points here would be arranged at the start, because knowing the end always gives a comforting suggestion that things are in hand. They would meet in an upstairs room at a pub, as this was not treason, only politics, and a fiddler would be in attendance, to play the well-known tune that would be repeated for each verse. The drawer was probably responsible for recording the text, and no doubt he sometimes got a bit muddled. Marvell puts himself at the end because he must not outshine his guests; they must feel that making up verse is an easy thing to do The poem is a series of random jeers and accusations against Clarendon, which is a likely result from the method. Having come so far, I realized that Marvell would have had to get his guests started, with a firm statement of the theme; a polite ducking away would not be enough. And indeed I had been mistaken about the first two verses; they are very strong and competent; but the first line of the poem is in flat prose, and the next two lines stumble on purpose. He would write them himself beforehand and give them to his stooge, who sat next to him; they state the theme extremely strongly. One must recall that Apollo is the god of plague (he starts the *Iliad* by sending a plague), and *brume* need only mean winter.

> When Clarindon had discern'd beforehand,
> (As the Cause can eas'ly foretel the Effect)
> At once three Deluges threatning our land;
> 'Twas the season he thought to turn Architect.
>
> Us *Mars*, and *Apollo*, and *Vulcan* consume;
> While he the betrayer of *England* and *Flander*,
> Like the Kingfisher chuseth to build in the Broom
> And nestles in flames like the Salamander.

None of the other MPs can work up anything near the lunacy of Marvell on the topic; they do not even mention that Clarendon had caused the Plague (presumably by black magic). The first line, I submit, must be intentionally prose; the 'Simpsonian' rhyme-word, off the beat, ends it with a complete deflation. It is stressed 'When...Clar ... Cern ... Fore'; how it is sung I do not know, but modern reciters have found that one can intone rather against than with a background of music. When Marvell comes on in person he is entirely in control of the metre, and accuses Clarendon of quite possible things such as commandeering materials for his palace. Someone said that the 'Ancient Mariner' makes one feel that the English language had been invented for the one purpose of writing that poem, and there is a verse here with something of the same power:

> His Wood would come in at the easier rate,
> So long as the Yards had a Deal or a Spar:
> His Friends in the Navy would not be ingrate,
> To grudge him some Timber who fram'd them the War.

Loony of course, but really very good poetry. Legouis remarks contentedly that '27 only out of 112 lines consist of anapaests' and it looks as if these are the seven quatrains contributed by Marvell, omitting the first line. If Legouis got so far, it seems a pity that he felt no further curiosity.

Clarendon was impeached in November, and after his fall no song against him was likely to be revived; so we may hope that the 'House-Warming' gives the original order of verses. As a rule, songs against the King would go on having new verses added. Also Marvell would not often join in communal composition; it was enough if he could set a fashion so that other people would do it. However, he would often be asked to improve such a poem, and evidently concentrated on getting more of a bang at the end; 'The Statue at Charing Cross' is an example, not at all consecutive, very uneven in capacity for scansion, and never feeling like Marvell till the last verse. (The statue is of Charles I.)

> So the Statue will up after all this delay,
> But to turn the face to Whitehall you must Shun;
> Tho of Brass, yet with grief it would melt him away,
> To behold every day such a Court, such a son.

The second line turns back to iambics for dramatic effect, and perhaps to keep in touch with the rhythmic confusion of the rest of the poem. Margoliouth reports very little ascription of it to Marvell, and this one verse is surely the only reason for giving it to him. 'The Statue in Stocks-Market' is a consecutive joke or argumentative reflection, pretty certainly by one author, but the last two verses are again notably better than the rest. The author may have asked Marvell to cocker it up, or he might have been able to imitate Marvell.

'The Kings Vowes', I would say, is the only poem other than the 'House Warming' which was written partly by Marvell in communal composition, taking turns round a table; and here the conditions are set by the first lines, so that writing the poem would be like taking part in a game. The date is 1670. This time there are only three guests, and they scan quite well; perhaps they are business men not MPs. The order is not perfect, but the Notes give evidence that one verse was added a year later, also strong evidence that the poem went on being sung, so a few changes of order are likely. The guests are rather brutal about the King, regarding him with contempt and anger; but Marvell finds him harmless and ridiculous, and pathetically bothered by his self-made problems. The distinction once noticed is very clear-cut, I think; and if you take the

Marvell verses alone, the poem feels soft; so here for once the method positively makes a poem better.

Here are the parts of the first draft which I believe to be Marvell's:

> When the Plate was at pawne, and the fob att low Ebb,
> And the Spider might weave in our Stomack its web;
>> Our Pockets as empty as braine;
>> Then Charles without acre
>> Made these Vowes to his Maker –
> If ere I see England again,

> 1
> I will have a Religion then all of my owne,
> Where Papist from Protestant shall not be knowne;
> But if it grow troublesome, I will have none.

> 7
> I will have a fine Son in makeing tho marrd
> If not o're a Kingdome, to raigne ore my Guard;
> And Successor be, if not to me, to Gerrard.

> 11
> But what ever it cost I will have a fine Whore,
> As bold as Alce Pierce and as faire as Jane Shore;
> And when I am weary of her, I'le have more.

> 15
> I will have a fine Tunick a Sash and a Vest,
> Tho' not rule like the Turk yet I will be so drest,
> And who knowes but the Mode may soon bring in the rest?

The sources vary a good deal in the order of verses. I accept the choice of Margoliouth, who says in his note: 'The text here printed is based on M 16, Which is the fullest version extant and good except for the last four verses.' So he did not choose it because he preferred this order. Probably there was one more verse by Marvell, ending the song, after one more by each guest; this final verse had the same purport as the final one in the edition, but was anapaestic and felt jollier. If the King would really abandon state affairs there would be no need to bother about him. Then Margoliouth lets drop that he would be pleased to relieve Marvell of this poem, but has not got enough evidence. I do not know why he should feel so; the poem is quite free from the self-deluding hatred of the attack on Clarendon. Up to this date, but not afterward, Marvell believed that some good use might be made of Charles, who at least was against religious persecution, and seemed otherwise unaggressive; laughing at him was a useful source of solidarity among anti-royalists but had best be treated as fun. Lord Gerrard actually had commanded the King's Guard till the recent appointment of Monmouth; Marvell probably backed Monmouth as the next king, and thought it pathetic for Charles to say, with rueful delicacy, that at least he can give the boy a job around the house. Verse 11 has the confident voice of a spoiled child, but a scrupulous child who has searched English history for precedents. The scheme of verse 15, to use Turkish dress as a psychological preparation for absolute rule, admits that he is a plotter but makes him a fatuous one. I should add that one of the other verses calls Buckingham the King's pimp, and it has been objected that Marvell would never have written a poem which said that – he always did his best for Buckingham, who had married the Maria of 'Appleton House'. No indeed, but Marvell could not censor the jokes made by others; this point is an argument for communal authorship. In the same way, he praises Buckingham in one of the verses he wrote for the House-Warming', and no one else would have done it, in such a poem.

K.H.D. Haley, in *William of Orange and the English Opposition* (1953), describes a struggle during the years 1672–4 to get a majority in Parliament against war with the Dutch; many MPs came to suspect that the King was taking French money to help the Papist cause, and that to let French Papists overrun Holland would be too dangerous. It is a pleasure to learn that Marvell (according to the King's spies) was the only MP with a code name for the correspondence with William of Orange; but it still seems possible that the busy activity of propaganda was not what brought about the decision. It came when the future James II announced that he was a Papist. In any case, Marvell was henceforward sternly disillusioned with Charles. In 1675, during a campaign to impeach the Prime Minister, Danby, he picked up a copy of 'The Kings Vowes', now five years old, and it seemed to him much too soft: he wrote some poetry at the foot of the page, without noticing that his new solemn rhythm would not fit the tune:

> Some one I will advance from mean descent,
> So high that he shall brave the Parliament,
> And all their bills for publick good prevent.

> And I will take his part to that degree
> That all his dareing crimes, what ere they be,
> Under my hand and Seal shall have Indemnity.
>
> I wholly will abandon State affaires,
> And pass my Time with Parrasites and Players,
> And Visit Nell when I shold be att Prayers.

Margoliouth very rightly prints this in his text, giving lower down the page the altered version in the *State Poems*, made casually by someone else for singing – 'And I will assert him to such a Degree, That all his foul Treasons tho' daring and high' and so on. But his comment is: 'The text at the end of M16 [the manuscript he accepts] is rather lame.' If Margoliouth was editing a sonnet sequence, and one of the sonnets turned out to be a limerick, would he say that the text was rather lame? These lines are majestic. And surely, it is only the leader of a communal song who would be treated so seriously as a contributor, and yet with such indifference as a poet, that his lines could be destroyed as poetry to fit them for the tune. The successive editors are queerly unable to realize what is happening.

This theory about the songs is useful if it lets us pick out and appreciate the bits by Marvell, but does not go very deep. The last poem by Marvell is 'A Dialogue between the Two Horses' (1675), not a song though in anapaests and, I think, clearly all his own. This provides an opportunity to reconsider the contempt usually expressed for the Satires. They are not about Nature, and hardly ever draw metaphors from Nature, therefore, we are told, they are prosy; and they are partisan, making no attempt to see both sides of a question, so they have no vision. Margoliouth even says that a flat analogy from bees in 'The Loyall Scot' is 'the last example we have of his poetry properly so called', but this mysterious propriety needs to be examined. It is true that the Satires do not expect their public to believe in fairies, who were no longer popular, but this limitation can be got round. The earlier poems, 'To his Coy Mistress' and 'The Coronet' for example, do not regularly and obviously sit on the fence; and if they do it in a subtle and secondary way, perhaps the 'Dialogue' does too. The horses are the mounts of the two statues of the kings who are so often discussed in these poems, and they represent public opinion, which is sick of the Stuarts, or at least the purpose of the poem is to make it so. But they are also very like horses; as they are herd animals, they discover from being together what they both feel, and they have none of the duty of courage natural to a flesheater or a military aristocrat, though they are strong when they are roused. Woolchurch and Charing are the stations of the two horses, but both they and their riders move freely at night. Charing, the steed of Old Charles, takes longer to warm up. The rhythm is highly dramatic; in the following quotation there are long pauses, for example, after 'Cromwell' and before 'a Tyrant's', and 'I am' gets two heavy stresses: whereas the previous break-through of Woolchurch runs like a spate:

> w. Truth's as Bold as a Lyon, I am not afraid;
> I'le prove every tittle of what I have said.
> Our riders are absent; who is't that can hear?
> Letts be true to ourselves; whom then need wee fear? ...
> CH. De Witt and Cromwell had each a brave soul.
> w. I freely declare it, I am for old Noll.
> CH. Tho' his Government did a Tyrants resemble,
> Hee made England great and it's enemies tremble

Woolchurch is wonderfully like a horse; you can hear him squeal. Surely it was very absurd of Legouis to say that this versification is exactly like the incompetence of 'The Statue at Charing Cross', and that both are part of a revival of Anglo-Saxon poetry?

Coming now to magic, of course you are not meant to believe in the talking statues of horses; they are political cartoons. But they are intended to work on you like magic; the author says so very clearly at the beginning and end. Talking horses come in the Bible as well as the classics, he says, and of course a prophecy from statues of horses will be even more reliable. In fact, the more they are like horses the more they are the voice of the people; and after making their final pronouncement ridiculous the author can turn and agree with what they say:

> CH. But canst thou Divine when thing shall be mended?
> w. When the Reign of the Line of the Stuarts is ended.
> CH. Then, England, Rejoyce, thy Redemption draws nigh;
> *Thy oppression togeather with Kingship shall dye.*
> w. A Commonwealth a Common-wealth wee proclaim to the Naccion;
> The Gods have repented the Kings Restoration. ...

Conclusion

But I should have told you, before the Jades parted
Both Gallopt to Whitehall and there Horribly farted,
Which Monarchys downfall portended much more
Than all that the beasts had spoken before. ...
Tho' Tyrants make Laws which they strictly proclaim
To conceal their own crimes and cover their shame,
Yet the beasts of the field or the stones in the wall
Will publish their faults and prophesy their fall.

I do not feel that there is any shortage of Natural Magic here.

Other People's Views

The preceding essay or lecture about 'populism' in Marvell was written for his tercentenary celebrations at Hull. I was already sure I had proved the marriage to be genuine, but the arguments about it would have been tiresome on such an occasion and it seemed better to describe the general attitude to Marvell's work for which belief in the marriage provides incidental support. After all, if this marriage had no significance, the legal arguments about it would be rather footling. Then, when the essays were published (Oxford, 1979), I found that another contributor, Professor John Kenyon, had provided two arguments favourable to my side, though he had not been arguing for it. Both concern the money affairs of Marvell, a topic which needs clearing out of the way before the main argument begins.

I had said what I could already to argue that he must have had a salary, and suggested that the idea of his starving rather than take bribes might be a result of his pretending among his supporters in London to be poorer than he was. Kenyon supports this by remarking that the city of Hull was rather heavily equipped to put pressure on the Government, so that Marvell was one of a team. A new Governor and Deputy Governor had naturally been imposed upon Hull, before the Cavalier Parliament was formed in January 1661, both of them military officers who had fought for the King. Their royalism did not mean that they would not play for their side; they wanted Hull to have control of its own militia, just as Milton had advised in *The Ready and Easy Way*. The Deputy Governor, Col. Gilbey, of course received a salary for his position, but very properly wanted to do some relevant work, and he became the chief MP for Hull; Marvell was strongly voted in as second MP but of course the man for the new central government had to come first. Lister, the Recorder of Hull, seems to have been in London pretty often during the sixties giving the two MPs his legal authority and advice; he of course had a salary. And then there was a more mysterious figure, Mr Stockdale the 'towns intelligencer', who would join them all when they visited some grandee as a delegation. I do not know who paid him, but he would make a decent appearance. It is a pleasure to think of the grandee asking: 'Who is that barefoot man, in rags, at the end of the row?' and being answered: 'Oh, excuse please. Just a left-over from Cromwell's time.' Hull did not want to give that impression at all; its citizens were working together, and had completely forgotten the passions of the Civil War. It could thus be a fairly open secret that Marvell was being paid by the firms interested to look after the business side, not out of the city taxes; the reason why his enemies do not mention it is that they do not consider it a scandal.

All the same, to fix up the working arrangement had required skill and an impressive manner. From the start, the letters of Marvell to the Corporation show him negotiating between the Mayor of Hull and its Governor and Deputy. Then in June '61 he sends a letter of splendid complaint, beginning: 'The bonds of civility between Col. Gilbey and myself being unhappily snapped in pieces', and ending:

In the mean time pity I beseech you my weakness for there are some things which men ought not, others which they cannot patiently suffer.

It is near to the challenge of a duellist, and yet it might almost be said by a Quaker. A brass hat whose side has been roundly defeated and yet, a dozen years later, finds himself back in power for reasons he does not understand, is likely to bluster, and needs treating in a high style. Just two weeks later, Marvell writes to the Mayor describing a partial victory, wholly due to himself, over the Governor and Deputy Governor in some question of a royal demand for patents. He earnestly demands the support of the Corporation in the later stages of the coming negotiations, and gives them hope because 'his Majesty is most fixedly honourable and true to that business'. A bracket after a mention of the Governor says 'concerning whose real affection to you you may be as certain as of his Majesty's affection to him', and even the Deputy gets a hopeful word: 'of whose endeavours therein you may be satisfied'. There is not a word about his quarrel with the Deputy. There is a masterfulness here, even a capacity to swagger, which we do not usually find reported in the accounts of his character.

In 1661 he was preparing to go to Holland on some unnamed ploy for Lord Carlisle, and after a year the Governor thought this would be a good time to get rid of him, but the Corporation merely asked him to return. Before leaving, he had written to the Hull branch of Trinity House, assuring them of his continued attention. By taking this trip, he says:

I do hereby make my Lord of Carlisle (who is a member of the Privy Council and one of those to whom your business is referred) absolutely yours.

Their chief business was to get another lighthouse at the mouth of the Humber, which was never achieved. Even if it had been true, this was rather a lordly way to talk. About ten years later, the Governor himself was sacked, for being a Papist, and the Duke of Monmouth was appointed instead. It was traditional (apparently) to present a new Governor with six pieces of gold, and Marvell was appointed to do it. Marvell writes afterward, to the Corporation itself, claiming to have saved the city from public shame (*Letters*, p. 138):

... I then delivered him the six broad pieces, telling him that I was deputed to blush on your behalf for the meanness of the present &c; but he took me off and said, he thanked you for it and took it as a token of your kindness. He had before I came in as I was told considered what to do with the gold and but that I had by all means prevented the offer, I had been in danger of being reimbursed with it ...

Clearly, the Corporation is lucky to have had Marvell on the job, as he is the one who knows how to handle royalty. He goes straight on to refuse the reward that they have sent him. At other times he would present himself as a poor man who preferred the company of other poor men, not as a ploy, merely because he was adroit. But such a man would have felt affronted, and would have shown it, if kept notably poorer than the rest of the team. After all, he had been fairly intimate with the previous ruler of the country.

It makes him a disagreeable kind of man, the reader may well reflect; but I expect he seldom turned that tap on; it was his resource for the occasional tight corner. Even so, it makes him seem bogus; could he really have earned a salary from a few business firms in Hull by nosing out inside business information? There is very little evidence for it. But then, letters about it would be very private, and not kept after they had been used. There is one case that slips through this net. Marvell wrote in March 1669 to his brother-in-law Edmond Popple, who was a Warden of the Trinity House at Hull, the chief authority of the port, asking for all previous papers about 'their business' to be sent to him, and urging greater secrecy (apparently he was still negotiating with the Government for the other lighthouse); then he adds, at the end of the brief message;

The Greenland Company here would fain have your town trade thither. You may have all immunity and propriety of post and not a farthing to be paid.

The letter was naturally kept among the Trinity House papers, as even the final bit concerned them; but Popple himself might have the first bite at the trade. I used to think it was a mild joke, as Greenland could not have much to offer, but it did have a few luxury goods, such as spermaceti and whalebone, and had been taken seriously enough to be made a monopoly of the Crown. Charles became increasingly unable to pay the interest on his debt to the banks, so he had to give up bits of Crown property. The separate Greenland monopoly had not been in operation after 1688, but the Greenland trade was not thrown open by statute till 1671. So Marvell was up to date in this glimpse of his activity – presumably the Greenland Company was new and wished to be secret till well established, and Marvell himself may have suggested a start in Hull.

Another point of Professor Kenyon, which was quite new to me, was that young Andrew, on the unexpected death of his father, would be ruined by the grand marriages of his sisters, so far from expecting any help from them. The father of such a daughter was expected to find the money for her dowry, which must be suitably large if her husband was rich; but arrangements would be made for the father to make a gradual payment, assuming a normal span of life. Young Andrew, when his father got drowned, would be expected to procure a salary with prospects as soon as possible and sacrifice himself by a large fixed quarterly payment. It was not that his sisters would ever need the money, since their husbands were sure to provide for them, but that they would lose face if their father's offer fell through. Andrew might be allowed to become a parson, because he seemed quite likely to get a well-paid job in the church; though that was always a gamble; but the steady reliable thing would be to sign up permanently with the firm of one of his in-laws. He refused to do either, being restless with an unknown ambition, and this is enough to explain the silence which envelops both his sisters; no doubt they also decided he was a bad character. He was willing to help the wine-shipping trade during the war, when it was in special difficulties, and he was receiving pay for that, as well as much opportunity for picking up knowledge, but a lawyer would not consider these casual earnings any ground for a loan to cover the dowries – for that he would need regular signed-up employment. And even though accepting this burden he could not use it for a marriage of his own.

The importance of this, I submit, is that subsistence-money for widows would be part of the settled furniture of his mind. He was not going to marry a woman who would make frivolous demands on him, as his sisters did; and he would make his choice without deference to the social world; but any real need of his wife he would attend to as thoroughly as any of them. This was established in his mind as a point of honour, but the need for it would be reinforced as a justification of his old refusal. As a young man, he would not sacrifice a possible carreer merely to save face for his sisters, but as a middle-aged one he would fulfil the reality behind the convention.

But could he have done it? The cost of an annuity is on a different scale from the occasional buying of fine clothes for special occasions, or a fine dinner for colleagues at an inn. I agree that he was still a fairly poor man when he achieved election to the Cavalier Parliament. But then he went on two trips abroad for Lord Carlisle, the first perhaps merely a trial run in Holland, allotted him because he knew Dutch, but the second as secretary and speech-writer for the King's emissary to Russia, Sweden and Denmark, taking nearly two years. There were always pickings on such a grand job, not all of them discreditable, and the King himself still felt able to spend lavishly. Even while behaving with moderation, Marvell could acquire a small nest-egg, enough to play the markets; and there was a 'trade boom' (Christopher Hill, *The Century of Revolution*, pp 185–92). A boom need not bring general prosperity, but it is a time when a man with a modest amount of capital and good inside advice, if he is not too greedy, can make quite a lot. And it was the regular business of Marvell, it was what he was paid his salary for, to get such advice (as in the case of Greenland). Hill considers that the boom went on all through the reign, but would agree that the Stop of the Exchequer, from 1672, was a disturbing factor. I suggest that Marvell felt free to play the markets during the ten years from 1665 to 1675, which were anyway the best years for his purpose. It was a game he was well fitted to play but after 1675 he became stern; historians often give 1675 as the date when the King began to exercise his skill, feeling the need to be serious, and it was when Marvell decided on his private war against the King. He needed to leave his wife already provided for, as he was risking execution or prolonged imprisonment and also he had a duty to help the gamble of his young friends from Hull. Very likely he split his nest-egg between them. The run on their bank began at the end of that year, and he could truthfully protest that he had nothing left (he wouldn't have had enough to make any difference, anyway). Presumably he would make it a joint annuity, with the housekeeper allowed to draw the income if he were for any reason not available, but while he could he would take it all himself. Bankers had been taking an interest in the mathematics of probability; Marvell and his wife were both over fifty, and the expectation of life was much shorter then than now. They would get quite good rates, and he aimed only at enough to live on. It is not hard to believe that he could reach it.

Three scraps of information have survived which favour this account, though not very strongly. He wrote to his nephew William Popple in July 1667 urging him to save and make investments so that he can retire; he was shipping wine at Bordeaux for his father's firm, and this bit of the letter is in Latin, presumably because it might appear disloyal. William had a wife and a child, and one might doubt whether he could save enough out of his salary; but he may have had extra resources from his relations. Anyhow, Marvell is thinking about retirement, rather early. Next, Tupper reports that Mrs Marvell once asked Nelthorpe whether Marvell had really got any money, and he said yes, 'to my knowledge' he had. So Marvell had not given the bank all he could. The third is the last item in the *Letters*, a fragment in Latin quoted by his first biographer Cooke: Marvell says he does not think death as important as not to die unprepared. This would be viewed as a pious reflection, meaning that he must guard against eternal torment by securing magical assistance from a priest, but Marvell would regard this idea as popish, and mean (quite as earnestly, though unselfishly) that he must take proper care for his surviving dependants. As he seemed to have no dependants, a reader might feel driven to accept the pious meaning, but secretly he had a wife, and meant taking care for her. He was always delighted by a sentence of this kind, meaning something good in his own intention, but likely to mislead an opponent.

These two items from Professor Kenyon's article gave helpful pointers late in the working-out, but I owe a greater and more long-term debt to the stubborn support of the marriage by Mrs Duncan-Jones, unpublished because she continued collecting evidence for it. It was she who first saw the importance of 'Palmer the bookseller', who stood in the pillory for distributing some of Marvell's satires. Tom Palmer gives a good deal more body to the story, as I will try to show, and one may hope that further details can be discovered about him.

II

The York University volume for the centenary was more far-flung, and exhibited an almost universal bafflement about the poetry of Marvell. I was asked to review the book, and now think, five years later, that it is right to reprint most of my text (there were no replies; if I hushed up replies that would be a bad thing). Much of the commentary amounts to defamation of character; perhaps one should not bother about that, but it is a very long way from understanding the poetry. It also gives a survey of the various interpretations of Marvell since the twenties. Thus my old friend B. Rajan (everbody named here is a Professor) has a firm background when he calls his lecture 'The aesthetics of inconclusiveness' and takes for granted that 'a controlled uncertainty is the objective' in all the major poems of Marvell. He recalls an edition by J. H. Summers which gave three incompatible readings for each case examined. Rajan lets drop that this has given rise to exasperation. It is also a good occasion for blasphemy; I think it proves that the grand American theory is all wrong. Marvell becomes a test case. The point where Rajan became incredible, I thought, was when he said that Marvell himself might be 'not displeased' at finding that his poems caused exasperation, or even, apparently, at hearing them called 'treacherous'. He would have become violently offended at that word.

Most of the critics I blame here are foreigners, so I had better bring in an Englishman early. The English have not the American theoretical drive, but this does not keep them pure. A comment on 'The Definition of Love' gives a typical example:

> And therefore her Decrees of Steel
> Us at the distant Poles have plac'd,
> (Though Loves whole World on us doth wheel)
> Not by themselves to be embrac'd.

A. J. Smith said in his lecture: 'That parenthesis so nicely takes off the

Donne mode as to be almost tongue in cheek.' The reservation *almost* makes no difference to the insinuation, merely insisting that the judgement of the critic is exquisite. He is sure that any knowing man at the time found the trope deliciously ridiculous, the silliest of all the Metaphysical pedantries, just as he does. But it was used by Carew, a smooth courtier if ever there was one, with splendid easiness, to introduce his best poem ('Those flowers, as in their causes, sleep'). Would Marvell still be jeering if he was imitating Carew? The cosy chortle of the snob is out of place here, because it assumes more knowledge than we have got. This pair of lovers has become the platonic ideal of such a thing, laid up in Heaven, from which all the standard properties of it, found in ordinary cases, derive; and the elevation is deserved because in this case the inherent readiness for self-sacrifice is forced to an extreme. Marvell does not use the trope elsewhere, but for once it was entirely suited. Surely it would be very *booksy* of Marvell, at this high moment, to distract attention onto a jeer at the style of Donne, who was not even a living rival? I grant that there is a touch of humour all along, because of the neatness of these wild assertions, but the persons in view to be laughed at are 'we', the lovers themselves, one of whom makes this cosmic claim. It is assumed that the situation is a familiar one. I take it that Marvell could not get married in the ordinary way because (although he had assisted Hull during the Civil War) he had refused to sign up with Popple's firm, so as to get a salary, reserving himself for higher things; but one does not need all that. Such obstacles were very frequent in life, though not described by love-poetry, so a reader at the time would not feel mystified. There had been at least one time when Marvell felt them keenly frustrating, though perhaps not just when he wrote the poem, and had consoled himself by reflecting that the situation was majestically familiar, a standard feature of human affairs.

These critics are often right in pointing out some nuance, but wrong when they yield to the craving to make it spicy. This is a bit hard to feel about C. A. Patrides, when he tells us that Marvell intended, at the end of 'Appleton House', to jeer at the young pupil of Marvell, who becomes a kind of goddess of the estate. As a Christian, explains the critic, he ought to depise her for being fallen like all the rest of us; and sure enough he 'associates her' with a comet, and the baneful parasite mistletoe, and (very indirectly) with a traitor-worm in an oak; so she is 'at least a threat'.

Come now, Marvell was a susceptible young man much impressed by the
estate, and had already written poems to girl children; there is no reason
to doubt that he was bowled over by the stolid well-meaning heiress. No
doubt he did not expect even her father to believe him when he described
her magical power, though her father was willing to toy with such ideas;
but Marvell was in no mood to jeer. Every detail that Patrides can find to
prove she was a witch is real, and there were real Christians too, bright
with craving to kill witches. Marvell was brave enough to ignore this
powerful trend of thought, which Patrides, apparently, endorses. All the
same, I think he does discover a slight under-current in the verse about
her eventual marriage; but he has got it upside-down; Marvell expected
her to be the victim not the wrong-doer:

> And, like a *sprig of Mistleto*,
> On the *Fairfacian Oak* does grow;
> Whence, for some universal good,
> The *Priest* shall cut the sacred Bud;
> While her *glad Parents* most rejoice,
> And make their *Destiny* their *Choice*.

When the time came, Fairfax saved his estates by marrying her to the rake
Buckingham, who neglected her shamefully. Her parents 'made their
destiny their choice' merely in the sense that they excused the deed 'with
necessity, the tyrant's plea'. I am glad to learn that Marvell wrote this
rather bold hint into his poem of flattery; but presumably at the time the
prophecy would seem very remote, and Marvell says it very tactfully. So
maybe the parents never noticed.

Two other moves to belittle Marvell call for an answer. R. Ellrodt,
speaking from France, describes an honest difficulty in getting an impression of Marvell, or even seeing the point of his poems, and decides that it
is 'tempting ... to consider Marvell as a poet mainly interested in the craft
of poetry'. He was so cool and detached that he could be at once a poet
and a politician, so here too he was purely aesthetic. The picture is very
unlike Marvell, but I hoped that this severe critic would at least admire
'The Coronet'. He grants that the poem shows a 'keen awareness of
impure motives', but adds

the discovery is not surprising, and the poem derives its power from the mastery
of form, not from any subtlety of psychological analysis.

The lack of any sense of reality here is majestic. But what other religious poet writing at the time in English, had any conception of this unsurprising thing? Who did afterwards, except Dr Johnson, and is he not enough to keep the minority vote from seeming trivial? It is an explosive poem, and perhaps Marvell was wise never to print it. To say that the power is in the form seemed to me a howler, even if meant as a compliment; if the technique is not used to say something, it is not used at all; but I am glad to have been made to realise that the poem does have an adequate form. It is a sonnet with an extra quatrain in the first part, leading in to the shock of the sestet, 'Alas I find the serpent old', and after the sestet and eight-line coda combines two other forms of sestet; it begins 'But thou who only', and continues line after line each with a sustained astonishment, as in the madrigals. A powerful form; but it was hammered out to carry a firm and passionate mental operation: it meant the end of his religious poetry. There seems to be a general unwillingness among critics to let Marvell mean what he said; B. K. Lewalski, who lectured on the religious poetry, thinks that the last line, '*May* crown thy feet ...' implies a permission for some types of religious poetry, just a few types, enough to permit everything that comes afterwards in the book. But before the fierce paradox of crowning the feet *these* must first *wither*, and their *frame* must be *shattered* too; it might have been argued that 'these' were not the simple flowers, only the towers perhaps, but the poem says both have to go. The order of poems in the book thus becomes a problem, and it had been pointed out that the publisher might see a slight precaution in putting the best religious poems first. The volume begins with three startlingly good ones, and continues with minor ones till the eighth, where the 'Nymph Complaining' presents a child who discovers the truths of religion independently. There are no further specifically religious poems, I suggest that Marvell did begin by writing religious poems, in considerable turmoil of mind, and we know that one of them was twice set to music; he was doing quite well at it, and when he said he was stopping he really stopped. After all, some are certainly out of order; no one believes that 'Tom May's Death' was written soon after 'Appleton House'. 'The Coronet' takes the Puritan suspicion of religious art to its final extremity, and you may find this crazy or perverse; but if you want the poem at all you do not want it castrated.

I was sorry to see that Christopher Hill, in his excellent survey of the political acts and contacts of Marvell, accepts the theory that 'Tom May's Death' was written or at least altered after the Restoration, when the corpse of May was thrown out of Westminster Abbey. He thinks that this 'makes it a less unpleasant poem ... and opens up the possibility of all sorts of ironical overtones'. It would become a disgusting poem, and the cowardice and the meanness of the turncoat would be thrust upon the public attention; the action could not even make him safer, because it would give many people an itch to reply. But if one accepts the obvious time-sequence the poem is not unpleasant at all. While still in his twenties, he arrives home romantically backing the side which had already lost the war; he comes to see faults on both sides (the 'Horatian Ode') and wishes not to make use of either side – at this stage he could feel violent irritation at a colleague who had cashed in by writing for the winners. He is then abruptly won over by admiration for General Fairfax, but the General himself has just resigned in protest against part of the Government policy, so Marvell is still allowed a balance of judgement. Even so, he has made a decisive swing, so far from continuing to teeter among ambiguities. Also, it is only assumed that he could not have prophesied the later casting out of the bones; well, I grant he was a bad hand at prophecy, but any Cavalier would have said as much. May died in September 1649, and by that time all the copies of the King's Book on sale were carrying the letter from Prince Charles promising his father to carry on with his policy. And the details about the carcass, how it will be eaten by birds, dogs and worms, and its bones will be broken, would apply equally to the body of Cromwell – if written in 1661. In December 1660 Marvell wrote to the Mayor of Hull that the body of Cromwell and three others, by a vote of the House, were to be 'drawn with all expedition possible, upon a hurdle to Tyburn, there to be hanged for a while and then buried under the gallows.'

> Thee *Cerberus* with all his Jawes shall gnash,
> *Megaera* thee with all her Serpents lash.
> Thou rivited unto *Ixion's* wheel
> Shalt break, and the perpetual Vulture feel.
> 'Tis just what Torments Poets ere did feign,
> Thou first Historically shouldst sustain.

Jolly enough in itself; he seems not to believe in any Hell at all. But if the lines were written after September 1661, when the bones of May were extruded, May would have lost his priority. Marvell had written about Cromwell with personal affection, and he was not at this time in a state of abject terror; he seems more concerned to preserve his dignity than his skin.

There are two magnificent lectures in the series, standing quite apart, by Ricks and Carey; and both these authors evidently find Marvell transparent – they are not puzzled by him, let alone betrayed. The poetry does say, as they both explain, that the human creature in the world is inherently puzzled or betrayed; but a reader of the poetry is granted, for the time, a more lofty viewpoint. The essays themselves made me feel I was reading two new poems by Marvell. Presumably the authors would not be able to answer many of the questions raised in the other essays, but such questions no longer seem important, and all those accusations as to character just melt away. Such a critic inherently claims to know what the author finds interesting, what he would be wanting to say; and this is justified (though of course it might need further justification) by giving an immediate satisfaction. The two lectures are much alike, but Ricks is concerned with the idea of being self-inwoven, as when the dew-drop 'round in itself encloses' or in the conceit 'mine own precipice I go'. I feared that the sad cult of solipsism was going to crop up; 'A poem should not mean, but be' has so often turned out to mean 'the ideal poem is about poetical techniques and jealous quarrels with other poets'; so it was a refreshing surprise when Ricks found the trope typical of civil war, and produced a group of recent Ulster poets who also make great use of it. I doubt whether the Civil War was a crucial influence on Marvell, because he can apply his method to such a variety of themes; but one can't deny that it fits in. Also this account of his mind allows him to be an excitable poet, usually writing from impulse and sometimes foolishly; he does not need to work out his standard effects, arranging a special point of view (this I think is what has made so many people recently find him a pig), because he finds them inherent in the world all the time.

Carey, in his Inaugural Lecture on becoming a Professor, announced a rigorous policy; there must be no more paraphrase, no reading in or spelling out, because all such tampering with a text was the work of vandals. I came in for some of the rough stuff myself, and thought he could have found stronger examples in what I wrote fifty years ago, though

I would never have intentionally gone beyond the intention of an author, either in his consciousness or his unconsciousness. But it struck me that the programme as he announced it was actually incompatible with teaching, let alone his own style of written criticism; it became a question whether he would achieve a Houdini-like reappearance. But here he is beside Ricks, both of them galumphing like the new dinosaurs, each of them the weight of ten elephants and yet as agile as a kitten. He takes the general theme that Marvell's poetry is about 'restriction – the condition of being thwarted, confined and enmeshed' (or perhaps this need not be more general than Ricks's theme; the drop of dew is not confined, only self-absorbed); but he is not himself confined to his theme. I quote a description of the forest birds in 'Appleton House':

> The arching Boughs unite between
> The Columnes of the Temple green;
> And underneath the winged Quires
> Echo about their tuned Fires.

The poem says no more about them. Carey says:

The clamorous and bewildering bird-filled grove is conveyed through the syntax. The birds do not sing, but echo, as if in the pulsating air echo extinguished song. And they 'echo' about themselves, flashing like fire through the grove, seemingly substanceless, with their noise not issuing from them but quivering in the atmosphere.

The syntax does seem deliberately blurred, so it is reasonable to expect that Marvell would be pleased to hear that it had conveyed so much. I think this a splendid reading-in, and can even agree that the birds flash across, though the nightingale in the next verse sits still, and there is no mention of flashing anywhere near. But such a reading may sometimes be wrong about the author's intention, or, even if the author did feel optimistic when he blurred the syntax, his hopes may sometimes fail. What you can say is that Ricks and Carey are deeply in sympathy with the author, knowing what he often wants to do, so that they can get a remarkable amount into their interpretation; it is a welcome advance on Carey's Inaugural.

One of the lectures is so malignant that it calls for a detailed rebuttal. This is by J. A. Wittreich, on Marvell's poem in defence of *Paradise Lost*, which was printed in its second edition (1674), the year of Milton's death.

Parker had attacked Milton as Marvell's friend while answering (1673) the first part of the *Rehearsal*, and anything drawing attention to Milton might encourage attacks upon him at that excited time. Wondering why Milton accepted such a faulty tribute, Wittreich admits that Milton would realise that 'history demanded of Marvell the kind of defence he provided'; this proves, I submit, that Wittreich has no reason for his view except the presumption that Marvell is treacherous. Marvell says he approached *Paradise Lost* with alarm, but found as he read on that it omits everything improper and includes all that is fit; as to the style, as usual it is majestic and soars above human reach. He had feared that Milton would be like blind Samson, groping the Temple posts in spite. Wittreich objects that Milton had denied that Samson was actuated by spite: but spite was what the royalists would call it. Marvell seems bold to admit alarm, but it makes him a more reassuring spokesman; and what a lot there had been to fear he does not tell. Presumably he knew that Milton was an Arian. Most readers would expect Milton to rebuke God for having failed to support the Commonwealth, and make a few cracks in favour of polygamy, but nothing worse; so Marvell's treatment is adroit. Wittreich then makes a graver attack; Marvell is belittling a rival. He 'invites a retrospective glance at his his own poetry' because 'Milton took the flight for which Marvell spent a life-time preparing'. Marvell invites no glance, and had positively renounced religious poetry. Wittreich says that Marvell presents himself as leader of a rival school because he goes on rhyming when Milton's preface on the next page of the 1674 edition tells him to stop. But Milton says 'in longer works especially', such as 'our best English tragedies'; of course one would continue rhyming in a brief verse compliment – not to do that would be pretentious. Indeed, Marvell does not present himself as a poet at all:

> Their Fancies like our bushy Points appear,
> The Poets tag them; we for fashion wear.
> I too transported by the *Mode* offend,
> And while I meant to *Praise* thee, must Commend.

'We' are the men-about-town, who of course can turn out a compliment, but have to follow the fashion, obeying the poets. Wittreich has already objected that 'commendation is the ultimate form of praise', and claimed the support of the OED; a commender 'places the person commended under his own protection'. A reader 'misses the wit of the couplet', says Wittreich, unless he realises that Marvell, regretting that he has to give excessive praise, insinuates that rhyme 'may sometimes be an advantage'. This example proves that the hold of Wittreich on the English language is an extremely shaky one, as might be expected. *Commend* is cold and dignified and usually describes a grading by a superior; Marvell says he has to use it for a rhyme, in place of a word that sounds warm and humble. There would be no wit in the nastiness invented by Wittreich.

So it is still going on; this case is on a par with the theory that the shepherdess in 'The Coronet' was a 'recherché bawd' (thus proving that the critic has no ear), and that the 'Nymph Complaining' is troubled by a slight exhaustion after enjoying all the wanton troopers. Carey was right to call such writers vandals, but it is hard to say where the line should be drawn: we certainly do not want a rule that critics must always white-wash authors. Perhaps it would be enough to ask that, when they make or imply a judgement about an author's character, they should supply evidence from his biography. Wittreich does that, but he invents it; still, his procedure is more humane than the refusal to admit help from biography, or any intention in the author.

The Marriage of Marvell

I

The article by Professor Fred S. Tupper, long and packed with information, which appeared in PMLA for 1938, has ever since been accepted as proof that Marvell's housekeeper was lying for gain when she claimed to be his widow. Both the early biographies, of 1726 and 1776, reject her claim, but the source they give, so far as they give any, is his family, the descendants of his two sisters, and a reader may take the rebuttal as a regular family hush-up. Tupper claimed to prove it from legal papers in the Record Office, relics of a prolonged law-suit which arose soon after Marvell's death. The character and inclinations of Marvell have long been found puzzling, and a more satisfactory picture of him emerges if the matter is cleared up. I say this earnestly, but Tupper said just the same, and we must fall back upon the use of reason.

Much of the article is written in the bullying 'worldly' style of Sergeant Buzfuz, and many of its arguments can be seen to be feeble at once. But Tupper had opened a new line of inquiry, and had already produced from it some useful additions to knowledge; I hope very much that some research man will at last go into these documents thoroughly. It would be too much to print them all, but all should be looked at and briefly reported upon: I was surprised by how much turned up in my timid peep. This was intended only to explode Tupper, a hope that was readily achieved. I asked at the Record Office for a selected few of the documents whose code-numbers are given in his foot-notes. When in this article I am quoting Tupper it would be pointless to give the code-number, but I give it on the occasion when I quote something he left out.

No records of the trials survive; the documents are 'depositions', a series of statements made by each of those concerned, taken down for the attention of the court; they are altered by the clerk into legal jargon intended to guard against contradiction or ambiguity, but that does not prevent them from being characteristic of the speakers. The voice of the housekeeper comes out particularly clearly, and should be heard first:

And though it be likewise true That the said Andrew Marvell was a Parliament
Man and a learned man, Yet it doth not follow but he might marry this
Defendant as in truth he did ... the difference in their Conditions might
be (as this Defendant believes it was) one reason why the said Mr Marvell
was pleased to have the marriage kept private And saith it is true that she
did not till after he was dead pretend or give out she was his wife, because
it was Contrary to what he had Engaged her to aforesaid But she did what
she could to Conceal the same And therefore she did sometimes Attend upon
him more like a Servant than Wife (which was the better to conceal their being
man and wife) and whilst the said Mr Nelthorp and this Defendant's husband
dwelt together in the house aforesaid, True it is she did not always set down
with them at Meals having sometimes other Occasions But she did very often
and so often as she pleased set down with them at Meals and Eat her Meat with
them.

Tupper appears to think that she sounds like a cheat here, but I think
she sounds very plain and true, as well as astonished and indignant. I can
hear her panting.

   This first part is meant to give the basic situation, but the feelings of
the expected reader should be accepted as part of that. In recent times
there has been a strong resistance against belief in the marriage, and at
least one of the reasons for it deserves respect. If the story is true, people
feel, Marvell was treating his wife badly, and doing it in a petty
underhand way; the story underrates his character. The class system, it
may well be claimed, was not applied so severely as to excuse him. I can
answer that he was a politician with unscrupulous enemies; the
quotation already given shows her being badgered coarsely about her
marriage after his death. Also, a marriage in the Minories could be
claimed by either party at any time; the choice of that place proves that
he did not intend to hush it up for ever. Probably he expected to retire
when the Stuarts were gone, and announce it then. Also, he is more
easily forgiven nowadays if his frame of mind is called neurotic, and he
may at least be called unreasonably afraid of his sisters, if he dare not
even mention them. The contrast is plain when he writes to his nephew
Popple, in Bordeaux for the wine trade (July 1675. *Letters*, p. 320):

Dear Will, present my kind love and service to your wife. O when will you have
arrived at what is necessary? Make other serviceable instruments, that you may
not be a drudge, but govern all by your understanding.

The polite message to the wife comes naturally when he thinks of saving up for retirement. Compare a letter to William's father and employer, at Trinity House in Hull, which ends (p. 275): 'Remember to all friends and Katy beside.' I thought this might be a timid olive-branch held out to the 'shrew' who was Edmond Popple's wife, but there is a simpler explanation. William had a young daughter Catherine, who had presumably come with her mother on a visit; they would sit among the wine-casks on the company's boat from Bordeaux to Hull, not bothering to stop at London. Marvell expects Katy to remember him, no doubt because he has sent some toy to Bordeaux, but they have not met so he cannot call her a friend. It is innocent and casual enough, but there is a suggestion that some in Hull are not friends, and no attempt at all to treat his sister Mary as a friend. She was four years older. He was then fifty-five. With so many letters, the cumulative effect is impressive.

Be that as it may, the chief thing is to explain the law-suit which emits so many sparks of information. In 1671, two Hull business men, Thompson and Nelthorpe, both connected to Marvell through the husbands of his sisters, started a London bank for traders to distant parts (Russia and India, for instance), and accepted two London partners, Page and Farrington, presumably to give further reserves of capital. The business seems to have gone on adequately but three years later they were leaders in some quarrel on the London Common Council; they opposed some policy of the King, and both of them were 'connected' with known anti-royalists. Tupper quotes a letter which says that their quarrel cannot be settled; only the King himself could settle it. He is rather prone to make a mystery, and ought to have told more about the letter (Is it from a well-informed man? Was he likely to be making a joke?); but he is clearly right to lay weight on the political background. The Hull bankers seem consistently young and brash; and Hull, which was firmly anti-royal in the Civil War, had been left feeling resentful and important. (It used to hold the main stock of gunpowder in the north of England, but this was moved at the Restoration to join the all-England supply centre, in the Little Minories, adjacent to the Tower.) Many banks were in trouble anyway. The King had borrowed large sums from the City and then refused to pay the interest, because his war with the Dutch created a 'national emergency'. The first year of this 'stay of the exchequer' was 1672, and then it was complete; in later years he paid a proportion of the interest. The immediate losers were large banks, but they had farmed out part of the loan to smaller ones, who could thus be pinched. Christopher Hill decided that the final result was to strengthen the banking system, by leaving only a few banks, all large; and this view is supported by a letter from Marvell to Sir Henry Thompson (4 December, 1675):

All the goldsmiths and bankers in Lombard St. have been for more than a week laid at by their creditors and so much money drawn from them that I believe it will never more find the same channel. And all so far as I can perceive on unnecessary surmises or upon an intention of some persons wholly to break all credit of that nature. It skirted upon our friends in Woolchurch market, but they proceed cocksure.

'Our friends' may be presumed to be Nelthorpe and Thompson, and Marvell does not yet regard them as singled out. According to Tupper, the fatal process had just started; the run upon their bank was from November 1675 to March 1676, when the bank failed, having paid out £60,000. Presumably this figure has been inflated by gossip, but it reflects a view that they had enough capital in the normal way, if they had not been unfairly set upon. Marvell decided, we may fairly suppose, that his friends were political martyrs, and to break the law in their favour was no more than a duty. This may be what Farrington means by cadging, but Marvell was taking a big risk, and the bankrupts could not pay him very much.

However, the third partner, Page, was bought out by Farrington, the fourth one; so the bankrupt Farrington must have had something he could use for money; also he must have thought there was still hope in the situation. One must realise, as he is the villain in this story, that he too thought his actions were fully justified; the brash men from Hull, when they coaxed him into the partnership, had given no hint that they meant to ruin the business by playing with politics or treason. He at once entered debtors' prison, from which 'he had his liberty to be in the city almost every day', but the summoners did not dare to fetch him to court as he was so brutal. He was still there in 1684, and one would like to know whether he ever got out. On the other hand Nelthorpe and Thompson, probably because they feared ill-treatment on political grounds, went into hiding in the parish of St Giles, which was a 'liberty' and could not be searched (though if caught they were not free from arrest). Marvell leased a house for them there in the name of his housekeeper, Mrs Palmer, and all four moved in together. It was in Great Russell Street, which now runs south of the British Museum. Presumably Marvell ran errands for them and brought them news; his living there cannot have added to the secrecy of their hiding-place , but perhaps he wanted to be with his housekeeper. They paid her rent. A price was put on their heads, but we do not hear of it being paid to anyone. In June 1677, when they had presumably been hiding for some time, Nelthorpe took £500 to a goldsmith (the trade still did some banking business on the side), and obtained a bill for it in the name of Marvell. At the eventual trial, no one denied that this bill was a device to keep the money from Nelthorpe's creditors. Only one bill was considered, but probably there were others (Tupper, p. 368) and this one was treated as a test case; it would seem pathetic to fight so long over £500 after losing £60,000. I shall write 'bills', assuming that more than one was at stake. The movements are so slow as to suggest shadow-boxing – perhaps the Government hoped the bankers would go into exile; we hear of Nelthorpe on the south coast, and Thompson on the Continent, but they came back. Evidently they, like Farrington, had some hope of a 'composition' with their creditors, for which money must be available though not directly liable to seizure, money such as the Nelthorpe bills.

This arrangement dragged on for about two years, and then Marvell visited Hull and caught malaria; he died of it after a few days' illness in Great Russell Street on 16 August 1678. Who now owned the bills taken out in his name? Then Nelthorpe died there, on 18 September; who now owned the bills taken out by Nelthorpe in the name of Marvell? Mrs Marvell still held the lease of the house, in the name of Mrs Palmer, and Thompson continued to pay her rent; he was still living there at the end of 1680, when he entered debtors' prison.

I shall try now to report what is asserted and not denied about the actions of Farrington, where there is so much disagreement, and also of the housekeeper. In the first stage, Farrington urged Mrs Nelthorpe not to demand the right to administer her husband's estate, but to let Farrington himself have it; Thompson also urged this but she was hard to persuade, and Farrington did not sign the document taking over the administration till the end of April 1679, seven months after the death of Nelthorpe. On the same day, so that it took only one leave-out day for the visit to the office, he entered a 'caveat' over the administration of Marvell's estate – if anyone applied for it, he must be informed. The

landlady did apply for it not long after, and found she had to plead with
Farrington, who agreed to her having it providing she accepted a lawyer
named by himself as her co-administrator. On these terms, she signed for
it at the end of September, five months later. Next year, she guaranteed
the text of the poems by 'my late dear husband', October 1680, though the
title-page of the edition says 1681; probably the delay was from doubt as
to which poems could be printed. The goldsmith claims that he had
already paid the £500 to Marvell before he died; Farrington goes to law
and quashes this pretence. The landlady's co-administrator, Greene,
recovers a debt for her son Tom, so the arrangement appears to be
working smoothly. But a storm is brewing up in later 1681; the landlady
has decided after all to claim the £500 for the Marvell estate. During
February 1682 both Farrington and Greene twice deny that the landlady
had been married to Marvell; in April she replies, in a deposition signed
jointly with the owners of the house, and gives the date and place of the
marriage. No more is heard of this. There was a trial in November, which
decided that all points were settled except the ownership of the bill; it was
treated as a test case. After further delay, the final trial was held in March
1684, and Farrington won; the bill was allotted to the Nelthorpe estate.
Farrington continued his litigations against other people. On 24
November 1687, Tupper discovered, the register of St Giles recorded the
death of Mary Palmer, Great Russell Street; so probably the ex-landlady
had stayed on in the house, continuing to use the name of her first
husband.

II

Such is the broad outline of the story, and it is not obvious that Farrington
and Mrs Marvell were working together in a plot for gain. No wonder
Tupper is sometimes unscrupulous. He writes, for example (p. 384):

Nothing could be more natural than for Mrs Palmer to have died nine years after
Marvell and three years after the collapse of her claims to his estate.

What the law had decided was that a bill made out by Nelthorpe to
Marvell, admittedly with the intention of keeping the money from
Nelthorpe's creditors, still belonged to the Nelthorpe estate. The judgement took for granted that Mrs Marvell remained in possession of her
husband's estate, and called her Mrs Marvell. Tupper himself had just

reported this, so what excuse could he give here? He had accepted the casual slander of Farrington, that Marvell 'never had any money except what he got by cadging', so perhaps he assumed there was nothing else in the Marvell estate beside the Nelthorpe bill; his remark was therefore, he would say, 'in effect, practically' true, though very misleading for his readers. But if there was nothing in the estate, why did she need a lawyer to help her administer it? One cannot easily believe that a man with four lodgings in London and a house in Hull left no money at all.

'Testimony is not altogether clear', begins Tupper with graceful moderation, 'regarding the time at which Mrs Palmer first declared herself to be the wife of Marvell' (p. 375). That is, Tupper recognises that Farrington cannot already have been training the landlady to act like a widow while Marvell was still alive, because his death was entirely unexpected: and yet no later date, if he settled on it, could be defended. There is no proof, he says, that she claimed her status at the deathbed, because the only evidence that she did is contradictory. It comes from Farrington himself, and Tupper does not attempt to show why Farrington might want this contradiction; he claims only to pick a legal loop-hole in the wording. 'On one occasion', Tupper does not deny, Farrington said:

... after the death of the said Andrew Marvell ... she the said Mary did pretend herself to be the widow and relict of the said Andrew Marvell and did several times with tears bewail the mean and low condition that the said Mr Marvell had left her ... and by such her cunning obtained several sums of money towards the charge of his funeral.

Also he admits 'another occasion' when Farrington says, more briefly, that the claim was made at the deathbed. 'But twice,' says Tupper, 'Farrington quite definitely asserts that Mrs Palmer did not claim to be Mrs Marvell till after he had filed the caveat'; and he quotes these two occasions, and they do not make any such assertion. As before one text is short, making only the essential point, and the other gives more detail:

And sometime after the said Mary did by insinuating and crafty speeches persuade your Orator she would be very serviceable to your Orator if he pleased to entrust her with any business and told your Orator she was married to the said Andrew Marvell though no other person knew it.

He does not say that he believed her, as the argument of Tupper assumes he did. The footnotes merely give the code numbers for the documents

that are being cited, but that is enough; they show that only two documents are cited here, and that each of them gives both halves of the
contradiction. This was what drove me to the Record Office; it seems
possible that Farrington might have contrived some elaborate confusion.
The answer was very simple. The full deposition was filed only twelve
days after the short one; clearly Farrington's indignation had gone on
boiling up. Both documents lead off with the two items just quoted, given
almost consecutively; it is plain that he thought them effective when put
together, because they make her look silly as well as dishonest. There is
no need to impute 'irony', in the sense of saying what he does not mean; he
does not claim to have been present at the death of Marvell. He has heard
that she then claimed to be his widow, and adds that she told him 'only we
know it' when she pleaded with him 'some time later'. There are no
different 'occasions' when Farrington said different things. And consider,
the official who wrote this document out was trained to guard against
ambiguity and confusion; he must have felt that the conjunction of these
two items was clear as it stood. For that matter, any child who can read a
cowboy story will understand it; some of them will also understand that
the trope is well fitted to the villain Farrington, who is always a sardonic
speaker though he does not crack jokes. Only a learned don, highly skilled
in such things, could contrive not to understand it. This part of the
Tupper argument collapses completely.

It is only fair, and of some interest, to consider how such a mistake
could happen to Tupper. A research man will often come home with
bulging notebooks and a sense that he deserves praise, only to be rebuffed
by current fashion: 'What is the good of all this work, if it does not save a
great poet from a degrading slander?' So he tries to re-interpret his notes.
Tupper would not have copied out the depositions in bulk; one is
confronted by endless trivial squabbling, written on stiff material with the
pages about a yard wide, impossible to spead out on the narrow desk,
much of it hard to read, and when I was there one was forbidden to write
except in pencil. Nowadays the documents could be reproduced, and I
hope this will be done for all of them; but Tupper would merely write
down short bits that gave useful information, and might easily forget how
they appeared on the page. He was not guilty of intentional deceit,
because that would be discovered as soon as the original was glanced at;
he could not foresee that the vaunted scholarship of international Eng.

Lit. would not look at it again for forty years. There must have been forty occasions during that time when some expert pursed his lips and delivered a considered judgement upon the question. Also, Tupper may have intended to make a final check-up but have found he could not; war was already considered imminent in 1938, the year of Munich. I was told that all such documents had spent the war in a disused tin-mine of North Wales, and some of the pages referred to by Tupper had become illegible at the edges because of damp. It is likely that this very large-scale precaution had already got under way before war was declared. Wherever I checked his copying, which of course was not my main purpose, it was exactly correct. The fatal weakness of Tupper is that he has no sense of character.

One might think that, with the removal of this one support, the whole edifice of Tupper collapses; but things are not so easy. What is proved is that Marvell's housekeeper claimed to be his widow as soon as he was dead; and the death was very unexpected, so if she was telling a lie she had not been taught to do it by Farrington. But these lessons had always seemed improbable; she would not learn her story from Farrington, but under some conditions she might invent it herself. If she had been the poet's mistress for ten years and more, sharing his life but with no other reward, and he had promised to leave her an annuity, explaining that he feared his sisters too much to marry her, and then was found dead, with no parting message, not even a kind word, leaving her nothing but solitude and destitution – she need not keep herself from denouncing him to the lodgers. And she might get something at least by claiming to be the widow; it was not so very untrue; if he hadn't married her he ought to have done. Marvell's doctor would be on the defensive (another doctor of the period, a bit later, blamed him for his treatment); probably he explained that Marvell had asked for a strong soporific. She would think that proved it was suicide; he had been too cowardly to face her. He had recognised two duties, one to her, and one to these silly young bankers, and they had coaxed him into throwing his whole nest-egg into the bottomless pit of their bank. To them she upbraided him. When Farrington turned up he saw how to manage her, and promised to keep her from want if she would help his plans, first by confessing to him alone that she had not married Marvell. Indeed, this may be more or less what happened, except that Farrington would be wrong in imagining that she had made the confession, or had made it sincerely. To imagine it would allow him to make plans with the servant without losing his superiority over her. But they probably did not reach this stage till six months later; he had an immediate use for her claim, but one that did not require contact with her.

It is not very surprising that Marvell had left her in the dark. Then and long before and after, it was usual for a husband to tell his wife as little as possible about his money affairs, and Marvell was a particularly secretive man. She would realise that he had a weakness for gambling, and for bold young men; the thought that he might save the whole bank by throwing in his tiny nest-egg at the crisis, thus winning their eternal gratitude and incidentally making his fortune, would tempt him strongly. But he was not such an ass, and anyhow could not undo the annuity. He had probably arranged it in 1675, through a banker who was a personal friend; but such a man could do little more than ensure that the routine of the bank was carried through correctly. He would not be told the secret address, and had no reason to expect that the housekeeper was tormented by anxiety – probably he waited for a message from her, realising that the matter might be delicate in more ways than one. The address of an MP need not be announced at his death, though a public funeral would betray his parish, and Farrington could then easily hunt out his partners at Marvell's address. But the place of death of Nelthorpe, a man with a price on his head, would necessarily be known to the police, and it would not seem nosy for the bank to send a man there asking for Mrs Palmer. However, no payment would be due till next quarter-day, about ten days after the death of Nelthorpe and six weeks after the death of Marvell, and the bank would probably wait till then. Mrs Marvell would have a pain-killer during this time because she was very over-worked, nursing Nelthorpe as well as cooking for Thompson and his wife, but she would be liable to accept bad advice at that time if it gave her any hope for the future. By the time the annuity arrived she had become more wary, and did not tell anyone, nor alter her moderate style of life (of course she held the lease of the house all along and received the rents). Farrington would probably realise that she was more comfortable about money now, but he would be too knowing to be suspicious; he would consider that women always say they are ruined, and later on, if treated firmly, turn out to have had something up their sleeves.

As to the lie that Farrington says Mrs Marvell told him, a claim that he was the first person she had told about her secret marriage, I suggest that Farrington constructed it economically. She did not say 'we' meaning only you and I, she said 'Only we in this doomed house know it, and I wish to God I could leave.' Maybe he hardly noticed he had played this trick; he thought all her talk was silly, anyway. As to why she spoke to him in a conniving manner, or why he says she did, that will be explained a bit later; but of course she was frightened of him, as everybody seems to have been.

This is maybe the first example of a procedure that will recur. Tupper always finds a bad motive for anything said or done by Mrs Marvell, and he does it entertainingly; so then he is safe in proposing quite wild motives, because his readers wish the new story could be true, even though their good sense tells them it cannot be. I have the more tedious duty of finding sober and well-intentioned motives for her, and when her motives appear positively saintly I have to tone them down, since the readers would not be gratified. I will be told that I am inventing details, or even conversations, with no evidence for them; but there is no evidence for the insinuations of Tupper either, although they are easier to invent. My plan at least shows that his arguments have no necessity about them. I also derive from the known facts a coherent story, with consistent characters; whereas he does not seem to know that any such attempt has ever been made by historians and biographers. Still, I could hardly call this a proof; the decisive thing is the legal evidence, which stands up behind both of us like a great rock.

The two 'occasions' when Farrington contradicted himself, or rather the one occasion when he opened his attack on Mrs Marvell, were quoted early in Tupper's essay; and they needed to be, because they were his excuse for ascribing no dates to his accusations. But they had an important extra function; they introduced the landlady as one who made 'insinuating and crafty speeches', and this spread a miasma all about her. One felt sure that she and her allies were up to no good, though in truth no other such quotation could have been found. But Tupper never even considers what effect it would have at the time. In his story, Farrington and the housekeeper had been accomplices for several years, and surely Farrington must have suspected earlier what he now asserts with such confidence, that she had never had any right to administer the Marvell estate. Would not the smell of this miasma be just as obvious to the lawyers who first read the document as the modern readers of Tupper?

Farrington would appear to be saying 'The woman tempted me', like Adam, which has hardly ever been found a useful excuse. He would not dare to talk so unless he were confident of his innocence; and indeed, he had regularly said he could prove in a court of law that the Nelthorpe bills belonged to the Nelthorpe estate. It was only to secure them for that estate without trouble that he had indulged the housekeeper with friendly help, and not till after the law had accepted her claim. Farrington was rather a brute, and was in a tight corner, but he was always a self-righteous man, who needs to be understood by his own lights.

This raises the question of how much his assertions in a deposition can be believed. Tupper has to believe him, as he provides most of the evidence for Tupper's side, though for Tupper's theory he has to be one of the villains. I agree so far; a man like that will decide it is right to tell one or two major lies, holding to them strictly, but he will recognise the need for economy in lies, and be very truthful in all else. He is an acute observer, and cannot have thought that all the details he mentions were to his own advantage.

We may believe then that Mrs Marvell did express indignation at not receiving an annuity when Marvell died. But in all her other surviving remarks about him, which are reported as made later, she speaks of him not only with love and admiration but with gratitude. This proves that the annuity did at last arrive; she might forgive him for failing her, but she would not forget, and she has none of the aristocratic ability to gloss over a scandal. Without this little income, and the resulting change in status, she could not have done all that she did; so there is no obstacle against believing in it.

I may now attempt to tell the story. Farrington would turn up at the hiding-place pretty soon after the death of Marvell. He would find Thompson in a pitiable state, chiefly afraid that Farrington would betray him for the price on his head, though his address was no longer a secret, but pretending to be upset about a social triviality. He had sent a polite letter of condolence to Marvell's sisters, and had mentioned, to lighten it a bit, that the landlady was claiming to be Marvell's widow, adding that she seemed to be a harmless old body, a bit cracked. A furious letter had arrived from Mrs Blaydes, the next-of-kin (probably he had made the mistake of writing to the more active but junior Mrs Popple); she said that any amount of harm might follow, and demanded an immediate retraction. This letter was still unanswered when Farrington arrived. He readily offered to save Thompson the trouble; such work, he would remark, had usually better be done by somebody not a relation. He wrote to Mrs Blaydes, enclosing an introduction from the prostrated Thompson, and agreeing with her that the matter should be taken seriously; but he undertook to save her from all trouble if she would post him a power of attorney, to handle her brother's affairs. He need not wait for the reply before asking for the key to Marvell's lock-up; any day now, he would point out, the police would be searching it, and might find papers very damaging to the firm, or at any rate to Thompson. Thompson was grateful for this good idea, and Mrs Marvell readily handed over the key, which she had found in Marvell's pockets (Thompson himself, of course, dared not leave the house by this time, and Mrs Marvell was too busy). Later on she recognised that this had been her one big mistake, but at the time she had no suspicion of 'the business gentlemen' who were her husband's friends, and relied on their advice. No one in the period would despise her for this, as Tupper does. When Nelthorpe realised he was dying he would become very anxious to get hold of the Nelthorpe bills and hand them to his wife, but till then the danger might not occur to him; after all, if captured he was liable to search; whereas the innocent MP had a private lock-up, so Marvell was the safest person to hold the bills. Probably he begged Farrington, from his sick-bed, to bring them back to him. Farrington pretended not to have found them. Meanwhile he strongly advised Mrs Marvell *not* to write to Mrs Blaydes herself, not yet anyway; let her calm down first. Mrs Marvell would be glad of this advice; she too had her pride. Her husband had always said that she could expect nothing from his sisters; only real need would drive her to beg from them. At present she still held the lease of the house and received rent from Thompson. The object of Farrington of course was to control any contact with Hull. Here one has to admire him; he had made himself master of the situation at electric speed, and could not have done it in any other way.

The lock-up was a room in a house occupied by a family called Shawe, in Maiden Lane, not a mile away from Great Russell Street. Presumably it was an attic room on the third floor, with a low ceiling fitted to the roof, and a view. Marvell got through a great deal of prose writing in his last years, much of it using quotations from official documents, which he would need to have handy, also he would need to have some undisturbed place for his work. Probably it also held some dangerous letters from Holland, not addressed to Marvell himself, and copies of political poems, some of them in his handwriting. Farrington would take them away, as he had promised to do, and a few other things which were more use to him. There would be a moderate supply of cash in case of emergency, and perhaps some records of investment in negotiable form; but the main source of money remaining there would be the Nelthorpe bills. This gave Farrington a strong reason for *not* wanting the housekeeper to be recognised as the widow; he would assume that either she or Mrs Blaydes would demand the money as the heir of Marvell, but Mrs Blaydes would never have heard of them, whereas Mrs Marvell could hardly not have done. As agent for Mrs Blaydes, he could assign them quietly to the Nelthorpe estate; if Mrs Marvell were recognised, he would need to be agent for her too. In the depositions, he does not deny, and she asserts, that he tried to induce Mrs Marvell to make him her administrator, and not demand the rights for herself. If they were accomplices, why did he work so hard against her from the start? If he believed the Marvell estate to be void, why was he so keen to control it? He had made an adroit use of the housekeeper at the start, to win over Mrs Blaydes; but from then on she was merely one of his obstacles.

After the annuity had come through, her frame of mind was rather odd but not unintelligible. She suspected Farrington and would not let him administer the Marvell estate, but she did not want to administer it herself either. And yet, as agent for Mrs Blaydes, whose claim she left unquestioned, was not Farrington controlling it already? Probably he had some plot up his sleeve which she could foil by refusal (he did indeed, he wanted the Nelthorpe bills). Also she felt a vast relief, and was recovering from shock; she wanted to have no more bother. It was very unlikely that her husband left an 'estate'; she knew he had meant to divide all he had between herself and the bankrupts. Any attempt to get more would look like blackmailing or begging from his sisters, and that she would give them no chance to insinuate. What he had provided was little but enough, and allowed her to keep her dignity.

There were two reasons for a general suspicion of Farrington, and both emerge in her depositions long after. When she had buried Nelthorpe and could get away for a little (hardly before) she went to Maiden Lane with cleaning equipment and the keys, a key to the front door as well as the attic room, probably, for a final clear-out. Though forewarned by what Farrington had reported, she was much shocked by the air of wreckage in the hide-out, empty except for waste paper scattered about the floor, as from a hurried search. Patiently collecting it, she had found a small tidy heap in the corner, the pre-Restoration poems, and this was all she could salvage. She tried to hope that Farrington was not guilty, but no one else could have got the key; and the irritation of her life in the coming months, carrying on with the housework though she had money in her pocket, would act as an eye-opener. Farrington and Mrs Nelthorpe frequently ate a meal at the house, with Thompson and his wife; it was cooked by Mrs Marvell, who waited at table. (They would not meet elsewhere, as Thompson was liable to arrest if he went outside.) The main business was a prolonged coaxing of Mrs Nelthorpe to give Farrington her rights of administration over the Nelthorpe estate; after the ladies had gone, the gentlemen would discuss progress over another bottle, brought in by Mrs Marvell, who might thus overhear quite a lot. When Farrington remembered her, he would make the same offer to her, with leering goodwill. Thompson supported both these requests. Both the widows resisted Farrington and yet neither would take out rights for herself. This deadlock all round lasted for six months, and would be increasingly tiresome for Mrs Marvell (for anyone in her position, but especially for one of her forthright character). At last Mrs Nelthorpe yielded to pressure and gave away her rights, and was somehow made to realise that Mrs Marvell was on the point of demanding hers. On the same day, near the end of April 1679, Farrington entered his claim to administer the Nelthorpe estate and his caveat against anyone claiming the Marvell estate. He was right; Mrs Marvell had changed her mind.

There might well be a simple worldly reason: she had found there actually was a Marvell estate, after all. Business letters for Marvell would arrive at Maiden Lane as they did before his death, and Mrs Shawe would collect them with her own (I gather that the post only took them so far as a local office). No doubt Farrington would arrive presenting his credentials as the agent of Marvell's next-of-kin, but Mrs Marvell had warned Mrs Shawe against him, and he was liable to start bullying as soon as he was crossed, which would put her firmly on the side of the servant long trusted by Marvell who had returned the keys and cleaned the attic. She would find that Marvell had made several wild-cat investments, not worth calling in to buy the annuity, and one or two of them (at that expensive time) would have done fairly well. Also there would be letters from people to whom he had made loans, asking for more time to repay, and some of these to her own knowledge had been intended as gifts, with the legal form only a decent pretence; they ought not to fall into the hands of Mrs Blaydes. She felt well able to handle such matters. However, all this is conjecture, whereas her other motive rests on solid ground. She wanted to bring out an edition of her husband's pre-Restoration poems, which Farrington had left with other harmless waste papers in the attic, and she would have to talk this over with somebody. In that closed circle it would at once get round to Farrington, who would seize the advantage. She had no title to print them, and he threatened to report her intention to the next-of-kin, who would certainly forbid it. Very rightly, she considered it a duty to her husband's memory to get them printed, even if she had to take over the administration herself.

Most recent critics, I suppose, would think it absurd to regard an ignorant old servant, probably not much good at reading, as the one person around at the time who could appreciate these delicate poems. But they were much out of fashion, and she was unaffected by fashion; or rather, she had had a mild taste for poetry when she was young, thirty or forty years earlier. Also she reacted fiercely to contempt, such as had been expressed by Farrington; if she had not, the poems would probably have been lost. There is a reason for thinking that she already meant to print them before her rights were recognised; she acted rapidly, in spite of the law's delays, as soon as she had got them.

We do not know the date when she first applied for these rights except that it was after April, but the investigation took time, and then an agreement with Farrington had to be reached; she signed the final document at the end of September. However, such a document did not come into operation till six months later (Tupper regularly gives the two dates), so she could not go to work confidently on the poems till the end of March, 1680. Only six months later, in October, she guaranteed the text of these poems by 'my late dear husband', and the language implies that she has gone over the proofs herself. Then there was a delay for another year over whether to print the Cromwell poems, but it seems clear that she had pressed forward against a series of obstacles as fast as she could. It is natural to suppose that this motive was already at work earlier.

The Nelthorpe bills would also be an important factor. Nelthorpe on his death-bed, forbidden to see his wife but nursed by Mrs Marvell, would almost certainly have begged her to search for them among Marvell's papers and allow Mrs Nelthorpe to inherit them; but he would probably not explain the legal situation. It was enough that the bills were almost certainly in Marvell's lock-up, and that the creditors would demand them unless they were passed on secretly. Farrington was determined to use them for the firm in its 'composition' with the creditors; that was why he was so keen to become administrator of the Nelthorpe estate. Mrs Marvell did not understand this; she thought he was merely doing his work as guardian, looking after Nelthorpe's widow, when he explained so urgently (after the law had recognised her as Marvell's widow) that she must not claim the bills for herself. She felt that the business gentlemen behaved very queerly, but her own course was plain; she ought to do what her husband had wanted to have done, in any case where he had left business unfinished.

This explains why she approached Farrington with 'insinuating and crafty speeches', as quoted earlier from his account, saying that she would be 'very serviceable' if entrusted with any business. No doubt she was afraid of him, as everyone else seems to have been, and she would want to hide that, so she would adopt an easy tone. She felt that the whole business of cheating creditors was much beneath her, but in this case she was prepared to connive at it; so now there was no reason why Farrington should not be friendly. She beamed at him, and the cheating gentleman actually had to gulp down this impudence from a pious old female servant. He is still irked by the incident two or three years later, when she has broken the agreement and he puts it at the head of his denunciation of her. We may be sure he had not invented it.

Why then did he allow her, free of charge, the lawyer Greene as co-administrator to help her with her legal business? and how could he 'make it a condition', after she had been accepted as Marvell's widow? He would consider her quite unfit to do the work alone, and if she ruined herself she would be likely to change her mind about the Nelthorpe bills; anyway, he had better be informed about what she was doing. He expected that there would be practically nothing in the Marvell estate, so that it would take little of Greene's time. Also there was a question of face; the grand family of Marvell had expressed dissatisfaction, and some concession should be made to them. But the important thing for Farrington was to save his own face with Mrs Blaydes. The official acceptance of the claim, he would admit in his next letter, was a setback, and informed opinion was confident it had been an error, but at least he had got one of his own men established beside the housekeeper, of equal status as an administrator, so that she realised that she must not go too far. Apparently Mrs Blaydes was satisfied. If she had paid for a London lawyer of her own, Farrington would realise, he would rapidly learn about the Nelthorpe bills, and she would have no scruple about demanding them for herself. It was not a bad settlement.

However, it barely lasted till Mrs Marvell had signed her guarantee for the edition. Then she changed her mind again, and demanded the Nelthorpe bills for herself. This was exasperating, and one cannot blame Farrington for losing his temper. Enough time had passed for the creditors to cool down, and for guarantees of money to be coaxed out from various sources; it seems likely that he had at last begun to negotiate with the creditors for a 'composition', or was ready to. With the ratting of Mrs Marvell all this collapsed, and Thompson was carried off to debtors' prison. We find Mrs Marvell protesting that she knew nothing about the arrest beforehand, which proves that she was accused of working against him; and her answer is not to the point, as the government must have known his address, and if they were determined to catch him they need only watch the door. What she had done was sabotage; she had wrecked the plan to save him. It is easy to suppose that she found herself short of money, but to find a high-minded reason seemed to me very difficult. One might almost think Tupper was right; right about her character, that is, not about his absurd plot.

So it was lucky for me that he quotes from a late deposition by Mrs Nelthorpe, which he does merely for evidence on a point of detail; I would not otherwise have found it, and it is the other main result from my timid visits to the Record Office. It was filed in November 1684, when all hope had fled; the court had awarded the Nelthorpe bills to the Nelthorpe estate, so Mrs Nelthorpe did not get anything. She is replying to further demands from Thompson, who is still in debtors' prison, and takes the opportunity for a survey: thus we learn something of what was said during those six months of coaxing her to give her rights to Farrington. He had told her that he was 'the principal creditor of the said Nelthorpe', and she had appreciated that the creditors ought to be considered (no one else considers them, but perhaps everyone knew that they were not widows and orphans but rich loyalist bankers trampling upon republican bankers). This was why Mrs Nelthorpe allowed him the administration, and not till too late did she find that he was merely a fellow bankrupt: he was now keeping the money for himself. Thompson, the other partner from Hull, and a cousin of her husband, ought to have acted in her interest; but he had urged her to submit to Farrington, and when she did 'the Complainant thanked the Defendant for permitting the said letters of administration to be granted to the said Farrington'. She recalls an occasion when Farrington had filed some bill demanding money from her, and 'the Complainant exhibited the said bill against this Defendant to vex and torment this Defendant'. Apparently he waved it in front of her, as if goading a bull; it is a scene from Dickens. What she finds shocking is the corruption of his character, but perhaps the chief deduction to make is that Farrington had some strong hold over him, making him afraid. Probably it was political, his signature to some anti-Stuart document; but he may simply have looked up to the bully as a protector. Clearly, she felt that he had been a better man when he was still in Hull.

This deposition itself comes too late to explain why Mrs Marvell changed her mind towards the end of 1680, but the cheat by Farrington which it recalls had come earlier, and the bitterness of Mrs Nelthorpe had grown ever since; probably he had begun by trying to fob her off with promises for next quarter. I suggest then that Mrs Marvell had at last had a good talk with Mrs Nelthorpe, and was astonished to learn that she would gain nothing from money paid into the Nelthorpe estate. Mrs Marvell had promised Farrington that she would sacrifice her claim, but she had done this merely because she was sure her husband would have intended Nelthorpe to get the money, or failing him, his wife and children: she felt fully justified in breaking the promise, if that meant defeating a rogue and carrying out her husband's intention. She would demand the money for herself and then, as soon as the law gave it to her, hand it over to Mrs Nelthorpe, and she told Mrs Nelthorpe so at once. The only question is why this talk came so late, and a simple answer would be that Farrington was soon going to cash the bills, for his deal with the creditors. Possibly Mrs Marvell might help in some way at this crisis, and it would be a comfort even to talk about the matter with someone else who was involved.

When Nelthorpe was dying, his wife was still not allowed to know the address. One morning she met Mrs Thompson, who told her he was going on all right, but she still felt anxious, and called at his doctor's house in the afternoon. There she found two notes, one telling her the address, the other that he was dead. She went to the house and found it empty, except for the corpse and Mrs Marvell, who had nursed both husbands into the grave. I expect after that they were on speaking terms. But the Thompsons wanted to keep them apart, and Mrs Nelthorpe could hardly go and natter in the kitchen, when she had been invited to the house only for a business discussion. After she had signed away her rights in the Nelthorpe estate she would no longer seem important. Also the status of Mrs Marvell had been rising; one did not discuss money affairs with the servants, but the editor of Marvell's poems was somehow different. Mrs Nelthorpe appeared gently vague, one must suppose, but underneath there was a lasting resentment at the way the Thompsons had treated her.

Her prose has a sad cool dignity, making her sound very unlike the others, who treated Mrs Marvell with contempt. She is plainly a lady, and Mrs Marvell would never be a lady, though it was something to be a person of independent means. Mrs Marvell would be bowled over by her, much flattered to receive the confidences of so high a being. The lady would at once reject, as quite impossible, the offer of Mrs Marvell; the whole plan had been iniquitous from the start; besides, she would point out, Marvell really was a creditor who had been robbed, perhaps the only one, and his widow deserved to have some recompense. It would make a most elegant scene, though rather a long one, and in the end the ladies would agree to go snacks, half and half. I expect that Mrs Nelthorpe had this plan in view when she arranged the conversation, and that it had occurred to Mrs Marvell fairly early. Thus the reader is not asked to think of her as positively saintly, but she behaved in the high-minded way which she would recognise as proper.

It is as well to keep in mind how Farrington would have answered this accusation, if the widows had dared to confront him with it. The creditors had worked up an absurdly large claim, and the only hope of getting out of debtors' prison, for both Thompson and Farrington, was to offer them a fairly large sum, in a form which they could not simply confiscate, with evidence to prove that this was the most they could expect. The Nelthorpe bills were particularly convenient, being in this form already; it might be claimed that Nelthorpe had another intention, to cheat his partners, but nothing in his conduct gave this slander any support. As to the accusation that Farrington was keeping money from the Nelthorpe estate for himself, instead of giving it to the creditors, there was no such contrast; he was saving all he could get for a 'composition' with the creditors, which would be greatly to his own interest, but also to Thompson's. Mrs Nelthorpe was receiving the usual dowry, arranged long beforehand, so she could not claim money which her husband had already forfeited as debt. It is hard to see what Mrs Nelthorpe's lawyer could have said in answer, unless he could produce evidence that this money was inherited and not gained through the firm. All the same, she had much better have consulted a lawyer; Farrington would be an unscrupulous man till he had fought his way out of debtors' prison. Maybe she thought she could do better without one. Maybe Farrington, during those six months of coaxing, despaired of making her understand the legal position, I am not concerned to defend her but to show that she could have a decisive influence upon Mrs Marvell.

Farrington was made angry by Mrs Marvell's refusal, and expressed it by wild assertions. One of them was his denial of her marriage, which he never made elsewhere, before or after. (He denied it twice, twice echoed by his jackal Greene, but all these came close together.) Of course, in making this negative assertion, I do not claim to have read all the documents; I do not need to, because Tupper had read them, seeking for support, and would report any he found. In the same document, Farrington accused the Morris couple of conniving with Mrs Marvell to cheat over the rents. This story is so farcical that to consider how it arose gives us interesting information. He must have noticed them about the house when he came to lunch with Thompson, glowering at them with suspicion but not inquiring who they were. Mrs Marvell could of course accommodate them, as two of her original lodgers were dead, and she was ready to oblige; the lease would be up next midsummer, and she hoped to stay on. The gaffe of Farrington was a help to her, as it put the Morris couple firmly onto her side, and they added their names to her rebuttal. But these minor points should not distract us from the main fact; it was loony of Farrington to accuse the Morris couple of cheating themselves, out of profits from their own house, on top of accusing Mrs Marvell of cheating herself – the lease was in her own name, and of course she pocketed the rents. He had only to ask Thompson, who was already at his side in debtors' prison. But he was in a temper, and loosing off at random.

Tupper does recognise a need to explain why Farrington never repeated his denial of the marriage (he might also consider why there is no surviving official reaction to it). He says that Farrington, 'on second thoughts', realised that it would do him no good to put Mrs Blaydes in the place of the housekeeper, because she too would demand the Nelthorpe bills, so he 'let the matter drop'. Tupper betrays ignorance of the law here. Mrs Marvell had been accused of perjury with intent to defraud, in an official deposition, and this was a criminal offence; the judge could not let it drop. I may be told that the law was often lax, and perhaps the judge could not be bothered; but we know he could be bothered. After the hearing in 1682, to consider the depositions, he decided that all questions had been cleared except one, whether the Nelthorpe bills belonged to the estate administered by Mrs Marvell; and he ordered a trial-at-law to settle that. In effect, the Nelthorpe bills were being treated as a test case, and he would not want such a trial to collapse merely through negligence.

There had already been a ruling on the question. Tupper has a different reason to explain why the housekeeper was accepted as Marvell's widow in 1679; he quotes an expert on legal history, who says that a formal oath was usually considered sufficient. That is, there would not be trouble about the status if nobody doubted it. In a case where anxiety had been expressed by a caveat, put in by the agent of the next-of-kin, concerning a prominent man (there had been widespread suspicion that Marvell was poisoned), by a fairly prominent and influential family, and then a very improbable claimaint appeared, surprisingly late – this type of case transferred to the Consistory Court, which examined the evidence. Mrs Marvell, when she is looking back at what happened during the pause while the law considered her case, remarks blithely:

The Plaintiff perceiving that the caveat was likely to be withdrawn did by himself and others very much endeavour to persuade this Defendant not to meddle with the administration of her husband's estate.

('The Plaintiff' here is Farrington.) She likes to speak as if she cannot imagine what they were fussing about, but one can deduce a little of what happened. Members of the public, going to the office, met a rather junior official, whose only decision in Mrs Marvell's case was that it must be referred up. Farrington would go to the same office, anxious and important and full of questions, but could only meet the same official, who genuinely did not know. But he was hearing lawyer's gossip, which he would not mind telling to a serious character such as Farrington. In short, the claim really was examined; therefore, a man was sent halfway across London to look at the church register; and the result was considered to be decisive.

This first examination only concerned property, which of course was serious enough, but the second attempt of Farrington three years later, accused Mrs Marvell of a crime. Farrington, when he could be got sober, must have been asked to explain it, and perhaps for the first time heard of the evidence from a church register, though not its date and place. He would doubt it, and the most obvious thing to doubt would be the signatures. For the second time a man would be sent halfway across London, but this time he was a somehow qualified expert carrying specimens of the signatures of both parties. He guarantees the entry as genuine; probably for no good reason, but what story could explain either of the signatures being false?

To sum up, there is no reason to believe that Farrington and Mrs Marvell were working together in a plot. The two surviving members of the firm, Farrington and Thompson, wanted the Nelthorpe bills to help in pacifying their creditors, but Farrington steadily maintained that such was their legal due, and, when he was driven to go to law about it, the law agreed with him. There is no occasion when he could be supposed to bribe the housekeeper for a pretence that she was Marvell's widow, and he was always opposed to her administering Marvell's estate. The whole story is so implausible that Tupper has to invent a hidden tie, some previous guilt which they have incurred together, so that they dared not 'go too far' in exposing one another; their relations are like Queen Elizabeth playing chess with the Spanish Ambassador. But in the surviving texts there is no sign of this mystery; they biff away at each other like two teenagers.

A marriage three centuries ago between two commoners is often hard to prove, and generally gets taken for granted. Even if one knows where to look, the record has fairly often not been preserved. But this marriage, thanks to the busy work of Farrington, had to pass through two official examinations. The evidence for it is remarkably strong.

III

That is the main argument for accepting the marriage, and it had better be put in a separate section, to keep it apart from trivialities. But Tupper brings up a number of other points, and I must not appear to ignore them. Besides, looking for an answer often clears up a bit of the picture.

The first of the other points has apparently been decisive in causing modern opinion to reject the marriage, but very unreasonably, it seems to me. The volume of the marriage register of the Little Minories covering this date is missing, and Tupper is very arch about it. Taking care to avoid assertion, he insinuates that the housekeeper herself carried the massy tome out of the church, using her other arm to scatter bribes among the vergers. Perhaps she calculated that the legal officials would hush up the absence of the ledger, fearing it might weaken the established order to let such a damaging rumour get about. But official opinion disapproved of the Little Minories. I do not know what would have happened if that register had been found missing, but it would not have been total silence.

Tupper does seem to have a dim idea that this story is improbable, because he tries to improve it. He suggests that the housekeeper arranged to have the trial of her case delayed for two years or so. By that time (1684) the old ledger had been filled, and a new one installed; perhaps the old one was kept in the parson's study, so that Mrs Marvell need only bribe one servant, and the loss need not be discovered immediately. But, in this church, the recently completed registers would be the ones most often called upon. Also, this one had not been lost. Also, none of the church registers would be consulted for the 1684 trial. The jolly report by Tupper is a mass of error.

The judge's decision after the first hearing (1682) was that nothing remained in doubt except whether the Nelthorpe bills belonged to the Marvell estate; for that, there must be a trial with a jury. This judge had heard or read the accusations of Farrington and Greene, and had rejected them; they were not put before the court in the trial-by-jury of 1684. Anyhow, the ledger from 1671 to 1684 is still extant, in the London Guildhall Library; the missing ledger goes from 1663 to 1671, so there would have been no help for Mrs Marvell in delaying the trial till 1684.

There are two other missing ledgers, from 1649 to 1658 and from 1659 to 1660; it can hardly be supposed that she savaged all of them. It is fair to remember that 1939 was the high summer of the detective story; Tupper has found a delicious clue, and feels sure his readers are with him; so he can kick up his heels a bit.

What is dislikeable is that he takes no interest in the Church of the Little Minories, a most curious institution, so he never wonders why a couple might choose to be married there. It was legally entitled to marry people secretly, that is, with no public announcement either before or after; the books were open to the public, but guarded, and a marriage would be hard to find unless one knew the date. Family interference with young lovers was frequent and much resented, as at other times, and the legal accident of the Little Minories gave some relief to a recognised need. No wonder a ledger at the Minories did not last for twenty years; when Mrs Marvell got married there it had (on average) one clandestine marriage every day, and two at the time when she is supposed to have robbed it. Such a marriage was hidden only in the sense that it was hard for an enemy to find; the woman concerned could claim it whenever she chose, no less than the man, and her proof was to tell the date of its entry.

There is a very informative *History of the Minories* (1907) by E. M. Tomlinson, who was vicar there, and had charge of the old registers, soon after the parish had been combined with St Botolph's Aldgate, wharfs and warehouses having displaced most of the old parishioners. It was a 'liberty' and adjoined the Tower, to the east of it. A nunnery had stood there, and Queen Elizabeth had bought the site, so that it was not governed by the City of London; it was an annexe to the Tower, chiefly employed in making cannon, and held the country's main store of gunpowder. Marriages there were performed by a clergyman, or they would not have been legal, but the incumbent at the Little Minories was not under control of the Bishop of London, being appointed and paid by the parish council. He did not publish 'banns of marriage'. A page in one of the ledgers has written on it 'Take care of this name of John Flight have been a Person to tear it out'; this shows that the ledger was open to the public, but also guarded – the public was watched. It also shows that the housekeeper need not have carried away the whole ledger; she had only to tear out one page and claim that her marriage had been entered there. She might then accuse Farrington of the atrocity. But the story would not get hushed up.

The object of a clandestine marriage was to delay the announcement, not to hide the truth for ever; that is why it was important to guard the old ledgers for at least a generation. The owner even of an entailed estate usually had a part which he could leave to his second son if he disliked the marriage of the first one; if this marriage were performed at the Little Minories, it need not be announced till the father was dead, and then also the legitimacy of the offspring (often important in a settlement of property) could be proved. Of course fathers were often difficult, and girls insistent upon marriage, in humbler walks of life; but a fair proportion of the clients of the Little Minories would be prominent enough to make themselves heard. The ledger to which Mrs Marvell appealed had lasted eight years, ending nine years before her deposition, so it would certify between two and three thousand clandestine marriages, and a large proportion of the clients would be needing its evidence after that lapse of time. Not all the people who had thus abruptly lost their respectability would keep their mouths shut. And the public would be keen to hear; whether such a church should be allowed to operate was a matter for debate. During the last year of his life, Marvell in a letter to the Hull Corporation (*Letters*, p. 211) reports that a bill sent from the Lords against clandestine marriages has been 'embezzled' in the Commons, and he copies out the oath by which he and all others present affirmed their innocence. He is always poker-faced to the Corporation but surely this scene would be considered very funny. A good deal of gossip from the period has survived, and the loss of an entire clandestine ledger would make a great noise, probably ending up as the plot of one of its heartless comedies. So we would have heard of it, I submit; and also, the house-keeper would not want her pathetic tale to be associated with coarse laughter. It would be much simpler for her to date her imaginary marriage a year earlier, soon after Marvell had got back from Russia, and place it in one of the churches that were completely destroyed, with all their records, in the Fire of London. For Marvell, of course, a marriage in the Minories was a good thing because it made certain that his wife would get her rights, though he could keep it secret out of fear of his sisters for as long as he chose – probably till he chose to retire. It may be answered that the housekeeper, if a cheat, would have wanted to give this impression, but even the simple version of the trick, tearing out a page, would have formidable difficulties for her; a servant could seldom go out of call.

It is E. M. Tomlinson who reports the two other gaps in the register, with their dates. They are likely all to have got lost in the same way, and the housekeeper could have no reason to burden herself with three of them. The Guildhall Librarian kindly wrote to me that a survey of the registers was carried out in 1831, and reported the Minories to be intact. In some cases the survey made mistakes, he added scrupulously; but anyone may add that this case was known to deserve special attention. There was a period of disuse before the parish was amalgamated with St Botolph's in 1899, and this is the most likely time for the loss of the ledgers, or at least two out of the three. Family pride might demand the suppression of one of them in the early eighteenth century, when the old system had been abolished and the incumbent would probably agree in reprobating it, but would hardly take a scattered three. It is gratuitous to suppose that the ledger in question here was stolen just at the time when it was most called upon, and therefore most carefully guarded, and that the loss, just at the time when it was of the greatest public interest, could be totally hushed up. I seem to be flogging a dead horse, but the ghost of this horse is what makes the historical critics feel so confident.

Also, it becomes natural to inquire why Tupper retained those very implausible arguments, to the effect that the officials could not be bothered to look at a marriage register in the town, or even send a servant to do it. How could it matter, then, if the register was lost? When Tupper discovered that the register is now missing, and made so much fun out of assuming it had been lost already, one might expect him to cut out the feeble alternative. But no, he is a sniper; he aims at exciting confusion and anxiety in the opponent, not at fulfilling a coherent plan.

In the dating of the story, it seems clear that he can be pinned down more than he wished. When Farrington entered the caveat he cannot only have been trying to pacify Mrs Blaydes; he was a man who looked ahead, and would be sure to consider the effects upon Mrs Marvell. If he was plotting with her, and yet knew her claim to be genuine, his behaviour becomes totally mysterious; because he could have no hold over her. We have to suppose that he believed her claim to be false, and yet expected it to succeed in spite of his caveat, so long as he did not play some trump card which would expose it. The effect of the caveat would be to challenge the law to disprove the false claim. But what trick could he have intended? When he at last denounces her and denies her marriage he has no secret to expose; it is again mere assertion. You may say that he could not tell this secret without endangering himself, but then we are high up in the clouds of fancy, and my own fancy refuses to play. He is much more likely to have been sure from the start that the housekeeper was in a delusion, perhaps caused by Marvell himself, as in so many comedies of the period, but perhaps merely crazy; so that he would be astonished when the law accepted the marriage despite his caveat. The habit of contempt would allow him to keep his own opinion; he would say: 'A very soft lot they are in those offices; I expect she went there and cried again.' Hence, when they quarrelled, he could bring his old opinion out in all its naked absurdity; but that did not matter, as he won his case all the same. It would take evidence, I think, to make one prefer the Tupper view.

Various minor points need to be considered. Tupper says that, if the housekeeper had been a genuine widow, she would have demanded her rights at once, and also would have written to her husband's sisters. It is ridiculous, he says, to suppose her prostrated by grief: 'she was up and about'. Yes indeed; after begging enough money to give her husband a decent funeral, even though believing he had betrayed her and left her destitute, she had settled down to nurse his friend Nelthorpe also into his grave. The jolly masculinity of Tupper is detestable here. However, he needs it for a contrast; Mrs Marvell, in her general defence of her claim, answered that she had written, later on, and had got an answer, but she had lost it. This would be about eight months later, when she met the obstacle of the caveat, and presumably Tupper means to suggest that she had then recently been induced to make her false claim (so she was lying when she said that Farrington at that time tried to coax her out of claiming her rights). She is obviously lying when she claims to have lost the letter, he says; she would have enough sense to know the value of this piece of evidence. His argument takes for granted that she is a cheat; if her claim was genuine, and the church register supported it, she would not need any such evidence. Also the circumstances have become different; if she had written at once it would have seemed a begging or blackmailing letter, but now she is inquiring into a persecution. Probably she would express certainty that Mrs Blaydes cannot have known what her agent was doing, thus enabling her to repent without loss of face, and she would explain that she needed her status to publish the wonderful poems of Andrew, which would enhance the family name. Mrs Blaydes would be horrified; wanting to publish more of that obscene subversive gabble – surely the woman could be stopped. Mrs Blaydes would be critical of the Stuarts, like all her circle, but would feel that such ideas should be presented with decent caution. Quite probably she was convinced that Andrew had married the woman, but that would make no difference. With grim courage, she answered that she did not indeed know all the steps which her servants had to take in protecting her against ridiculous and disgusting cheats, but she fully endorsed them. Mrs Marvell destroyed the letter, not caring to have it read out in court, and reflecting that Andrew had always warned her against his sisters. Farrington was furious at the whole affair, and denied that either of these letters had ever been written; he had always tried to discourage any contact between Mrs Marvell and Hull.

There is one point, I ought to admit, where Tupper catches out Mrs Marvell in a lie. Several years after the death, she denied in a deposition that she had begged money from the lodgers to pay for the funeral. The Hull Corporation voted a handsome allowance for it at once, sent to Marvell's doctor as the quickest method, and though it was too late for the actual ceremony there could be an early repayment to the lodgers. Nelthorpe and Thompson ought to have helped with the funeral, as Marvell had taken a big risk for them, but probably they expected to be repaid by Hull and made the landlady sign a paper about it. Maybe at that moment she was not considering what would happen next, but it was true enough to say that she had not begged from them; in this deposition, she was defending her dignity, which would justify putting truth to a considerable strain. Tupper uses her denial to insinuate that the deathbed scene described by Farrington never occurred. One might argue instead that the raising of this question so long after suggests that it had become well known, one of her exploits. Tupper and Farrington are alike in that both regard it as contemptible, which most people would not. By the way, the £50 given by Hull for a memorial went to the next-of-kin, Mrs Blaydes, as there was no hurry about that; if anyone embezzled this quite handsome sum, it was not Mrs Marvell.

When the law allows her the administration of her husband's estate, she accepts a lawyer appointed by Farrington as her co-administrator. I have tried to show that this was sensible (there could be little point in refusing

his help, after she had decided to give him what she understood him to
want from her); and have now only to consider the reaction of Tupper.
He is exultant; of course she could have done the work herself, like
anyone else; she accepted Greene 'because they forced her to'. The
plural suggests a whole gang of villains, battening upon the riches of the
Marvell estate, though perhaps it is only meant to include Thompson. A
woman did not usually take on this work, as the case of Mrs Nelthorpe is
enough to show; let alone a female servant. As to the legal affairs of
Marvell, we only hear of one of his ploys, and the judge treated it as a
test case. I do not believe that Tupper could have handled them, and I
certainly wouldn't have tried myself. The idea does occur to Mrs
Marvell that it was odd to accept help from her opponent, or more
probably the objection was put to her, and she answers with an example,
of a case where she caught Greene trying to defraud her:

by this Defendant's taking advice upon this draft of an answer the Petitioner's
design was defeated, and the Defendant got a new answer drawn up.

Even when she spots something wrong, she knows that all she can do is
pay another lawyer to put it right. She seems particularly competent
here. Of course it is assumed that she has a little money in hand.

Tupper also finds it very suspicious that she did not know the date of
her supposed husband's death. If she didn't, that would not prove
anything; she was not at all the type to set aside days for private devotion:
but the evidence is very thin. Apparently she said '16th' the first time,
which was correct, and '10th' the second, and after that refused to be
precise; it sounds as if she merely got rattled, under repeated ques-
tioning, and some friend may well have warned her against asserting
needless details. But there are errors in the text which cannot be her
own; when she is telling how she gave the keys of the study to someone,
he is given as 'F...'. This cannot have been handed to the bench,
and can still less be a report of what she said. I take it that a copy of
each deposition would be made while it was being hammered out (it
was plainly not a literal report), and the copy would be kept in the
files, giving us all that remains, but necessary corrections might be
made in the master text before it was handed to the bench. The extra
'proof' by Tupper would be almost too footling to mention if it did not
illustrate this point of routine. It also suggests an unappeased doubt in

the mind of Tupper, driving him on to produce one 'decisive' proof after another.

However, he sounds really confident about another argument of the same type. Mrs Marvell, he finds, 'confessed' that her claim was false by allowing people to go on calling her Mrs Palmer. Well, even nowadays, she would have no way to prevent them; but also there has been a slight change of social custom. In the seventeenth century, a widow of two husbands, with children only by the first one, often did revert to the name of her children. Consider the patron of Shakespeare, who gave his mother a splendid tomb calling her the Countess of Southampton, though she had married two subsequent husbands, one for money and one for pleasure, both of them only knights. She was the mother of the reigning Earl. The situation of Mrs Marvell has at least one point of likeness; her children would be insistent that she should stick to the name of their father, rejecting the name of a family which had insulted and rejected her. And Mrs Marvell herself, though she would be forthright enough to impose it on her few intimates, would find the effort needlessly painful; at every mention, they would say that he had treated her badly, and she would repeat that he had done all he could, while feeling in her heart that a man ought not to be so much afraid of his sisters. Tupper exultantly quotes from a letter of Thompson which remarks incidentally that 'Mrs Palm' has just fetched a letter from the post. There is a smudge above the word 'Palm' and Tupper explains it as a contraction sign: this makes the remark of Thompson a proof that he believed her to be Mrs Palmer. But consider, she came round collecting the rent, and in a comedy of the period 'Mrs Palm' would be just the name for her. Tupper is wildly out of touch when he regards the detail as a proof. Thompson did not care about the question at all.

Coming now to the later life of Mrs Marvell, I have to feel that, in the rather grubby but necessary work of controversy, I am liable to forget the positive achievements of Tupper. He discovered in the records of St Giles' Church that a Mary Palmer of Great Russell Street was buried there in 1687; giving of course a strong suggestion that Mrs Marvell had lived on quietly in the same house. It would be bad luck if this was another Mary Palmer, but not astronomically improbable; the name is not un-common, and Great Russell is quite a long street, perhaps more crowded when it was part of a refuge for petty criminals, and free from the British

Museum, than it is now. There were no street-numbers. I accept the attribution as readily as Tupper does, but this is because it fits in well with each of the different pictures that we have formed. He suggests that the Morrises may not have wanted their house back, so then the housekeeper 'could have lived on there, collecting rents'. Presumably he realised that she would pay these rents to the owners; she herself would be earning what Marvell had said he was paying her, £10 a year, and would still do the cooking, in a resort of criminals where she had no friends. One can now appreciate the sour grease of Tupper's charity, in his cooing remark earlier – 'nothing could be more natural' than that she should die there pretty quickly. None of this is probable. The Morrises say they want their house back, and say nothing about leasing it again: they are willing to sign their support for Mrs Marvell to the wild accusations of Farrington, although they need not have bothered about the accusation against themselves; and it is hard to see how they could enter the mind of Farrington, unless he had met them in their house on one of his visits. They might well hope to get other rich mugs as lodgers, hoping to hide from the police; but with one such lodger, or even two, they would not have to leave the house themselves. Surely it would be wiser to stay within call. I suggest that they had been camping out in the attic of a friend settled further up the street, for a moderate rent, not too uncomfortably, and had been driven to this unusual step by a sudden demand for a lump sum of money – in most such cases, it would be because a near relation had got into trouble. Five years is a long time, and they would be thankful to be let off the last half-year of it. They would feel they had got out of a scrape, and would not be at all inclined to take the risk of a large new commitment, which might drive them from their house again.

So they would not hire Mrs Marvell as a servant; she would be too demanding. There was already a slavey in the kitchen, it is let drop somewhere in Tupper's essay, and no doubt she went on doing the basic work through all the stages of the story. One could not expect Mrs Marvell to take her place; she would at least have to eat with the family. It might be thought that a discredited cheat must endure anything; but Mrs Marvell remarks that all her children had been well planted out, so she could draw upon them if she must, though she would regard it as a last resort. Hence she could be firm in her demands. And then, all old people are a liability, though nowadays the risk has been put ten years or so later;

they start dying, and take to their beds. Mrs Marvell was over sixty; it would be more sensible to appoint an unsuspecting vigorous young girl. Of course the Morrises would give her a good character, for employment elsewhere.

But if she came as a paying guest, maybe paying only twice as much as her keep, on the understanding that she would help around the house in ways that she already knew, she would be a great stand-by. It would not much matter if she took to her bed; she would eat less, and the money would keep rolling in. In this anti-government parish she would be well thought of, in a mild way, having had an interesting past. She had expected the Morrises, living in a bad neighbourhood, to be bad people, but she had an affectionate nature and had recognised good feeling in them; and her son Tom, who had advanced views, was much in their favour; and really, though it seemed rather dreadful, she had nowhere else to go. She died, not in shame or despair, but while placidly expecting the happy ending, only a year away, of the final collapse of the Stuarts. As so often, some bug happened to intrude.

I have kept till the end some passages in the report of Tupper which have probably made two or three generations of readers turn against the housekeeper, though it is doubtful whether he gave them space with that intention. They are merely what he would expect. In her reply of Farrington's major attack, when he denies the marriage, she accuses him of robbing Marvell's study in Maiden Lane, and describes with eager excitement how she had seen it stuffed with 'hampers trunks bonds bills and other goods', also 'money jewels bonds bills and otherwise to a good value' (Tupper, p. 374). It might be the cave of Aladdin or the dragon Fafner. She is obviously lying, and the mere thought of so much money seems to go to her head. Just so a false widow might behave. It need not be denied that the true widow was excitable; one needs to consider what she was excited about. Farrington had accused her of petty cheating over the rents (Tupper, p. 379), and these law-courts, like those in which Cicero performed, were not good at calling witnesses to clear up side-issues; the standard reply was to play the loud *tu quoque*, and so she would be advised. But also she had painful feelings about this lock-up. She ought not to have given Farrington the key to it, soon after the death, when she knew so little about him; he had pretty certainly stolen something, though she could not be sure what. The truth was, Marvell did not allow her to enter his study;

it was the place where he must not be distracted. Mrs Marvell could not admit this, as it would make her seem even less like a real wife; also perhaps she needed to impress the Morris couple, who were her co-signatories for this document, with her financial stability – she wanted to stay on as their paying guest. So she glorified the study; lying to defend her dignity would seem to her more respectable than any other kind.

All the same, I expect she was remembering something real; she was not an imaginative woman, though vehement in her reaction to actual troubles or successes. Marvell, as seems evident, found it a necessary kindness to keep things from her, and probably her children did that too. But it was also worth while to put on a show for her, as she would enter into it so warmly. Obviously he did not as a rule keep bags of gold in his lock-up; he was in close touch with the emergence of modern banking. But there was one occasion when he could have such things there without serious inconvenience; when he was collecting his various assets to buy the joint annuity for himself and his wife. This was in 1675, probably, and he would feel it as rather a sacrifice, because playing the markets was fun, but also as a dedication, or a private declaration of war on the King; he was now going to take serious risks, and must make sure his wife was safe. But on her side the occasion was purely one of rejoicing, and well symbolised by allowing her to visit the lock-up. The capital now to be devoted to the annuity would be spread out in an eye-catching form, and great scripts in legal handwriting would alternate with actual piles of gold. Very out of date, but the one spectator of the show received a lasting impression from it. Of course she knew that it had not remained there till Marvell died, and then got stolen by Farrington, but it came readily to her mind when she wanted to make the most of the thieving by Farrington. It gave her a deep respect for Marvell, even if he had taken most of the money away from her and wasted it of his own accord on those horrible bankers, as she still sometimes suspected. This visit to the study is the only glimpse we have of their life together.

IV

To establish the marriage is of no great consequence to literature, as it came so long after his best poetry, though I do think it saves Marvell from a scandal – Tupper seems to presume that he remained virgin through-out, but gives the impression that he treated his mistress very shabbily. It also opens a wider horizon, and the most prominent landmark that comes into view is Tom Palmer the bookseller. I learn this through the researches of Mrs Duncan-Jones, who has been collecting details about it for many years. She permits me to cite the main points

Marvell started writing verse again a few weeks after his marriage, in 1667, breaking a silence of nine years, and in most poets one would expect to find some connection between the two. Here there is none on the surface; he was a public-spirited man, very conscious of his audience, and the current trouble fitted his talents exactly. He could hardly avoid joining in. Both of his poems of that year can be dated to its later half, after the Dutch had come up the Medway; both are very externalised and 'masculine', perhaps in the sense of cultivating and depending upon warm support from a male political group. But the 'Last Instructions' is nearly 1,000 lines long, written within three months apparently, and the 'House-Warming', trivial as it seems, must have cost a good deal of time in coaxing and grooming the five MPs to take part. Marvell was working under great pressure, feeling that the crisis gave a unique opportunity. A poet at such a time has to draw upon the impulses he has in easy reach, fresh and ready; that is why the poetry gives us our nearest source of evidence about his state of mind. And there is one very queer passage in the 'Last Instructions', long, prominent and repeated four years after, which at least calls for explanation.

The circumstances of the poem should first be recalled. The Fleet had been laid up in March, because the King could not pay the crew, or for any other upkeep, while England was supposed to be at war with Holland. The Dutch occupied Sheerness on 10 June and on 12 June sailed up the Medway, which had been considered inviolable; they towed away the flagship and burned another ship, equally large, but did no harm to civilians. It was a snub rather than a disaster. But it struck the public mind as a great eye-opener, an exposure. The absurd Waller, in 1666, had brought out a poem call 'Instructions To A Painter', on how to illustrate the 'posture and progress' of the King's Navy, led by his brother against the Dutch. The results for the Navy were so bad that four successive parodies called 'Advice to a Painter', probably by one unknown author, were made available during 1667; indeed, according to the title-page of the book, they were actually printed before the end of that year, together with 'Clarendon's House-Warming', 'by an unknown author' – this was probably a joke hinting that it was communal, as a false authorship had been given for the main four. Wood reports that the printer stood in the pillory for it (*Poems*, p. 269). Margoliouth, whose notes are particularly good in this jungle, decides that Marvell wrote none of the four parodies called 'Advice' but started writing his 'Last Instructions' after he had read the first two; the third describes the Dutch in the Medway, and Marvell is clearly independent on that topic. His poem leads up to the scene of public shame.

A mild contradiction is inherent in the poem. The fit reader is glad to have the greed, idleness and dishonesty of the King made manifest, and is ready to laugh at them; but he is appalled by the national shame which they have caused. However, as little harm has been done, one is not keen to blame other people (except, of course, top people, tainted by the King, courtiers and such); so the common sailors who joined the enemy to get their overdue pay are regarded with positive sympathy:

> Our seamen, whom no danger's shape could fright
> Unpaid, refuse to mount our ships for spite;
> Or to their fellows swim on board the Dutch,
> Which show the tempting metal in their clutch.

But the jovial tone could not be extended to officers; at least one heroic officer was needed, to offset the poltroons of the court, and he was found at once. The first surviving reference seems to come in a letter from Sir William Temple, stationed in Brussels, during August, saying he wished Cowley were still alive to write a poem about the heroic action of Captain Douglas (*Poems*, p. 284); he had stood and burnt in one of our ships at Chatham, when his soldiers left him, because it should never be said, a Douglas quitted his post without order. If Temple heard this story so soon in Brussels, the recognition in London that it fitted a propaganda need must have been very quick. Marvell did not invent the heroism of Douglas, and his public would need to have it treated extravagantly. Even here, one might argue, he is entirely concentrated on his political duty; if the result is in bad taste, as a literary critic might say, that does not lie on his conscience. But he could not have supplied this poetry if it had not welled up; and from what, a biographer needs to inquire? Here are the crucial lines:

... modest Beauty yet his Sex did veil,
While envious Virgins hope he is a Male.
His yellow Locks curl back themselves to seek,
Nor other Courtship knew but to his cheek. ...
Fixed on his Ship, he faced that horrid Day,
And wondered much at those that run away. ...
Much him the Honours of his ancient Race
Inspire, nor would he his own deeds deface.
And secret Joy, in his calm Soul does rise,
That Monk looks on to see how Douglas dies.
Like a glad Lover, the fierce Flames he meets,
And tries his first embraces in their sheets.
His shape exact, which the bright flames infold,
Like the Sun's statue stands of burnished Gold.
Round the transparent Fire about him glows
As the clear Amber on the Bee does close;
And, as on Angel's heads their glories shine,
His burning Locks adorn his Face Divine.
But, when in his immortal Mind he felt
His altering Form, and soldered Limbs to melt,
Down on the Dock he laid himself, and died,
With his dear Sword reposing by his Side.
And on the flaming Plank, so rests his Head,
As one that's warmed himself and gone to Bed.

I find this disgusting, and all too likely to well up from the worst
perversion, that of Gilles de Rais, the craving to gloat over the torturing
of a tender innocent. Mrs Duncan-Jones was quite right, in her Academy
lecture, to point out the strangeness of it, but (I think) not nearly
censorious enough. And of course it is not a matter of mere clumsiness,
such as one finds in much of the verse mistakenly ascribed to Marvell;
this bit of work is highly finished and glowing, conscious of its power; and
the last line quoted is screwed up a bit tighter in 'The Loyal Scot':

As one that Hugs himself in a warm bed.

This kind of 'paradox' would be familiar to the first readers, from
descriptions of religious martyrdoms, mostly by Papist authors (though
not Crashaw), so might be accepted as conventional; Marvell is so very
anti-papist that it is surprising to have him echo the technique here,
except that applying it to a military officer, who is definitely not ordered to

become a martyr, gives a further surprise. And they might regard the passage as a string of 'conceits', but there is too much intimacy of feeling in it for that; it is another case where Marvell dissolves the conceit of his period into the much later style of Romantic poetry. In the basic examples, the reader is expected to believe that the martyr enjoyed being burnt, and there are some very striking, though sober, reports of what a religious ecstasy can achieve; but even so the recital excites a fascinated horror, as the reader knows he would have felt otherwise, and there have been times when it induced a craving to watch the burning of heretics. But the first readers of Marvell would not be tempted to believe in the miracle, as it was so remote from what was expected from a soldier; it would be just a stimulant to them, mustard and pepper, to the effect 'He was frightfully keen'.

Still, the effect could hardly be achieved without the insistence that he was a glowing virgin, presumed to be already tormented by desire. His chief reason for restraining it, apparently, is that he was enthusiastic about his military duties, but also he is in love with his commanding officer, who was a hard-headed political worthy, General Monk. To be caught by the flames is already a kind of orgasm, but there is a yet greater pleasure in knowing that the general himself has arrived and will see him burn. One would like to hear the comments on this passage by the officers' mess which had included Douglas. He would not himself have claimed to be a virgin; his widow petitioned for a prize ship in compensation but received only £100, very inadequate; still, she probably brought trouble on the senior officer who had failed to release Graham. I expect he really was both a very brave man and also very indignant with the brass hats. It was quite gratuitous for Marvell to insist he was a tender virgin.

The case is so bad as to excite grave suspicion against the subconsciousness of the poet, and here I am keen to whitewash his character, a thing the Victorian biographers are often blamed for doing to their subjects. I hope to escape blame for this explanation because the Victorians would think that it blackened his character. In pursuit of his very high-minded political intrigues he needed a young man to work for him, and found one who was eager to learn how to cheat and to hate the king and so forth, and very grateful to be given the chance, and his mother was grateful too; and yet what would he get in the end, thought Marvell, except the monstrous cruelties of Charles's agents? So would Marvell himself, but he knew it, whereas somehow he could not make the child know. Up to this point it might all be decorous, but he needs to be in love with the young man, and feel guilty about it at least to the extent that he is afraid his mother may find out, because otherwise he could feel no need to make the whole passage about Captain Douglas reek with an improbable virginity. Probably the actual sexual privation had not been severe for Marvell – young Tom would make no bones about allowing him minor pleasures, and once he was taken to bed by the grateful mother he would find he had none to spare; though he would continue to feel a very decent regret about exposing Tom to risk. Thus one might possibly have deduced the whole story from the verses themselves, but of course it is better to have evidence.

In this period, there was a small row of bookstalls inside Westminster Hall, supplying recent books or pamphlets which might be tempting for lawyers and other types likely to go there. It is hard to realise that Charles II did not allow newspapers, though Cromwell had done; there were private 'newsletters', sent to country houses, but surely the ban would be evaded for the public too as far as possible, and word of mouth was not forbidden – the scene is hard to envisage. These stalls were supplied and staffed by regular bookshops in the city, with larger stocks of course, and these shops were owned by members of the Stationers' Company. But there was one maverick booth, run by a person usually described as 'Palmer the bookseller'; he was not a member of the Stationers' Company, nor backed by one, but he himself acted as a publisher, inducing printers to supply him with material which would only be available at his booth, unless he chose to grant it to someone else. The other men in the row were presumably also minor figures, sent out to get a bit of experience; a booth would help to advertise a shop, but would seldom achieve great sales. They would not be startled to find Palmer a young man, because they would assume he had a backer, just as they had, but presumably an MP, as it wasn't a shop. He sold a good deal of anti-government stuff under the very nose of the government before he was nabbed. It is hard to see who had both the authority and the impudence to put him there except Marvell.

He is first metioned in 1664, when Marvell was on his tour to Russia, so he had somehow been launched before Marvell left England, a year earlier. This is not surprising. Marvell had not been free to choose his

lodging under the Commonwealth, either as a tutor or a minor official
(Milton when totally blind had been rather meanly turned out from his
official rooms), and still, while getting himself established in the Cavalier
Parliament, he would have to be careful; but in 1662, when just over
forty, he would have the first intoxicating pleasure of choosing where to
live in England. Within a year or two, he was settled; Mrs Palmer was a
very sympathetic type, and the occasional visits of her son gave him great
hopes. One can be fairly definite about the dates. Marvell would fear
ridicule if he married a woman older than himself, and would not want
her young enough to produce further children; two years younger than
himself would be best. Tupper reports Mrs Marvell as remarking contentedly that all her children have been well planted out, and it is
unlikely that this could have been done without the help of Marvell. Her
words imply more than two, and he would not take on more than three.
We know she had one son called Tom, because Greene collected a debt
for him some time after Marvell was dead; this implies having money to
lend, and the bookseller when nabbed is mentioned as Thomas. This
was the elder son probably, and Marvell had long been sick of the
subject of dowries, but could stand a low-class dowry for one daughter.
If Mrs Palmer had her first child when she was twenty, and it was Tom,
he would be twenty-one when first mentioned, twenty-three when his
mother married again, and not quite thirty in 1671 when pilloried for
publishing what her husband chose. This exposure did not kill him or
degrade him, as he is again mentioned in 1675; but probably he was just
employed by an anti-Stuart publishing firm, with a mild respect for him
as an old-time martyr.

Some of his publications can be found in Plomer's *Dictionary of
Booksellers and Printers*, also in *Anonymous and Pseudonymous Books* (both
on the open shelves of the British Museum). An early one, probably the
most important for propaganda, gave all four of the 'Directions to a
Painter', even yet of unknown authorship but here ascribed to Denham,
and 'Clarendon's House-Warming', described as 'By an Unknown
Author'. The date on the title-page is 1667, which might extend into the
next year but still means quick work. It was of course unlicensed; the
printer stood in the pillory for it, but the publisher and the authors were
not found. Marvell's 'Last Instructions' to this painter made a better
poem, and if this Tom Palmer was Marvell's son-in-law and his agent

(as I maintain) it seems odd that he did not print that. But Marvell was just entering this field, and had a valuable position to lose; also, the public might well be keener to have this series, which Marvell had only imitated; he was genuinely modest about his verse; and he would explain that he had established a cover-publisher for the public good, not for himself only. Publication was found so dangerous after 1667 that a regular system was developed for making and distributing manuscript copies, especially by Shaftesbury, who sent them to other cities; but the method was easier and cheaper inside London, and the main duty of Marvell was to swing votes in the House of Commons. Tom Palmer was eventually caught and sent to the pillory on 15 March 1671 and this is firmly reported in the State Papers (also on the open shelves of the BM) and they vary, but probably there were a number of accusations. One says that he had 'circulated the manuscript of a pamphlet called *Advice to a Painter*, in which their Majesties and many of the nobility were maligned' (*Poems*, p. 289). There had indeed been a recent pamphlet, called *Further Advice* etc., which is short and very obscure, seeming only intended for other members of Parliament, so that even the editor 'cannot elucidate the allusions' at some points, and the insults for the king and his nobles have become a perfunctory routine. Surely there was no occasion here for the under-the-counter publicity that Tom was skilled to purvey; Marvell almost certainly wrote this tiresome pamphlet, but seems to have become convinced by it that he ought to be aiming at a larger audience. I suggest that Palmer was still circulating copies of the grand 'Last Instructions to a Painter' (of 1667; in either case, the newsletter has got the title slightly wrong). This poem was much admired; it was printed as soon as possible, in the first year after the Stuarts had gone; but no manuscripts have survived. There is also a great shortage of the old almanacs (some of them published by Palmer), not because they were ignored but because they were passed from hand to hand and worn out; and the 'Last Instructions' would be a manuscript of a thousand lines, always liable to fall apart. That it is hard to imagine Palmer at work, under the eyes of jealous colleagues, I cannot deny; many of them would be in sympathy, but he could not trust them all. Of course the impudence of the thing, its sheer improbability, would be a help; and he might merely receive a note and hand back an address. But to catch him out required something very definite; he had published the speech of Lord Lucas, made on 22 February 1671 in the Lords (*Letters*, p. 308). Marvell writes to his nephew that it was a fervent bold speech, attacking the government, and copies were going about everywhere, and Lucas when shown one said that part of it was not his; so the Lords voted it should be burned as a libel by the hangman; 'and the Sport was, the Hangman burned the Lords' Order with it' writes Marvell – a feeble joke, as they could easily sign another. He never talks about Sport like this; he is trying to hide his involvement even from his nephew.

Another newsletter, which seems anxious to make clear that Palmer had a thorough punishment, says that he was taken to pillories in four quarters of the town, and suffered heavy fines, and the usual treatment. This I am afraid means that he was flogged, which was always a severe process, and the mere sight of him after being flogged would affect Marvell extremely. The pillory was an appeal to the public, and many in the crowd would be in favour of Palmer, but that would not stop the rude boys who came for the fun of throwing rotten eggs, or not quickly enough. However, we need not collate the reports and believe that he was pilloried twice, ten days apart; it would probably have killed him (they were astonished, and rather awed, to find that they could not kill Titus Oates by flogging him). After this exposure, he would lose his privileged booth in Westminster Hall; the procedure would very likely take a year or two, but meanwhile he could not go there. He is still publishing in 1675, so even if not Marvell's son-in-law, he is not dead; and if he is Marvell's son-in-law his mother's lawyer is collecting a debt for him around 1680, when he is (on my estimate) around thirty-seven, so he is rich enough to be lending money. He had been planted out, as his mother comically but quite truly said; he would be working for anti-Stuart publishers, with the prestige of the pillory behind him.

At the time when he stood there, Marvell was writing 'The Loyal Scot', and he transferred into that the whole verse paragraph about Graham in the fire, gearing it up a bit. I must again confess that the external, the political, reasons were decisively strong for making the poet act as he did; that his private emotions also fitted the case would be a mere accident – it cannot even explain why the poetry is so good, in this later case, as it had been written before. And to throw it in again as if this kind of stuff wasn't really a poem, and nobody would remember it from four years ago, is almost contemptuous. He was not feeling like that.

What he had foreseen had come true, and he would now have to take some decisive further step. He must still keep his temper, and try what could be done by negotiation, but that must be done in prose; the easy convincing prose of a gentleman. After marrying a Mrs Palmer he started writing verse again; after a male Palmer had been tormented in his service he started writing prose, and his prose was admired far more than his verse for the next two centuries. The first part of his *Rehearsal* came out in 1672, and it is a very elaborate piece of writing; he must have begun it in the previous year. To assert that neither Palmer had any influence on Marvell, as appears now to be usual, means straining coincidence rather far. If Tupper is to be allowed the entry in St Giles' Church of the death of a Mary Palmer, somewhere in Great Russell Street, surely my side may claim the far more detailed evidence of a relation with Tom Palmer.

One should not impose a tone of doom upon their relation, which they would have treated largely as fun, and it did not end tragically. The publication of *The Nenushtan* by Joseph Wilson of Beverley, who proposed not merely the abolition of all liturgy but the actual tearing down of York Minster, cannot have seemed to Marvell a practical step towards a political settlement. Wilson, as we look back, seems to have been in a hopeless position; he had lost his parish under Cromwell, and yet, though still determined to tear down York Minster, he expected Charles to give him Hessle back; though he would not mind taking Leeds. Everybody seems to have treated him with great forbearance, as when Marvell writes to the Mayor of Hull: 'I am sorry to hear that Mr Wilson has been so refractory' (*Letters*, p. 15, for 1660). It is quite in accordance with this tone to allow the old man a publication of his book in London, which would give him great satisfaction, though its only effect would be to give the establishment a tease. The title-page has no name for the author, and I suspected some trick there, but the *Anonymous Books* makes the matter plain; Joseph Wilson had accepted a legal precaution, but did not at all mind having it leak out that the Rev. J. Wilson was the author. But then it was found that there was another person of the same name and title, in Chester. We have to leave them in their difficulty. Probably the two members of Hull were the only people in the House who had ever heard of this author, and his book cannot have been a great money-spinner, so the incident is quite strong evidence that Marvell was using and supporting Palmer. Marvell of course had no intention of tearing down York Minster; he thought that printing the book was fun, and perhaps, remotely, a warning.

The same rather puzzling aroma clings to the 'House-warming', which apparently leads off by accusing Clarendon of causing the Plague and the Fire. (Maybe young Palmer was his stooge, and sang the first two verses; but more likely the party was for Members only.) None of the guests follow his lead here, and Marvell himself, at about the same time, was saying in the House that Clarendon ought not to be penalised in any way, or even examined, but simply dismissed; and at the end of the 'Last Instructions', which he was writing at the same time, he regards the dismissal of Clarendon as merely one of the results of the nightmares of the guilty king, who will treat him as a scapegoat like the unfortunate Pett. Historians usually say that Clarendon was the last anchor for Charles, who behaved worse after he was gone; and that Clarendon had not been in any way responsible for the treacheries and disasters of the reign of Charles. There has been much doubt about this king; he spent a lot more money on fighting the Dutch than the French gave him to do it, and he might feel as a patriot, without any religious bias, that our Protestant brothers in Holland were simply our chief trade rivals. Marvell tried hard to induce Parliament to stop a war with Holland in 1674, and they did; the peace treaty was not glorious, but incidentally changed New Holland into New York. Few Americans will blame Charles for this. The Dutch language carries much good sense, but it is hardly flexible enough to unify a continent. Anyhow, it seems clear that Marvell, in this powerful attack on Clarendon, was adopting a familiar democratic procedure; he pretended to be ahead of his colleagues in what they wanted to do, or to be leading them, whereas really he wanted the leadership so as to do other things, in his case good ones, though he never had much political judgement. What is notable is that he now feels able to become a leader of men, which he had not done before.

This change would be at least supported by his marriage, and gives me an occasion to round off remarks about his sexual constitution; which may seem tiresome now, but it was readily discussed at the time. He is reported as saying that he would not drink with a man unless he would trust him with his life, and also as being accustomed to drink alone, over his books. We may readily believe that he talked in epigrams, which are misleading when reported; and he might merely be boasting that he carried secrets about business and politics. But these would be fairly easy to keep. When men get drunk together they often become affectionate, but do not want to make love, only to boast about their successes with women; and Marvell would long have felt that his embarrassment at this stage was itself a betrayal. He did not want to appear unresponsive, nor sexually timid, nor impotent, nor yet chaste by an effort of piety such as both friends would reject, and anyway he had few successes to boast of; but they were with young men, so that a true answer would amount to a demand for a perhaps unwelcome degree of confidence. This is presumably what A. E. Housman meant by the splendid line: 'Ask me no more, for fear I should reply'. But now, with a secret marriage behind him, he could answer with conviction that he regretted being unable to answer, but he had vowed secrecy to a lady. (Probably there was a time when she was only his mistress, and forbad him to tell; but now they were married, and he forbad her to tell.) It would sound rather swagger, an intrigue with a countess perhaps, but he could carry that off. Also (I expect) he had been much relieved to find that his reactions when in bed with Mrs Palmer were entirely normal; his previous experience had been very mangling. So he now felt equipped to get drunk with men, and thus coax them into doing what he wanted. The resulting poem won approval, as it is in four of the surviving manuscripts and was reprinted after the Stuarts had gone, though rather late (1697); but it is likely that he found the procedure disagreeable, as he only repeated it once, in 1671, when he was again eager for activity. Of course, he may have induced other drinkers to compose group poems, and that may have been his chief intention. He was a restlessly busy man, who cannot have spent much time in pubs.

The feelings of Mrs Marvell should next be considered, especially in her plans for the basic edition of his poems. Her recorded remarks say nothing about politics, and could not be expected to; but if her son Tom was getting a good job, and a good training, out of his help for the political schemes of Marvell, she would be warmly in favour, as she always sounds. Her capture of Marvell had been an immense relief for her anxieties as a mother; if her first husband had lived (he owned a tennis court in Westminster, and young Tom would eavesdrop on conversations there between important figures) their future could have been arranged; but there was no cushioning for the widow, as there is now, and though she could earn enough to feed them at present they could only grow up to be beasts of burden. Or worse: Tom, for one, would revolt and take to bad courses. So she was immensely in favour of Marvell, and his political plans, such as getting rid of the king, though she was naturally rather vague about them. After he had died, and she had received the annuity, she thought it her chief duty to carry out his intentions. Or go beyond them; he was so modest that he might not have expected his poetry written before the Restoration to be published, but it clearly ought to be, to honour his name, as it had most fortunately been left to her by the ignorant contempt of Farrington. She had had a mild taste for poetry when she was a girl, and the idea that such poetry had become out of date, which was now thrust upon her, seemed to her nonsense. She had heard him speak with careless contempt for his propaganda verses, written since their marriage, and anyhow they would be dangerous to print and hard to select, but this tidy collection of his earlier poetry he could not have wanted to remain ignored. Of course it should be printed as a whole.

The usual story here is that the cheating landlady was merely brought in to sign her name, while Farrington arranged a publication so as to bolster up his fiction of her widowhood. To whom could it need bolstering up, except the lawyers? But they had granted her the status and its rights two years before. It is hard to understand how Farrington could pay for anything while he was in debtors' prison, but he certainly would not want to be lavish about this edition, and lavish is the first thing you feel about it. If Farrington had published the poems, so as to encourage the friends of the housekeeper into supporting her claim, surely he would need to do it quickly and cheaply. The belated extravagant edition allows a year between the signed assurance by the sponsor (15 October 1680) and the title-page (1681).

The Restoration had brought in a very sharp change of literary fashion, and the earlier poetry of Marvell had become out of date. Of course, too, said the publisher, any praise of Cromwell must go out. Mrs Marvell, as she listened to him, became convinced that the entire text must be printed. The advance reports about Titus Oates had convinced her wise husband that the Stuarts would very soon be overthrown, and she and Tom were sure of it too; why need she bother about their restrictions? But as it turned out, the edition did not include the three poems about Cromwell, and the Stuarts remained in power for another ten years.

Legouis says in his biography of Marvell, assuming of course that the bogus wife can be ignored, that

The publisher had indeed thought of including in his collection the pieces in honour of Cromwell, possibly relying on the Whig fervour of the Parliament that met in October 1680 (the brief preface 'To the Reader' is dated the 15th of that month); but a dissolution soon followed, and the publisher's heart failed him; in the printing he stopped halfway through the 'Poem upon the death of O.C.', and this piece, like the 'An Horatian Ode' and 'The First Anniversary', disappeared from the copies put on sale.

This makes the publisher look pretty raw. He was Robert Boulter, described as experienced and capable; rather on the side of Marvell politically, as one would expect, but not likely to run a great risk with little to gain. Consider now: the main contention of 'The First Anniversary' is that Cromwell has proved himself so much better than any king, whether judged by a human or a divine standard, that he makes all real kings look farcical. This is said in general, but it was bound to apply mainly to Charles, who claimed to have been already King of England when it was written. The censorship was not in being just then, as it needed to be revived by a parliament, but the king's officials would be quite ready to act in such a case, and any judge not already committed against Charles would think the insult a plain one. A publisher would not haver and wonder, and wait to hear whether Parliament was dissolved, before deciding that he could not print it. Certainly, this was an important dissolution; the King played a trick to make it a dramatic surprise, when his opponents thought him cornered, and he never called a Parliament again. A further subsidy from Louis had arrived, just enough to keep him afloat, and afterwards the rise of foreign trade, since he had a traditional claim on the customs, made him able to manage so long as he avoided wars. Automatically, he had ended Parliamentary opposition, and this of course threw the opposing parliament men into dismay. But it would not have much effect on a publisher, whereas the dry description of the changes in Margoliouth's 'General Note on the Text' (*Poems*, p. 206) gives an impression of panic.

The two crippled copies of the book are only concerned to remove the final poem, on the death of Cromwell; the British Museum copy gets rid of the final two thirds of it, the other one all of it, printing one substitute page, to retain the end of the previous poem, as was done in the copies put on sale. But the affectionate farewell, in which traditional rhetoric could be discounted, was much less subversive than the other two printed together in the book, ending about ten pages before the farewell began. Presumably, the man who ordered these changes had not yet realised the presence of the more dangerous poems, which would be harder to get rid of. One might possibly argue that he first set the printers the easier task of the change at the end, and they began by muddling even that; but they were not as feeble as this theory makes out. Much more probably, he just demanded to have the final poem removed, at first making no suggestions about how to do it; and the printers were already rather disgruntled – Mrs Marvell had been giving them orders, under the pretence that Boulter had changed his mind.

Boulter would coax her till she at last agreed, as he supposed, that to print the Cromwell poems would be sheer waste of effort, as the book would be suppressed at once. She would feel, one might expect, that she had failed in her chief duty, that of getting the Cromwell poems into print. Even after being caught out, she may have planned for the success which she eventually achieved. Why, after all, did Boulter's firm hang on to the two abortive copies? They would take a lot of explaining, if his office came in for a police search, perhaps on some quite different ground. He might reckon that he could laugh them off, explaining that he had kept them as curiosities; but they would be an extra risk, and he would not really have felt proud of them. Mrs Marvell, I suggest, when she accepted the inevitable, had insisted that he must retain one or two copies of the missing poems, in secret, so that they could be printed when the Stuarts had gone. He promised, not wanting to make a determined enemy, and hoping she would even yet pay some more of his bill; perhaps at the time he even meant to keep his promise. But afterwards he would reflect that it was a very impudent demand, after she had shown herself so grossly untrustworthy, and would put him to a definite risk, probably for a long time. As a compromise, he would keep those two half-baked copies, which at least did not look like a conspiracy.

Why Cooke did not ask the publishing firm if they had scraps for his edition of 1726 I cannot tell, but it was the height of the Augustan period and he cared more for Marvell's politics than his poetry. By 1776, when Thompson was completing his edition, there was more interest in old poetry, but the publishing firm had probably dissolved, selling off its curios into private hands. Still, he found a variety of extra poems (many of them plainly not by Marvell) just as his edition was going to press, and added them at the end of the third volume. He claimed that some had the authority of family manuscripts, but his remarks are very confused, and Margoliouth, who displays great patience in dealing with this exasperating editor, says: 'He may have printed the Cromwell poems from manuscript, but he does not say so' (*Poems*, p. 212). The three cases are unalike. 'The First Anniversary' (of the Protectorship of Cromwell) was printed in 1655, when it was topical, but did not name the author, and reprints after the Stuarts had gone ascribed it to Waller. There is a bounce and hopefulness about it that make it agreeable reading, but this is within the reach of Waller too, and the only reason for ascribing it to Marvell is the botched edition in the British Museum. Thompson is no judge of authorship himself, but it sounds as if he is reporting someone who had looked at this text. And indeed, it would be natural for one of the grandchildren of Marvell's sisters, mocking at the prejudices of granny, to scout round on a visit to London for relics of their now famous ancestor. Of course Boulter would be gone, but any publisher who took over from him would be likely to hold on to his curios, from a dangerous time. The grandchild, arriving a year or two after Cooke's edition had aroused a mild interest in the topic (1726), would pay somebody to copy out the two middle poems but ignore the botched final one, even if they found the text containing half of it, as the family had got that already.

This theory, I should explain, gets round the difficulty of supposing that there could be family archives containing any of Marvell's poems, though in his lifetime no relation would have wanted them. But there is one exception: the poem on the death of Cromwell. Marvell had expected this to appear in an elegant volume with two other poets, and then found himself jostled out by Waller. It would be a painful snub; he, unlike Waller, really was writing out of personal contact and affection but must not boast of it; his admiring nephew William Popple, who gets some very lively letters at the end of the volume of letters, was then only eighteen, and seems never to have liked any poetry at all, but he was quite able to realise that uncle needed a soother. The young man would also despise Waller as a known coward. He asked permission to copy out the poem which he had been looking forward to reading in print, and showed uncle that he had really copied it. He probably never looked at it again, but he left it among his papers. Here Thompson actually could have claimed a family archive which was contemporary. Marvell was a secretive man, especially about his poems, especially after a snub, and it is hard to invent any other occasion when he would allow a copy.

We come now to the only good poem of the three, the 'Horatian Ode'. Here the historical approach is bound to be difficult, because what we admire in the poem is its capacity to see both sides of the question, which at the time would be liable to exasperate both parties; and Marvell himself would be ashamed of the bits in favour of the King, in case they were evidence of a juvenile confusion which nearly made him join the wrong side. I hope too he no longer wished that Cromwell had tried to conquer all Europe and dethrone the Pope. Maybe he showed the poem to Fairfax, in a confessional mood, but he would not show it to anyone afterwards. Probably these objections did not occur to his widow at all, and indeed they are far from obvious. She would think of the political poems as carrying the most important part of his message, so that being forced to leave them out of the book meant that all her efforts had failed. It was far worse than being snubbed and out of pocket. I think she would make one final effort to preserve them.

How did the two botched texts come to be preserved? They can hardly have been filched from Boulter's office by someone who wanted the forbidden poems to be printed, because in less than ten years Dutch William came, and a mass of such poems got printed, many of them ascribed to Marvell though very bad. If Mrs Marvell had lived another two years, we may expect, she would have got it done herself, from the documents which had been returned to her. On the other hand, it would not be surprising if Boulter himself felt that he had had enough of Mrs Marvell. I suggest that she extracted a promise from Boulter, who would be both indignant and impressed, that he would always keep in his office a copy of the rejected poems, so that they were preserved for better times. For the sake of peace he would agree at the moment, but afterwards thought it a fair compromise to keep only the botched texts.

She had behaved outrageously, and was now demanding that he should take a permanent risk; his office might be searched at any time. The advantage of these texts was that they could be laughed off; the searcher could be told that they were mementoes of a slight triumph by the firm, evading a promise. Still, in the one case of the 'Horatian Ode', the untutored behaviour of Mrs Marvell worked out as a triumph on her side, though she could not have imagined it would take a century.

Finally, a deduction may be put forward about the death of Marvell, which at the time was found curious. It came immediately after a visit to Hull, apparently the first since his marriage, at which he and his colleague Col. Gilby were given a modest banquet in the Town Hall, with the mayor and several aldermen; 'meat and wines' were provided. On 29 July, the Bench Book reports, 'the Court and Mr Marvell held several discourses about the town's affairs' (it does not mention Deputy Governor Gilby), and the death came in London on 18 August, not quite three weeks later. One would expect them to hear him soon after he arrived, so this made a short visit according to the custom of the time. There is no sign of a quarrel; on the other hand, there is a considerable silence. Tupper is good about the suspicion of poison, quoting a rival doctor who examined the case at once; this man blames Marvell's doctor for over-dosing, but is sure that he died of an ague. That disease no longer troubles northern Europe, so contemporaries of Marvell knew more about it than we do. However, it seems to have been the same as malaria, though carried by a more northern species of mosquito. Its southern cousin travels very little, seldom even crossing a slight rise of ground between two marshes; that is why the disease could be eradicated from northern Europe before the part played by the mosquito was understood – any marsh found to be dangerous was drained. There are reports of mass migration from a drained marsh, but not into a walled city; Marvell could not simply have caught malaria in Hull. Probably there were marshes known to be dangerous within a mile or two of Hull, and Marvell would be given the routine warning; just possibly, he was taken out with other city officials to consider drainage plans, but then there would be thorough precautions. Any risk he took would be taken alone.

It would be part of his work, both what the firms paid him for and what he did from public spirit, to get advance rumours of the Titus

Oates plot, which was elaborately prepared; and it would be his official
duty to inform the city of Hull. The details could not be sent by letter, so
he had to come home for it, which he had long been making excuses to
aviod. He was now feeling very hopeful. There is a report of his final
speech to the Commons, shortly before this visit north, which the
reporter probably makes sound sillier than it was, but on the kindest
view it is a series of laborious hints that some great event may be
expected. He and his friends were confident that Charles could soon be
thrown out, and he felt sure that Hull would be willing to co-operate, if
spoken to behind closed doors.

He met with a great shock. Hull thought it would take another ten
years to get rid of the Stuarts, and were not going to get their feet wet
meanwhile. (Ten years was what it actually took, and they could not be
quite so accurate, but they could come near it.) The excitements of a
London mob, though no doubt necessary, were mere machinery; how
much solid opinion, across the country, had been won over? Wait till
Charles's brother inherited; then the dynasty would drop like ripe fruit.
Meanwhile his in-laws were asking what good he had done to Thompson and Nelthorpe, with all his fuss? He had merely put them in a
different prison, and from all accounts not a healthier one. (Of course, if
the Revolution came quick enough, they could be brought out among
the heroes who had prepared for it, but not after ten more years.) As he
had probably heard, the Government now had proof that he had written
Mr Smirke and suchlike; he might expect to spend these ten years in jail.
And, though it was a less august disaster, his sisters had wormed the
secret of his marriage out of him as soon as they got him into a corner,
and kept on expressing their indignation.

Marvell was a stocky fighting type, though a deskworker of course, and
had been threatened with trouble on the tour to Russia for hitting out;
but he genuinely wanted peace, and would prefer to walk away from a
duel if the rules permitted. I suggest that he walked out from an evening
party at a house in Hull, and used his eminence to walk out through a
gate of the city, and walked for what remained of the night, indifferent to
the fatal marshes; and returned at dawn to take the first coach back to
London. As the coach jolted slowly on, and he got more and more

feverish, he would reflect on how thoroughly tricky his situation had become, on every side. When he at last got home, irritated all over, and his doctor suggested a risky medicine, as the 'tertiary' returned, warning him that it would cause a long deep sleep, he accepted that eagerly. Nobody expected to die from the familiar ague, tiresome though it was; that was no problem. But from a real deep sleep he would expect to wake up, as often before, suddenly seeing a way out, knowing what to do.

DRYDEN

A Deist Tract

There is no decisive proof that Dryden wrote the letter signed 'A.W.',
but for various concurring reasons the attribution is more likely than
not, so that the onus of disproof lies with the opponent. The question
is of literary interest because the poetical side of Dryden, his power to
make general remarks about all mankind with an air of exalted public
spirit, which was warmly appreciated in his tragic heroes, depends upon
the frank Deism of his treatment (imagine a character on his stage
telling Montezuma or Aurung-Zebe that they will automatically go to
Hell unless they are baptized). He would have written the tract between
1675 and 1678, and if you suppose him committed to this extent,
though privately, you understand his later development much better,
and may even give him credit for behaving well when teased. The whole
attempt of that time to bring Enlightenment into the Church of England
has its charm; I particularly like the rueful remarks let drop by the
Deist Archbishop Tillotson, when he was not deploying the powerful
double-talk of his oratory. The tract was first printed in *The Oracles
of Reason* (1693) by Charles Blount, as one of the letters which had
been sent to him, and was first attributed to Dryden in a Deist collection of 1745. A small book was published in 1747 answering the arguments of the tract, but no one denied its authorship; and this could
hardly happen unless the claim were true. Someone around seventy
would have said: 'My father wrote it; he was a much abler man' or 'That
whitewashed pig wrote it, who cheated my uncle'. The whole movement
had been a great subject for leisurely upper-class gossip. Blount would
be scrupulous about keeping the secret of his friend from print, but
would have seen no harm in telling his inner circle the name of their
great ally, if indeed Dryden had not announced it at one of his country-
house visits. Nowadays the attribution, if mentioned at all, is passed off
as a giggle, like saying that *Don Juan* was written by Queen Victoria in
her girlhood; but the presumption that Dryden had always been devoted
to the Incarnation is a very recent fashion. Sir Walter Scott thought it
obvious that he had been a Deist when he wrote his earlier plays, and

Coleridge became prone to give lengthy warnings against the Deism of Tillotson.

This topic is unfinished business for me. I had an article in the 1970 *Essays in Criticism*, pointing out a passage in *Religio Laici* where Dryden says you can ignore the belief that Jesus is God and still not go to Hell; and I actually wrote that we do not know the names of Dryden's Deist friends because of the Stuart religious persecution. A letter in answer came from Mr Phillip Harth, who rebuked my ignorance in general but did not let on that he had written a book, *Contexts of Dryden's Thought* (1968), containing much useful news. I came across the Deist Charles Blount for myself in the DNB, and was astonished by what emerges if you follow him up in the catalogue of the British Museum; you are thrown into the hubbub of a literary party. I was led to read Harth by the grand California edition of Dryden (Vol. II, 1972), which is very tight-lipped about the poem, anxious no doubt not to weaken the faith of the children by a careless word, but repeatedly refers (anxious also for truth) to the *Contexts*. He despises his Deists grimly, and expects them to be criminals in other ways beside the main one; but never mind, he has broken the ice, a needed procedure, even if the first result is cold water. His research is what convinced me that Dryden wrote this tract himself.

It was not considered a minor work in its time. Mr Harth describes a manuscript carefully prepared for distribution years before it could be published; he says it is the earliest Deist pamphlet he has been able to find (p. 113). The *Oracles* was the first publication of Blount after he had succeeded in getting rid of the Licensing Laws, under Dutch William; so he would give of his best, and the letter may have arrived long before. Blount himself has been proposed as the author, but the deception would be very unlike him; he was prone to encourage other men to write on these subjects, but not shy about using his own name. The letter ends 'Your friend without reserve, A.W.', which he would not care to invent. (Anonymous Wit we may read it, as a mnemonic for the initials.) By the time the letter was printed, Dryden had been a Papist for seven years, so he would no longer feel responsible for it; but his feelings might be hurt, and he might again be jeered at. Blount would certainly not wish to betray the old confidence. The reprint in 1745 is a selection of material from the *Oracles*, but the letter from A.W. has a special position on the title-page:

An essay by the celebrated poet John Dryden, Esq., to prove that Natural Religion is alone necessary to salvation, in opposition to all Divine Revelation. NB. This last piece contains the strongest argument against the Necessity and Advantages of a Divine Revelation yet published.

In the preface, the editor claims that he has been 'credibly informed by a gentleman of great learning and integrity' that Dryden wrote the letter. A second edition came out next year, and the year after that brought a refutation, of this letter only: you could not say that the affair is treated with silent contempt; and yet nobody questions the attribution. Presumably it was hard to deny.

As Mr Harth points out, the tract has an important point of likeness to the poem. Lord Herbert in his original *Religio Laici* (and in an earlier book) had said that we ought to worship the Supreme Authority chiefly by 'virtue joined with piety', but both A.W. and Dryden express this more warmly as 'prayer and praise'. Mr Harth deduces that Dryden worked from a copy of the tract, most probably borrowed from Blount himself. They were certainly acquainted, and it would not take great intimacy to borrow a tract; still, it presumes that Blount did not suspect Dryden of being a police spy. What is more important, I think, is that the same questions seem crucial to both Dryden and A.W., especially whether the justice of God towards the Red Indians can be defended. No proof can be won from this, but Dryden had long considered such questions in his plays, and did not need to learn of them from A.W. In the poem he had come upon an answer to them, not an ambitious answer, merely enough to allow Deists to become reconciled with the State Church, and help to support it.

I ought perhaps to add something about the style of the tract, as we literary critics are accustomed to tell authorship from that. It is written in the impersonal prose style which was then being developed. Dryden had acquired a grand style, whether or not from Tillotson as he said, which shows the careless ease of a gentleman, and is therefore exasperating for anyone who wants to refute the argument of his Preface or Dialogue; but this had to be arranged with labour, whereas in the tract he argues with direct force. One could say that it is like his arguing in verse, because he regularly quotes and answers an opponent. There are minor slips in the writing, repeated exactly in the edition of fifty years later, such as Dryden would have put right if he had seen his proofs. I have a difficulty in judging the argument, because it seems to me so plainly true; I cannot see why everyone else did not say it. An entirely forgotten man might easily have written the tract. But, of the well-known writers of the time, Dryden is the only plausible one.

I am now to tell the mildly entertaining story which had been hushed up, till at last Mr Harth bravely laid it bare. Only a few months after Dryden published his *Religio Laici*, presenting himself as a loyal Anglican, the well-known Deist Charles Blount brought out a prose work with the same title, earnestly thanking his friend Dryden for giving such valuable help to the honest side, which might well help to preserve the nation; and explaining that this title is what Lord Herbert of Cherbury had used when he first presented the theory of Deism. His own book, he says, merely helps the work forward with some practical deductions. As Mr Harth and his friends maintain that Dryden was always devoted to the doctrine of the Incarnation (the one thing that the poem does undoubtedly call unnecessary) he has to explain that this was a malicious trick by Blount, who 'must have known' that the poem is actually 'a severe attack on the Deists'. This claim, I do think, cannot survive reading the poem; the Deists are told, not that any one of their opinions is wrong, but merely that their opinions derive from the revelation made by God to Adam at his creation, which was handed down to the sons of Noah and hence to the Red Indians and all. The mission of Jesus Christ became necessary because the original revelation got so confused. Thus the poem is a statesmanlike attempt at reconciliation; the Deists need offer very little (if the Anglicans agree) to become loyal members of the State Church and free from their heavy liabilities. Blount of course knew that he was making fun of a false pretension, but only in an innocent way, because no civilized person would think any worse of Dryden for understanding this. Blount too was not opposed to having a State Church, and only wanted to make its tenets less discreditable. The insinuations of Blount, says Mr Harth, must have been very embarrassing for Dryden, who had already defended himself energetically against charges of atheism or impiety in his Preface to *Tyrannic Love* (1669), and still claimed to regard such defence as a duty even so late as the Preface to the *Hind and Panther* Part III; he has inserted, he says there:

that defence of myself, to which every honest man is bound, when injuriously attacked in print.

Mr Harth proves too much here. We can all imagine how the great satirist must have written a smashing reply; he was not only good at answering back, but he made it a point of honour. And yet he never printed anything about Blount at all, except a mild compliment in his old age, while introducing a group of translators. Surely this refutes the position of Mr Harth. Dryden was a bit shy of answering lords, it may be confessed, but Blount, though quite high among landed gentry, was not a lord. There are only two solutions; either Dryden dared not reply, because he could be made to look so ridiculous, or he did not consider himself insulted. In conversation he would claim the second, but the first was pretty certainly among the factors which cooled him down.

We are next to consider the Preface to *Tyrannic Love*, where Dryden had appeared indignant at the accusation of infidelity. He does indeed claim, in a bullying manner, that his view of Christianity is the right one, and that the Head of the Church of England agrees with him. It was probably true that Charles had encouraged him to write about Christianity in this vein; when the plot of Titus Oates was at last exposed, it turned out that a clergyman had been detailed to collect authenticated examples of what Charles said about Christianity, so that after he had been murdered he could be proved to have been unfit to be head of the Church (DNB). Dryden is trying to outface any doubts about his orthodoxy, or simply shout them down; and he needed to do this *because* they were so likely to arise.

The play makes a Christian saint convert a pagan philosopher, in a prominent debate, without any mention of the crucifixion, or the atonement, or even the name of Jesus Christ. I do not think the name occurs anywhere, though I would not care to read the play again to make sure. It is driven home that the greed of the heroine for a heavenly crown is precisely like the greed of other characters for an earthly one; fair enough, I daresay, but very near the edge of satire on the ideals which are being praised. This of course is a frequent result of Dryden's heroic technique, delighting in extremes; but it does not usually create so much strain as it does here. I think success had gone to his head rather. There is no need to suppose he had as yet a settled doctrine about Deism; he is writing for the

court of Charles II, and accepting its sceptical tone, also its taste for the
sweeping high-minded gesture. As to the King himself, his main opinion
seems to have been a rather sympathetic one, that God is not as black as he
is painted.

Mr Harth lays down in his preface that 'religious ideas in the plays are
to be explained ... by an understanding of the part they play in revealing
characters or in supplying the motivation for dramatic action'; hence they
cannot be used at all as evidence for the opinions which the author either
held himself or intended to recommend to others. Mr Harth will make no
mention of them in his book. I ought to report this scruple prominently,
because otherwise Mr Harth is liable to appear simply dishonest; it was
comic impudence for Dryden to present the play as a specifically
Christian one, and he expected his audience to be aware of it. They could
not foresee that W. K. Wimsatt was going to make a law forbidding them
to grasp the intention of an author. We should observe here a secondary
ill-effect of the Wimsatt Law, which operates very often though not
inevitably; the effort to ignore the author's Intention makes the critic
impute to him some wrong Intention. Mr Harth clearly feels allowed to
deduce from Dryden's Preface that he felt angry at having unorthodox
opinions imputed to him, so he assumes that he intended to express
orthodox ones, which nobody could think as a result of a direct experience
of the play.

A great change in Dryden's life, though he pluckily delayed the
recognition of it by keeping his temper, was marked by *The Rehearsal*
(1671). It is a good joke against him, and partly deserved, but it is also
against the expansive sentiments in his tragedies, which they need.
Perhaps it was rather a relief to be thrown out of Rochester's circle, as the
young men could be alarmingly disagreeable in their cups, but one must
realize that Dryden felt a romantic admiration for them. Rochester had
been born in 1647, Dryden in 1631, and it is remarkable that he had been
accepted at all. Some jackals in Oxford seized the occasion to bring out a
jeering pamphlet, pointing out 'solecisms' in the poetry of the plays; and at
this moment Charles Blount entered the life of Dryden, with a pamphlet
in answer. Taking the examples in order, he explains why the poet had
needed the variation from the usual formula which had excited the
jackals' contempt, and he can do this every time. It seems to me a most
impressive piece of work, which would be remarkable from anyone in the

period, and Blount was only nineteen. Mr Harth comments furiously: 'That juvenile effort was only the beginning of a succession of public compliments' which he supposes to have embarrassed Dryden. Dryden was not at all shy about compliments, and I expect he went and stayed at the country house pretty soon, as the lad turned out to be a respectable character. He was needing a new group of friends. (Both this literary work by Blount, defending Dryden, and the preface to Blount's *Religio Laici*, are now available in *Dryden, the Critical Heritage* by J. and E. Kinsley, 1971; but the brief tract signed A. W. must still be read in *The Oracles of Reason*.)

The father of Charles Blount had made a journey in Moslem countries and written a well-known book about it, later sitting on advisory trade committees under both Cromwell and Charles II. Charles was a younger son, but at the age of eighteen was provided with an acceptable wife and an adequate estate, including his own country house. He had been educated at home to save him from the immorality of the public schools. His father agreed in general with his religious opinions, and made minor contributions to his books. He printed nothing for some years after his defence of Dryden, and then opened a series of semi-clandestine short books with *Anima Mundi* (1679); this does not encourage the doctrine of immortality, but also shows that it is not universal among mankind (which Deists said it was). A rather quaint incident followed this publication; the first edition was burnt in London by some confident jack-in-office during the absence of the Bishop of London, but as soon as the Bishop came back another edition was printed and published. It shows the family was well thought of, even among the higher clergy. Indeed the whole movement was very upper-class; so far, Dryden would have no feeling of disloyalty in joining it. The effect was to make it dangerously ignorant of working-class movements of feeling.

An excellent recent *Life* of Bishop Wilkins (1970) by Barbara Shapiro estimates that if he had lived another twenty years (he died in 1672), being such an able negotiator, he would have become Archbishop of Canterbury and made the Anglican Church Unitarian. Very likely he intended so, but if he did he was mistaken; and when his disciple Tillotson accepted the office in 1692 he did it only to keep the peace. The Titus Oates affair had made evident what these characters ought to have know before, the extreme vehemence and suspiciousness of popular protestantism in the cities. It made a confused and prolonged row, starting in 1678; by 1679 Dryden would already realize that the Deists could not win. After that, he wrote political satires planned to discourage any vehement change in the present workable arrangement. Blount himself continued to speak up for the ideal; but he gives Dryden credit for taking part in a bold attempt to hold back the mob (Preface to his *Religio Laici*):

... And therefore; Sir, at this time, when the name of Christ is used to palliate so great villanies and Treasons, under the pretext of God's cause, against both King and Government, I thought I could do no less than snatch up all *weapons* that might defend the *Publick*, and hope I have not lighted upon one with a *Double Edge*.... I designed this Treatise of mine to be only an Addition or rather the Consequence, of yours; encouraging men to live up to the *Virtue* of that *Doctrine* which you preach. Which, with your Pardon for the present, and Friendship for the future, is the highest Ambition of / Sir, Your most faithful Friend, and Servant, C.B.

I expect that every word of this is from the heart, though of course he also knew that the situation was funny. The Latitudinarians inside the Church were in very much the same position as Blount (and Dryden was presenting himself as one); we hear the same exalted tone when Joseph Glanvil praises them, in 1676, saying 'they took notice what *unworthy and dishonourable* opinions were published abroad concerning God, to the disparagement of all his attributes, and discouragement of virtuous endeavour' as when Gildon, writing about Blount after his death, says 'He rejected any doctrine opposed to the perfection of God, but the age was too corrupt to suffer his virtuous endeavours'.

I wish I had room to describe the elegant trick by which he got the censorship abolished; it ought to be more widely known. His strange death came in the following year. His wife died, and he wanted to marry her sister, but here he encountered the Mosaic Law against marrying a Deceased Wife's Sister; he had already written against its being an English law, pointing out that in one book of the Old Testament the practice is enjoined as a duty. Having found that the Archbishop could not help him (or had trouble enough already) he shot himself, and died a month or two later in the lady's arms (he had also written in favour of suicide on due occasion). We are told that she felt remorse, so she must have realized it was possible to have a scholarly revival of a pagan-Roman marriage, at a grand party, and then take his name by deed poll; nobody she cared to meet would have despised her for that. It shows that the Blount milieu was conventional to a stifling degree, however freely they thought; after that death, he need not be regarded as an intriguing revolutionary.

Pope mentions his death as still well known, in the *Epilogue to the Satires*, but the argument hardly allows him to give his own opinion. 'We admire sin in the rich, and punish it in the poor' is his formula:

> If Blount despatched himself, he played the man!

– and so on; Blount's act is *usually* admired. Pope's later career, which in this poem he is looking back upon, had entirely depended upon the success of Blount in getting rid of the Licensing Laws (indeed, most of the grand literary record of the eighteenth century depended upon it) so Pope would behave badly if he jeered at Blount. A disgusting footnote is added in later editions, full of lies:

> Author of a foolish impious book called The Oracles of Reason, who being in love with a near kinswoman of his, and rejected, gave himself a stab in the arm, as pretending to kill himself, of the consequence of which he really died.

I was relieved to find that this first appears in the Warburton edition of 1753, after the death of Pope, so we need not blame Pope for it. Maybe the Bishop badgered him into agreeing to it while he was dying; but probably not, as he died in 1744. The 1745 reprinting of parts of *The Oracles of Reason* would be what made burying the book in ridicule seem to the Bishop a pious duty. The plan was successful, as Blount is seldom mentioned afterwards.

If not by Dryden, the tract would have been written soon after Wolseley's publication of 1672, to which it refers; but Dryden went on meeting that author, and I think only gradually reached a sufficiently theoretical frame of mind. *Tyrannic Love* (1669) and the two parts of the *Conquest of Granada* (1670) mark the peak of the public enthusiasm for his kind of heroic drama, and the *Rehearsal* appeared in 1671 – it had long been planned, first aimed at D'Avenant apparently, and many people had added jokes, but now was the time for it, the breaking of the wave. Dryden made no reply, perhaps because the attack was sponsored by lords, but he engaged in a tiresome quarrel with Settle, defending his *Conquest of Granada*, during 1673. In 1675 he brought out *Aurung-Zebe*, the last of his heroic plays in rhyme, generally considered the best of them; but the dedication when it was printed said that he had 'never felt himself very fit for tragedy', and that, as to comedy, many people in his time had written funnier ones. An author who talks like that is usually preparing to break out in another line. There seems to be a pause before he brings out *All For*

Love in 1678, his best unrhymed tragedy. In 1679, while the Titus Oates affair is getting heavy, he brings out an adaptation of *Troilus and Cressida*, and at the end of the year he is beaten up by hired toughs. It was time to begin writing political satires.

Dryden and Rochester still seem on good terms in 1672, at the dedication of *Marriage à la Mode*, the year after *The Rehearsal*; and Rochester in April 1676 (*The Rochester-Savile Letters*, ed. J. H. Wilson) at least affects to think that Dryden is the one making the quarrel: 'You write me word, that I'm out of favour with a certain poet, whom I have ever admired for the disproportion of him and his attributes: He is a rarity which I cannot but be fond of, as one would be of a hog that could fiddle, or a singing owl.' The famous threat of 'Black Will with a cudgel' then crosses his mind; probably he had nothing to do with the actual beating-up three years later, but it was always a real enough threat. Within a year he is writing (or at least accepting) a sort of dismissal of Dryden, without enmity, in *A Farewell to the Poets* (Poem LVII in Pinto's edition):

> In the head of the gang John Dryden appeared,
> That ancient grave wit, so long lov'd, and fear'd,
> But Apollo had heard a story i'th'town
> Of his quitting the Muses to wear the black gown;
> And so gave him leave now his poetry's done
> To let him turn priest, now Reeve is turned nun.

Various critics, C. S. Lewis perhaps in the most perceptive and needling way, have pointed out a coarseness and self-defeating clumsiness in Dryden's work; but one must distinguish this from any failure of intelligence or understanding. He is pretending to live in the magical world of the poets 'before the flood' (before the Civil War), and allowing his contemporary readers to pretend with him, though he can never feel really at home in it. He knows that a good deal has been lost, but knows how to make do with what survives. That is why he can flatter so shamelessly, imputing godhead with such frigid elaboration – he was in a make-believe situation anyway. Rochester does not think him a fool but surprisingly clever, a talking animal; and what he says is what they all want to hear, though not from him. This account is perhaps rather a literary myth (Donne could be just as frigid) but it is a myth that Dryden subscribed to, how thoroughly one cannot be sure; and he was a conscientious man-of-letters, considering how the literature could be kept up, as hardly any other English poet has been.

Mr Harth might claim the verses of Rochester as evidence that Dryden had become a pious Anglican, and no doubt he did talk things over with Latitudinarian parsons; but surely, if he had already become positively Anglican in 1676, as he was in 1682, he would not have taken six years to mention it in print – he explained himself very freely, especially in the prefaces. On the other hand, a serious bout of Deism he would need to keep quiet about, and this I think was the period when he wrote the pamphlet. Meanwhile his occasional writing treats in a grave manner the support of the lawful Government and the prevention of civil war; there was no need to be surprised at finding him sober and right-thinking when *Absalom* came out (1681). But there were always people who suspected him, and Luttrell wrote 'atheistical' on one of the surviving copies of the first edition of *Religio Laici* (1682). It is true that the political change was the first to be shown, and perhaps the religious one was little more than a scheme for a concordat.

He has avoided any hint of capitulation. The book he sets out to praise was considered frightening; it had recently been burnt in Paris, and a letter survives from the diarist Evelyn to a Bishop, warning him of the extreme danger of letting an English translation be printed. It was held to prove that the text of the Bible was untrustworthy. Dryden does not make much of this, treating it as a matter of course where so many priests have been concerned; so far from weakening his faith, the book has convinced him that the Bible has 'divine authority'. At least, Mr Harth says he 'stresses' (p. 193) ...

Simon's achievement in restoring the Scriptures from ancient error ... and implies that it reinforces the divine authority of the Bible. Indeed, he declares that his notions in the first half of *Religio Laici*, including his proofs that the scriptures are the repository of divine revelation, were bred by reading Simon's book.

Dryden compliments the translator halfway through the poem, as he turns to consider the author of the book, and welcome his arguments. So far, Dryden says, he has been speaking his own mind:

> Yet what they are, even these crude thoughts were bred
> By reading that, which better thou hast read:
> The Matchless Author's work ...

This does not commit Dryden to very much; and the next paragraph begins by telling us that 'Some, who have his secret meaning guessed, / Have found our Author not too *much* a *Priest*'. I agree that the official meaning would have to be that he sounded like a secret Protestant; but surely most readers could reflect that he was likely to be a secret Deist, and that Dryden himself feels a bit insinuating here.

Mr Harth, it soon turns out, though he was ready to welcome the theological confession of Dryden, is convinced that his compliment was insincere or at least that he had not yet found out how shocking the book really is. Now surely, a man who has been a Court wit at the side of Rochester may be idle and ignorant, but if he comes out with a mildly surprising paradox he is likely to know what he is saying. Besides, translating poetry from Latin and Greek was a long-term interest for Dryden, and he published some of this work the following year; the problems of translating texts of great political importance out of Hebrew would excite his curiosity. Simon talks about it in the right way for Dryden; thus, after merely touching on the question whether the Old Testament foreshadows the doctrine of the Trinity, he remarks (as with a graceful sigh) 'there is nothing more intricate in Scripture than the pronouns'. The book is in a plain terse style, effectively translated into English; and the index is very full and clear. Starting from that, Dryden would find himself among his central interests at once (I agree that he probably did not read the whole book, if that is all). The book says that Calvin's burning alive of Servetus had been the crucial event of the Reformation, in terms of political effect, by arresting it halfway; but that its intellectual development had gone straight on from Servetus through Laelius Socinus – that is, to the Deists (Book III Chap. xvi). 'He at once exploded the Mysteries of the Trinity, the Incarnation, Original Sin, and Grace'. Both Socinians and Protestants argue from Bible texts, neither defeating the other, and 'what is altogether strange is, that they both of them own the Scriptures to be plain and easy to be understood'. This argument is reported in the poem, followed at once by Dryden's own conclusion, that belief in the Incarnation is not necessary to avoid going to Hell. (Otherwise he could not maintain 'God would not leave mankind without a way'.) Here he was not merely trying to boost the sales of a dull book to oblige his publisher.

Simon does not give any reason for preferring either Anglicanism or Socinianism, but he does allow a good deal of freedom in the interpretation of the text, such as might allow the Bible to appear the best spokesman for the universal voice of mankind. The first fathers, he says (Book III, Chap. viii), thought that literal sense 'agreed only with the Synagogue', so they 'considered rather the Mystical Explanations'; indeed St Augustine (or Cardinal Perron?) observes that the same piece of scripture may be differently explained, and 'the Providence of God has given these many or several senses to the Holy Scriptures; but I doubt he stretches this principle too far. ... I doubt not but there are many places in the Bible, where God has been pleased to have different senses set down, but it is necessary that these places should be marked out, and the reasons that we have to give different explanations to these places ...'. It is heady stuff, especially for an author and translator, and probably did make Dryden feel a certain awe for the ancient text. The sentiment is jollied along by scholarly jokes, which Dryden would feel as anti-Puritan, on the ignorance of the tongues concerned which was almost standard among Luther, Calvin and their likes (Book II, Chap. xxiii): 'Luther blames himself sometimes for having too much followed the Rabbins; but we ought to pardon him a fault he was in no way guilty of, since he never understood how to read their books'. I expect Dryden read a good deal of this, wondering more and more about the secret meaning of the author.

The heroic couplet is perhaps a narrow instrument, but his mastery of it is so great that it betrays feelings he had meant to conceal – or else, its merit is that even while expressing one part of his mind forcibly it expresses contrasted feelings which he is only pretending to conceal. Whatever the cause, he sounds forced or phoney in the following couplet (it begins a paragraph):

> Then for the style, majestic and divine:
> It speaks no less than God in every line.

But we must not assume that he lies when he sounds like that; all we know is that he is trying to put something over on his audience, rather uneasily. The change in public literary taste, since the Bible had been published, had been extremely rapid and severe; it must have been usual to hear tittering in the churches, in the towns at any rate, when the required passages were read out. Some of the reports of Hebrew barbarity would deserve it, but often the text was being misunderstood, and Dryden was uniquely well equipped to know why the titters were wrong. Yet it would be bad tactics for Dryden to discuss the findings of Simon at length; what he needs to do is to give a blanket assurance, that Simon's work on the Bible leaves it intact and therefore ought not to be persecuted (Mr Harth agrees, p. 176, that Simon is now recognized as 'the founder of modern biblical criticism'). Dryden is embarrassed, in the honourable manner which became habitual for the Church of England, because he is working for a tacit compromise agreement, rightly believing that all the alternatives in view are worse ones.

I am next to consider the argument that Dryden had never heard of Lord Herbert's *Religio Laici*, so that he would be completely staggered when Blount published a third book of the same name, saying that he had taken the title from Herbert. Mr Harth says 'It seems unlikely that Dryden would consciously have adopted the title of a deistic book and risked giving the impression of having imitated, rather than answered, Lord Herbert's book.' Turning Dryden into a booby is carried to a wild extreme here. He would be certain to know about a scandalously heretical lord, whose last and worst publication was not yet twenty years old. For that matter, he would know that there had been a series of other books with similar titles, and would decide whether the resulting flavour gave him what he required. The over-all impression from *Religio Medici* etc. was broad-minded but not scandalous. And Mr Harth himself reports the proof that Dryden did know the final positively anti-Christian work of Herbert. He reflects there, looking back on the vast scope of his discovery, 'I have often thought myself more happy than Archimedes', and Dryden echoes this directly:

> The Deist thinks he stands on firmer ground,
> Cries Eureka, the mighty secret's found.

You might answer that Archimedes was tiresomely familiar in this role, so that two writers could easily think of him independently; but the system of Deism claims to point out the universal sentiments of mankind, and when Herbert regards it as a clever invention he betrays its basic absurdity. Dryden would not have thought of the comparison for himself – he insists that his approach is a common-sense one, and seems to realize here that the Deist looks comical.

There is one bit of textual evidence in the tract that Dryden wrote it, the paragraph about Sir Charles Wolseley. This landowner had been prominent under Cromwell, and Sir Robert Howard, a brother of Dryden's wife, a royalist like the rest of the family, introduced him to Dryden as the man who had saved him during that time. The introduction probably came before 1668, when Howard and Dryden had a disagreement. Howard had recommended Wolseley to the King at the Restoration, probably among other sponsors, so that he was allowed to keep his estate. He then gave up politics and wrote little books in favour of the Anglican position. One about the *Absurdity of Atheism* (1669) was a popular success, with a second edition within the year and an enlargement in 1675, but his follow-up in 1672, *The Reasonableness of Scripture Belief*, has no second edition. Mr Harth maintains that the poem of Dryden followed this book in order, detail by detail. Also he manages to find one fellow-preacher, a Nonconformist, who praises the work of Wolseley. The book has no chapters, headings, or index, and hardly seems to claim to have any order; it suggests a jovial though lengthy address to his cottagers in the village church. Fun is extracted from the sex-lives of sybils, houris, etc. (implying 'we learned men have fine opportunities to learn about such things'). Indeed, he is so frankly concerned to be on good terms with the audience that he sounds like a cheat when probably he is merely ingenuous, as in the eerie sentence: 'The eclipse of the Sun upon the Crucifixion of our Saviour (which, considering the position of the moon at that time,was prodigiously supernatural) was mentioned by many heathen writers which Eusebius says he himself had read.' Eusebius lays down that a Christian historian *ought* to provide evidence for his religion, wherever it is conspicuously lacking. You may answer that it is easy for us now to read the famous bits of Gibbon, the only source for my learning here; but Gibbon reports a number of earlier historians who had lamented the absurd lack of tact shown by Eusebius (and remarks that Pliny would have been sure to mention this eclipse). I suspect that Wolseley was rather an embarrassment to better-informed theologians. But he was on the right side; he said that the Creator had made a revelation to Adam, and that a Divine Revelation can only be trusted 'When what is taught agrees with Nature's laws'. No wonder he was a friend of Tillotson. We happen to know that Dryden stayed at his country house in 1680, but he had probably given Dryden a copy of the *Reasonableness* in 1672, fresh from the printer. The first and only edition would be ten years old when the poem was written, and Wolseley is not mentioned in it, but I expect Mr Harth is right about the order; Dryden might well find the book on his shelves and use it to remind him of the main heads. No other Deist would be likely to cite Wolseley as an authority.

The brief paragraph in the tract shows a curious mixture of feeling; warm approval is followed by abrupt withdrawal, but in a bracket, as if shyly:

Sir Charles Wolseley tells us, what is most true, that Mankind in all ages has applied to God, as guilty and offenders; that all have agreed an Expiation was necessary but looked to him for the Revelation of it. Therefore they used several Sacrifices and Lustrations, which they had, or thought they had, revealed. (This is so weak an argument for a Revealed Religion that it serves rather to destroy it.)

When Dryden deals with this question in the poem it is not very clear which side he has settled upon. The pagans, he is explaining, got into a wicked muddle about sacrifice, though they ought to have known better from the original revelation of the Creator to Adam, and therefore it was necessary for Christ to come on his mission. To expiate their conviction of sin, these pagans made animal and even human sacrifices, actually imagining they could bribe the Father by a Vicarious Atonement:

> Nor did *Remorse*, to *Expiate Sin*, prescribe,
> But slew their fellow Creatures for a Bribe.
> The guiltless Victim groan'd for their Offence;
> And *Cruelty* and *Blood*, was *Penitence*.

'Ah, at how cheap a rate the rich might sin.' Such objections could apply to the standard theology of the Redemption, whether in Aquinas or Calvin; and many of Dryden's first readers would take the line about the rich as a glance at the Papist Indulgences. And then again, surely Dryden did not think that Jesus had a mission to abolish the sacrifices in the Temple? The man who answered the tract in 1747 asserted roundly that nobody except Christians had ever felt a guilty need to be reconciled to their God, so that this impulse was wholly acquired through revelation. Probably this man, if confronted with the Psalms, would have said they didn't count (against his argument) because they too were inspired; but his classical education ought to have given him examples which are at least hard to explain away. (There is a very clear and strong example from the dawn of history – see *The Land of Shinar*, Leonard Cottrell, p. 150.) And yet there is clearly much sense in his retort; a yearning for unclouded intimacy with God is not universal, when you examine the anthropological data. The subject is genuinely confusing.

In the second passage, from the poem, Dryden is not simply accepting an argument for Christianity which in the tract he had called a bad one; we cannot be sure that he has changed his mind at all. It is clear from the affected jauntiness of the couplets that he feels uneasy about his relation to the reader; at least, it was clear to me (*Essays in Criticism*, 1970) before any reason for it had emerged. The tone is like his claim for the style of the (English) Bible which 'speaks no less than God in every line', and both are like the easy charms of Wolseley, when he is presuming upon the confidence of his reader. But why need Dryden bring this subject forward at all, if it embarrassed him? The critic is driven back to consider the main lines of interest of the author.

Dryden is always ready to ascribe high thoughts to the Noble Savage – he had invented the phrase; so he agrees with Wolseley (in the tract) that the aim of primitive religion is to win back the love of the Creator. All mankind agree with the Deists at bottom, the Deists maintained; but they would agree that the bottom is a great way down, and that men are often sadly confused. However Wolseley went on to insinuate, as many Christian apologists have done since, that the pagan sacrifices prove that the Crucifixion meets a basic need of the human soul. This argument Dryden when a Deist of course would not stand; indeed, the chief object in becoming a Deist was to keep at bay this barbarous conception of God. But when he has become a Christian, and has catered for the noble savage well enough by allowing him a share in the revelation to Adam, he can cheerfully say that the pagan sacrifices were very bad; they prove that the coming of Jesus was needed to restore the original revelation. His description of them amounts to a parody of the doctrine of Redemption; but he believed that he was offering (though unobtrusively) an alternative doctrine which was not barbaric, as I shall try to show; thus a tacit parody of the barbarous orthodoxy would fit in with the main plan. To be allowed to admit that most of primitive religion is not so high-minded as Deists made it appear would no doubt also be a relief to the ex-Deist. To sum up, the poem has an intimate and rather contorted relation to the tract at this point, hard to understand unless he had written the tract himself some years earlier. With Blount holding the text of the tract, and probably many of their mutual friends knowing about it (witness the copy planned for circulation), Dryden might well have found it too embarrassing to argue with Blount in public.

In trying to form an impression of the impact of such a poem, one needs to have some idea of the frame of mind of its intended readers. The British Museum Library is good at binding up anonymous pamphlets, and finding strategic places for them in the Catalogue; and the ones in rebuttal of Blount, especially the set listed as '701.i.10', give an illuminating picture. 'A True Son of the Church' writes on 'The Charge of Socinianism against Dr Tillotson, and G. Blount's *Great is Diana of the Ephesians*' (*Diana* came out in 1680, and has much the same material as *The Golden Bough*). Evidently the True Son was already uneasy, before he read these authors, about the likeness between the Christian sacrifice and the heathen ones; otherwise he would not have become so indignant about what Tillotson had meant for a soother (it is the very soother Wolseley had offered, thus irritating Dryden). Tillotson had suggested that God had arranged the Crucifixion because it would remind the pagans of their own rituals, which were already fitted to the depths of their natures:

As if he was incarnate for no other end but to make people *wonder* and Gaze, and because of the Mystery forsooth! And that he was Crucified, only to outdo *Rawhead and Bloody Bones*, the Inhumanity of the Pagan Sacrifices! That is, to cure the *Wickedness* and *Folly* of Men, by over-acting them in both

Plainly, the demand of the Christian God for appeasement *ought* to mean something much better, but this man never suggests what it can be; he merely knows that Tillotson has trodden on a sore place. He compares the passage to one in Charles Blount about the same painful topic. Some apologists had explained that the Crucifixion was planned to end all human sacrifice; the horrible thing could never be done again, after it had been accepted by Jesus. Blount answered that burning heretics alive, in order to appease God, gives precisely the same evil pleasure and merely changes its name. The True Son denounces this too, but he feels as usual that the open heretic is less bad than the false priest:

he does not go so far as his master Dr Tillotson, to make the Sacrifice of Christ, and other institutions of the Christian Religion, to be only a Compliance with the *Wicked* and *Diabolical* Fancies of Men, in the Bloody Sacrifices of Beasts and Human Kind, etc.

('etc.' is used here to include the Godhead of Jesus). These two quotations, I submit, are enough to show that the deepest objection to Christianity, that is, the doubt whether a God who could be satisfied or appeased by a Crucifixion was a good God, or a safe guide to follow, was very present in the minds of these people, though not expressed so clearly or so often as by the Romantics a century later. It had only recently entered their minds. That splended work *The Decline of Hell* (D. P. Walker, 1964) quotes the intelligent Bayle reporting with mild surprise that he feels a 'je ne sais quoi', as if it had diffused into his study with the air, 'qui choque' at the belief that God makes the blessed in Heaven enjoy gloating over the tortures of the damned (p. 30). Because of their impalpable origin, such feelings might attack even loyal churchmen; hence the danger of people 'boring from within', which was often suspected and sometimes occurred. Deists liked to say that reactionary priests tricked the people into superstition, but they lived among enlightened priests, rather timidly trying to trick the people into giving it up. No wonder the True Son is more indignant with Tillotson than with Blount, who at one point 'shows great respect for the *Socinians*, because they show nothing of Christianity but the name.... Whereas I can tell you, Sir Positive (and ask your Priestcraft at Lambeth if it be not true) that the *Socinians* do differ....' Much effort was dvoted to defining these technical terms, with little success. It would be wrong to end with this picture of Tillotson as a snakelike intriguer. About a month before he died, there were a number of questions of policy to be reviewed, one of them about the Athanasian Creed: 'I wish we were well rid of it,' he wrote cosily. The complete selflessness of this, while knowing his own release to be so near, makes it deserve a high place among Last Words.

Mr Harth tells us that Dryden was merely ignorant when he supposed there was any problem about the justice of God, as the question had long before been officially settled. I expect Dryden would have answered that Mr Harth is too ready to be fobbed off by an official reply. St Thomas Aquinas, in a well-known passage, had laid down that even an ignorant savage might be saved 'if he followed the guidance of natural reason in seeking good and avoiding evil', because 'God might by internal inspiration reveal to him what had to be believed'. He does not explain just how much would have to be believed, but one would expect from analogous cases that he must at least know the name of Jesus, in some recognizable linguistic form, and probably know how to bear witness by crossing himself. Most Anglican authorities thought it would take a special miracle. But Tillotson, being a Latitudinarian, did not consider that any vision or instruction would be required : 'such men might be accepted by that Lamb of God, which, in respect of the virtue and the efficacy of it, is said "to have been slain before the foundation of the world" '. I do not know what use had been made of this text before (Rev. 13. 8); as Tillotson uses it, none of us need have heard of Jesus, and yet we might be saved, not through nature, but by the justifying grace of his Atonement. This (I submit) is clearly what Dryden meant to imply, in one of those passages of the poem which carry warmth and conviction:

> And though no Name be for Salvation known
> But that of his Eternal Son alone,
> Who knows how far transcending Goodness can
> Extend the *Merits* of *that Son* to Man?

The theoretical difference may appear slight but the practical one is large. Mr Harth seems to approach these debates as a Public Relations Officer, not as a member of the public who might get caught when the concessions were interpreted; and the ear alone should be enough to tell a literary critic that the tender courtesy of Aquinas here is a fob-off. A Papist missionary in an up-country district could report, and probably would, that no such case had emerged from the neighbouring tribesmen; but the Latitudinarian missionary next door to him could not even estimate the frequency of these salvations. Also the lines just quoted, if you give sufficient weight to the rhyme-word *known*, may even suggest that a different Redeemer could be known to the men on the moon (each Redeemer would be an avatar of the Lamb slain before the foundation of the world). This would be particularly subversive, because almost every sect had felt the need, like a quack doctor, to market the only cure; but the Anglicans held the honourable distinction of leaving the claim in doubt. If the Church of England would allow a communicant to go as far as this, there could be little reason for a Deist to expose himself to persecution.

But it was widely felt, and surely with some reason, that here was where the boundary lay, and that Dryden and Tillotson were themselves on the Deist side of it.

The Hindu conception of an avatar is likely to have been important here, though it might be described as merely a way of not bothering about the status of Jesus. Dryden is sure to have known about the *Life* of Apollonius of Tyana, written by a Philostratus between AD 200 and 240. He appears as an extremely high-minded philosopher, like Jesus in every way except that his father did not get satisfied by having him crucified. He was 'divinely begotten' by Proteus, who told his mother when the time came that she was 'about to bring Proteus himself to birth'. This of course would not be said in earlier times about a son of Zeus or Poseidon. Traditional Romans had long been complaining about the importation of 'oriental' religions, and now Christians were making the same complaint; in this detail, I suggest Philostratus probably was influenced by Hinduism.

We may now turn to the deeper objection. It seems natural to ask what prevents Blount from saying, as Shelley did: 'The more we reverence the Son who endured, the more we must execrate the Father who was satisfied by his pain.' It does get said, by Lord Herbert of Cherbury, but in a very mumbling way, and in Latin, and in Amsterdam, and after he was dead; probably he feared persecution for it: 'How could Adam's sin have been so terrible that his descendants, innocent of his crime and in no way approving of it, could be so delivered up to eternal torment that, after so many centuries, God could only be placated by a more than human victim?' The priests, he goes on, had better explain themselves in a manner intelligible to the layman (if they can contrive to think of anything decent to say, he does not add). Now, it is a most unexpected thing, but Dryden's poem carries an answer to this query, one which is still current and appears to be his own invention.

I was often abashed, reading C. S. Lewis while I was writing *Milton's God*, by the awe and wonder with which he treats the doctrine of the Atonement as meaning that God himself endured torture for the sake of man; he seems to have assumed that this was the traditional interpretation. There can be no possible complaint against such a doctrine; it clears the Father absolutely, and deserves the astonishment with which Lewis surrounds it. To be sure, the reason why the Crucifixion was needed at all is now an even deeper mystery since the Father cannot be supposed to demand it; and I may be told that no Christian had ever ascribed to him a bad motive for demanding it. But the effect of the change is to give assurance that he had no bad motive, and the suspicion of one is (plainly, I think) very liable to nestle at the back of a Christian's mind, where it does him harm. The usual explanation is that disobedience to God's laws had offended his dignity, and that he has a duty to keep up his dignity; but this is hard to distinguish from spitefulness. It might be a valid argument for a human king, who can actually lose his dignity, but surely God could not. And yet this idea that the Father suffered, when it is considered by theologians, is greeted with execration as an extreme offence to his dignity. They do consider it, because a group of theologians existed during the third century called the Patripassians, perhaps only so called in mockery by their victorious opponents. Their main aim was to insist upon the unity of the Godhead; at that date, Christians might still be mocked by pagans for making Jesus a second God. The authors of *The Encyclopaedia of Religion and Ethics* are generous-minded men, keen to recognize merit, but they do not report any quotation even hinting at a moral interest felt by the Patripassians in the doctrine they are named after. It cannot have occured to them that they were altering the motives of the Father from suspicious ones to very good ones; or they would have made enough of this point, in their desperate theological battles, to win some clumsy refutation from those who report their defeat. The heresy itself is explicitly rejected by Aquinas, and by Hooker, for example, in passing. Having no body, the Father is incapable of bodily pain; this seems to be the basic argument. But he is certainly able to appreciate pain; the Son, having a perfect constitution fashioned miraculously by the Holy Ghost, had an extremely acute sensitiveness to pain, and this made a notable addition to the gratification of the Father (*Summa Theologica*, Part III, Question 46, Article 6). Hooker is not luscious about it in this way, being preoccupied with the difficulty of getting a formulation that stands on the knife-edge, but for him too the transcendentalism of Lewis is a closed book (*Polity*, Book v, Chap. 51). I do not remember that the belief gets suggested even as a wild fancy among all the conceits of the Metaphysicals. And yet Dryden takes it for granted when he defends the Atonement, implying 'If you join us Anglicans, and find the Father too oppressive, you are entitled to imagine ...' – a wholly innocent process of Redemption:

See God descending in thy Human Frame;
Th' *offended*, suff'ring in the' *Offenders* Name:
All thy Misdeeds to him imputed see,
And all his Righteousness devolv'd on thee.

Surely, nobody ever said that the Son was offended by the eating of the apple. Dryden had consistently avoided expressing any sympathy with the central plot of the Christian drama, but here he has to recognize it; so he assumes that the Father suffered too. There is unlikely to be any learned source for the idea; I expect he had got it from his old nurse when he was a child. The peculiar horror of the orthodoxy of the holy-lawyers did not enter the popular mind except when it had been whipped up into hysteria.

I do not deny that other paradoxes about the Trinity were quite frequent, as when Crashaw remarks in his version of the *Dies Irae*, 'But thou giv'st leave (dread Lord) that we / Take shelter from thy self, in thee', or when Dryden after he has become a Papist says that no act of belief seems hard after accepting the Incarnation – 'that the great Maker of the world could die'; but that the Person who required the appease-ment also suffered the pain does not get said, even as a conceit, and was known to be a heresy.

One might expect, however, that someone else within earshot of Dryden was thinking along those lines at the time, and a likely one is Thomas Firmin (1632–97). This was another friend of Tillotson, a wealthy business man and philanthropist, who wrote very little himself but commissioned a 'History of the Unitarians' by various hands, apparently the first use in print of this term. A *Life* of him (under *Firmin* in the British Museum Catalogue), published in 1798 'by one of his most intimate acquaintance', is anxious to explain that these people were practically Anglicans, indeed the difference of doctrine was hardly more than a verbal misunderstanding. 'Jesus is Man ...'

in respect of his reasonable Soul and human Body, God, in respect of God in him.... the Divinity was and is always in Christ, illuminating, conducting, and actuating him ... the Persons are internal relations of the Deity to itself ... the three are internally conscious to each other's thought ...

This system of belief is 'what he and his party call Unitarian, but others Socinian' – though according to Dryden 'the bold Socinian' said 'He's but Man'. The DNB4 (article signed A.G) says that Firmin 'never departed from the Communion of the Church of England, but put a Sabellian sense upon the public forms'; he had a plan for allowing Deists to use Anglican churches for their meetings. The *Life* often uses the term 'Sabellian', but never defines it. The two extreme theories about Jesus seem to get confused here, and oddly enough the same confusion clings to the memory of Sabellius himself, a disciple of the Patripassians in the generation after them. He was still being cursed by a Council of Rome about 380 for having said that the Father is the same as the Son, and yet he is reported to have denied that the Father was tortured by the Crucifixion (perhaps for fear of getting tortured himself), and even that the Son existed at all before his human birth. It was Heraclitus the Obscure, another member of the same group, who expressed the view celebrated in *Ulysses*, that the Creator . . .

when it pleased him to undergo generation, having been begotten, himself became his own Son, not another's.

It is thus hard to be sure what was in the mind of Firmin, when he sat in church interpreting the liturgy in a Sabellian sense; but at least we cannot presume that such men were all 'materialists', following Hobbes, as is now usually supposed. Perhaps they merely felt that Sabellius had justified freedom of conjecture.

We would probably be taking a different view of Dryden's *Religio Laici* if Charles II had lived a few years more. When he died, Dryden was lining up the first versions of *Albion and Albanius* and *King Arthur*. Having accepted the Church of which his King was the head, he was prepared to offer worship such as the first Charles had received, and he would have struggled to make the ritual sufficiently popular. Dryden was working on an ambitious programme when Charles yet again did the inconvenient thing; and one can understand that continued loyalty to the Stuarts may have struck him as the only dignified exit after the collapse of his hopes. Maybe we had a lucky escape.

Looking Back

'A Deist Tract by Dryden' reprints the second of two articles about Dryden, in *Essays in Criticism* for 1970 and 1975; naturally, most of the arguments in the first one had to be worked into the second, after so long a gap; so the first one need not be reprinted. And yet, as often happens in controversy, the starting-point had become ignored. I had set out to say: 'The whole tone and style of Dryden prove that he is not churchy, as the neo-Christians pretend; his moral position is that of the Enlightenment.' What then are we to make of his last fifteen years, when he writes in much the same style as a converted Papist? His behaviour has long been recognized as a puzzle, and what little I can add comes mostly from the first article.

Near the end of *Religio Laici* we find him in his normal state of muscular vigour about priests:

> When want of learning kept the *laymen* low,
> And none but *Priests* were *Authoriz'd* to *know*;
> When what small knowledge was, in them did dwell;
> And he a God, that could but *Read* or *Spell*;
> Then *Mother Church* did mightily prevail;
> She parcel'd out the Bible by *retail:*
> *But still expounded* what She *sold* or *gave*;
> To keep it in *her power* to *Damn* and *Save*.

This tone of plain-man jeering in Dryden, so very unseraphical one would think, cannot simply be ignored in an estimate of his religious views. To be sure, it was then usual – Coleridge called it the blackguardism of the Restoration style; but nobody else could do it so well, and the leader of a fashion must be supposed to have an emotional commitment to it. And another fashion which he led, we should remember, is the Heroic Drama. Noble sacrifices were fully in his line of sentiment; it was only the peculiar lay-out of the sacrifice of the Son to the Father which he would not have used in a play of his own. It would be wrong to deduce that he had no heart; his heart could be stirred by large public issues, and this was the root of his dramatic power. Consider *The Indian Emperor* (1667), his first tragedy, written when he was about thirty-five, which established his

reputation. The extreme highmindedness and enlightenment of Montezuma, already made clear in the first act, evoke astonished admiration in
the last scene of the play. There he is racked on the stage by 'Spaniards,
and a Christian priest' to make him hand over the remaining gold of the
Aztecs, and the priest ridiculously argues that he has a duty to give this
gold to the Christians, because their endurance as martyrs proves their
religion to be true:

CHR. PR. But we by martydom our faith avow.
MONT.   You do no more than I for ours do now.
           To prove religion true –
           If either wit or sufferings would suffice,
           All faiths afford the constant and the wise.

It is clear from the break in the couplets that the audience was meant to
wait for this as a tremendous hit, and indeed the gonglike reverberation of
Dryden is never more splendid. Montezuma is fully abreast of the theory
that God cannot have left him without a way – 'all must know enough for
happiness' – and is at once ready to mock the assertion that the Pope is
unerring – 'Man, and not err?' In the first act he kneels to Cortez as a god,
thinking his courage and endurance superhuman, so he would have been
quite ready to accept the God of his conqueror, had he not also met
contemptible Christians such as the Priest. Here for the first time the
enlightened Anglican would meet a theological puzzle. It had been
agreed, as only fair, that Indians who had had no opportunity to hear of
Jesus might go to Heaven if they were good enough; but we see Montezuma just at the time when he rejects this opportunity, and the least
impious reason would be that he finds the religion to be preached by bad
men. Yet the audience must expect him to go to Heaven, when he kills
himself a few minutes later ('O powers divine, Take my last thanks').
Dryden made a bold innovation on the first night, handing a printed
pamphlet round the audience (he was mocked for it in *The Rehearsal*); the
last paragraph reads:

The difference of their religion from ours, I have taken from the story itself;
and that which you find of it in the first and fifth acts, touching the sufferings and
constancy of Montezuma in his opinions, I have only illustrated, not altered, from
those who have written of it.

We tend to think of the Tragedy of Admiration as admittedly unreal, aimed at describing almost farcical characters, but here the young Dryden is labouring to authenticate his anecdote, like Wordsworth with a legend about a cottager. He is showing generous public spirit, a thing which is somehow felt as particularly manly; and it is a tone of feeling which he never lost. But he never came to write in this ringing way about Redemption through Crucifixion; he can argue for the conception, but it is outside his sympathy.

And yet, only five years later than *Religio Laici*, though now under a Papist king, he is writing *The Hind and the Panther*, mostly theological argument, but attempts are sometimes made to grant the symbolic animals a breath of life. In III. 145 the Hind tells the Panther that any form of Protestantism is liable to make people doubt the divinity of Jesus, which will involve them in eternal torture. Sources of evidence are discussed for about 150 lines, by which time the Panther has been brought to agree that it would be better to have an infallible judge, but where, it asks, can you find one? 'The Dame' feels that this offers her a decisive retort:

> And looking upward to her kindred sky
> As once her Saviour own'd his Deity,
> Pronounced his word – *she whom you seek am I.*
> Nor less amazed this voice the Panther heard
> Than were those Jews to hear a god declar'd
> Then thus the matron modestly renewed:...

I said that Dryden was showing his famous clumsiness here, as he presumably expected reverence for 'this simpering herbivore'; but my sarcasm was stupid, almost like Leavis. Actually, the lines are a rare breath of poetry in that dismal mass of grumbles against all the opponents of Rome. How he expected them to be read is another matter. Consciously or not, they presume that the theological differences between Anglicans and Papists concern matters beyond our knowledge; we are like children when we think about them, and nursery talk is the best we have. Of course this attitude makes persecution look especially wicked, and maybe Dryden, as he thought all priests wanted to do it, and was himself a strong royalist, thought that all sects should be controlled by the secular arm. When he wrote he cannot yet have seen much of the administration of James II. Anyway, such an attitude is highly Deist, assuming that all religions hold something of the truth though much obscured. An opponent at the time, in a letter which has happened to survive (*Life of Dryden*, C. E. Ward, p. 233), remarks that it is a miracle to move 'from a declared patron of Atheism to a zealous champion for Catholicism' – except that it shows what *that* is really like. (Atheism was often used to mean not believing that Jesus was God.) No doubt he chiefly means that Dryden had been bought.

This would not be very bad, in a man who thought it a duty to support his king, especially a new one, and thought nothing of the points of doctrine concerned. Also there was a strong personal pressure on Dryden. He had married a lady of aristocratic birth and social prominence, who became converted to Rome, maybe first as a matter of fashion but in earnest later; and to her the arrival of James II was an awaited opportunity. Her husband had never stood in her way (there was some talk abut her having lovers, but the three boys were admittedly his), and now his conversion brought her a house in the newly erected Gerrard Street, not half a mile north of St James's Park, and perhaps actually in earshot of Charles's cormorant. We hear of her taking a charitable interest in young men who had been made Fellows of Oxford colleges by direct order of the new King; naturally they crept away to London, feeling miserable, as often as they could. Anything to do with this project would sound like doom to Dryden; James II, he would feel, could not have hit on anything more certain to estrange all respectable opinion. And yet he would feel more 'undemocratic' than ever; Puritans had always annoyed him, and those recent Protestant mobs, yelling to murder anyone pointed at by Titus Oates, had left a scar on his mind. He could plug away at writing his sectarian gibes quite conscientiously.

No one has been puzzled at his joining Rome to gratify the new king, though various critics have tried to excuse it, as I have been doing. But why did he stick to it for the rest of his life, twelve years of fines, disabilities, and casual insult, in a hopeless cause? It was the dignified thing to do, but surely dignity might have been placated at less cost. And yet there was some point in his asking, with a glance at his old mentor Tillotson, what there was that he could change back to. He might indeed have announced himself as a Deist, but that would bring worse penalties than he had already, and much tiresome quarrelling which would probably involve old friends. As it was, he could be as rude to priests as ever. Near the end of his life, he modernised the English of the *Parson's Tale*, out of piety no doubt; but he remarked in a letter that he was still free:

if I shall think fit hereafter, to describe another sort of priest, such as are more easily to be found than the Good Parson; such as have given the last blow to Christianity in this age, by a practice so contrary to their doctrine.

Not much can be deduced from this, as it is only a heightened form of what he had long been saying; but he is still using a standard Deist line of talk.

There was also a simple line of argument, which probably decided the last action of Charles II: that the cats said all prots would go to Hell, but the prots (or some Anglicans at least) admitted that some cats would not. It was therefore safer to become a cat at the end. This is not cynical; in moods when such people really did believe in God, they accepted the ample evidence that he was like a capricious earthly king. In Dryden the argument would probably take one step further back. A dying man has weakened resistance to superstitious terrors, and is often tormented by fear of Hell; as an insurance against that, it is as well to secure in advance the attentions of an expert. It is no discredit to Dryden that he was capable of thinking like that, probably to defend a choice which he had already made on other grounds. Here the decisive factor, it seems plain, was his wife. The collapse of James, though it had been widely foreseen, would be a great shock to her, and meant the end of all her hopes. She had become demanding and tiresome and had lost her beauty, but she had opened doors for him and he felt some gratitude; also, deeper than that, she was a romantic ideal, the kind of woman he wrote comedies about. He could not break with her now, even though it might be a way of saving her from the worst consequences of her folly; he would not care to break with the sons she had misled. He felt that everything had gone badly wrong; his voice is ringing with manly conviction at the close of his life, and of his century:

> 'Tis well an old age is out,

– though the stage performance is apparently meant to be comical. He would stick to the maxim with which he ended *Religio Laici*:

> For points obscure are of small use to learn:
> But *Common quiet* is *Mankind's concern*.

FIELDING

Tom Jones

I had been meaning to write about *Tom Jones* before, but this essay bears
the marks of shock at what I found said about the book by recent literary
critics, and my students at Sheffield; I had to consider why I find the book
so much better than they do. Middleton Murry was working from the
same impulse of defence in the chief of the *Unprofessional Essays* (1956)
written shortly before he died; I agree with him so much that we chose a
lot of the same quotations, but he was still thinking of Fielding as just
'essentially healthy' or something like that, and I think the defence should
be larger. Of American critics, I remember a detailed treatment of the plot
by a Chicago Aristotelian, who praised what may be called the calculations
behind the structure; I thought this was just and sensible, but assumed the
basic impulse behind the book to be pretty trivial. English critics tend to
bother about *Tom Jones* more than American ones and also to wince away
from it more, because it is supposed to be so frightfully English, and they
are rightly uneasy about national self-praise; besides, he is hearty and they
tend to be anti-hearty. What nobody will recognize, I feel, is that Fielding
set out to preach a doctrine in *Tom Jones* (1749), and said so, a highminded
though perhaps abstruse one. As he said after the attacks on *Joseph
Andrews* (1742) that he would not write another novel, we may suppose
that he wouldn't have written *Tom Jones* without at least finding for
himself the excuse that he had this important further thing to say. Modern
critics tend to assume both (a) that it isn't artistic to preach any doctrine
and (b) that the only highminded doctrine to preach is despair and
contempt for the world; I think the combination produces a critical blind
spot, so I hope there is some general interest in this attempt to defend *Tom
Jones*, even for those who would not mark the book high anyhow.

Fielding, then, is regarded with a mixture of acceptance and contempt,
as a worthy old boy who did the basic engineering for the novel because he
invented the clockwork plot, but tiresomely boisterous, 'broad' to the
point of being insensitive to fine shades, lacking in any of the higher
aspirations, and hampered by a style which keeps his prosy common-
sense temperament always to the fore. Looking for a way out of this clump

of prejudices, I think the style is the best place to start. If you take an interest in Fielding's opinions, which he seems to be expressing with bluff directness, you can get to the point of reading *Tom Jones* with fascinated curiosity, baffled to make out what he really does think about the filial duties of a daughter, or the inherent virtues of a gentleman, or the Christian command of chastity. To leap to ambiguity for a solution may seem Empson's routine paradox, particularly absurd in the case of Fielding; but in a way, which means for a special kind of ambiguity, it has always been recognized about him. His readers have always felt sure that he is somehow recommending the behaviour of Tom Jones, whether they called the result healthy or immoral; whereas the book makes plenty of firm assertions that Tom is doing wrong. The reason why this situation can arise is that the style of Fielding is a habitual double irony; or rather, he moves the gears of his car up to that as soon as the road lets it use its strength. This form, though logically rather complicated, needs a show of lightness and carelessness whether it is being used to cheat or not; for that matter, some speakers convey it all the time by a curl of the tongue in their tone of voice. Indeed, I understand that some Americans regard every upper-class English voice as doing that, however unintentionally; to divide the national honours, I should think the reason for the suspicion is that every tough American voice is doing it too. Single irony presumes a censor; the ironist (A) is fooling a tyrant (B) while appealing to the judgement of a person addressed (C). For double irony A shows both B and C that he understands both their positions; B can no longer forbid direct utterance, but I think can always be picked out as holding the more official or straight-faced belief. In real life this is easier than single irony (because people aren't such fools as you think), so that we do not always notice its logical structure. Presumably A hopes that each of B and C will think 'He is secretly on my side, and only pretends to sympathize with the other'; but A may hold some wise balanced position between them, or contrariwise may be be feeling 'a plague on both your houses'. The trick is liable to be unpopular, and perhaps literary critics despise its evasiveness, so that when they talk about irony they generally seem to mean something else; but a moderate amount of it is felt to be balanced and unfussy. The definition may seem too narrow, but if you generalize the term to cover almost any complex state of mind it ceases to be useful. I do not want to make large claims for 'double irony', but rather to narrow it down enough to show why it is peculiarly fitted for *Tom Jones*.

There it serves a purpose so fundamental that it can come to seem as massive as the style of Gibbon, who seems to have realized this in his sentence of praise. He had already, in Chapter xxxii of the *Decline and Fall*, describing a Byzantine palace intrigue, compared it in a footnote to a passage of *Tom Jones*, 'the romance of a great master, which may be considered the history of human nature'. This would be about 1780; in 1789, discussing ancestors at the beginning of his *Autobiography*, for example the claim of Fielding's family to be related to the Hapsburgs, he said, 'But the romance of *Tom Jones*, that exquisite picture of human manners, will outlive the palace of the Escurial and the imperial eagle of the House of Austria.' This has more to do with Fielding than one might think, especially with his repeated claim, admitted to be rather comic but a major source of his nerve, that he was capable of making a broad survey because he was an aristocrat and had known high life from within. I take it that Gibbon meant his own irony not merely to attack the Christians (in that use it is 'single') but to rise to a grand survey of the strangeness of human affairs. Of course both use it for protection against rival moralists, but its major use is to express the balance of their judgement. Fielding is already doing this in *Joseph Andrews*, but there the process seems genuinely casual. In *Tom Jones* he is expressing a theory about ethics, and the ironies are made to interlock with the progress of the demonstration. The titanic plot, which has been praised or found tiresome taken alone, was devised to illustrate the theory, and the screws of the engine of his style are engaging the sea. That is, the feeling that he is proving a case is what gives *Tom Jones* its radiance, making it immensely better, I think, than the other two novels (though perhaps there is merely less discovery about proving the sad truths of *Amelia*); it builds up like Euclid. Modern critics seem unable to feel this, apparently because it is forbidden by their aesthetic principles, even when Fielding tells them he is doing it; whereas Dr Johnson and Sir John Hawkins, for example, took it seriously at once, and complained bitterly that the book had an immoral purpose. It certainly becomes much more interesting if you attend to its thesis; even if the thesis retains the shimmering mystery of a mirage.

Consider for example what Fielding says (XII, 8) when he is reflecting over what happened when Sophia caught Tom in bed with Mrs Waters at the Upton Inn, and incidentally telling us that that wasn't the decisive reason why Sophia rode away in anger, never likely to meet him again:

I am not obliged to reconcile every matter to the received notions concerning truth and nature. But if this was never so easy to do, perhaps it might be more prudent in me to avoid it. For instance, as the fact before us now stands, without any comment of mine upon it, though it may at first sight offend some readers, yet, upon more mature consideration, it must please all; for wise and good men may consider what happened to Jones at Upton as a just punishment for his wickedness in regard to women, of which it was indeed the immediate consequence; and silly and bad persons may comfort themselves in their vices by flattering their own hearts that the characters of men are owing rather to accident than to virtue. Now, perhaps the reflections which we should be here inclined to draw would alike contradict both these conclusions, and would show that these incidents contribute only to confirm the great, useful, and uncommon doctrine which it is the whole purpose of this work to inculculate, and which we must not fill up our pages by frequently repeating, as an ordinary parson fills up his sermon repeating his text at the end of every paragraph.

He does, as I understand, partly tell us the doctrine elsewhere, but never defines it as his central thesis; perhaps he chooses to put the claim here because XII is a rather desultory book, fitting in various incidents which the plot or the thesis will require later, and conveying the slowness of travel before the rush of London begins in XIII. To say 'the fact before us' makes Fielding the judge, and his readers the jury. He rather frequently warns them that they may not be able to understand him, and I think this leaves the modern critic, who assumes he meant nothing, looking rather comical. Perhaps this critic would say it is Empson who fails to see the joke of Fielding's self-deprecating irony; I answer that the irony of the book is double, here as elsewhere. Fielding realizes that any man who puts forward a general ethical theory implies a claim to have very wide ethical experience, therefore should be ready to laugh at his own pretensions; but also he isn't likely to mean nothing when he jeers at you for failing to see his point. Actually, the modern critic does know what kind of thing the secret is; but he has been badgered by neo-classicism and neo-Christianity and what not, whereas the secret is humanist, liberal, materialist, recommending happiness on earth and so forth, so he assumes it is dull, or the worldly advice of a flippant libertine.

Nobody would want to argue such points who had felt the tone of the book; it is glowing with the noble beauty of its gospel, which Fielding indeed would be prepared to claim as the original Gospel. The prose of generalized moral argument may strike us as formal, but it was also used by Shelley, who would also appeal to the Gospels to defend a moral novelty, as would Blake; an idea that the Romantics were original there seems to confuse people nowadays very much. When Fielding goes really high in *Tom Jones* his prose is like an archangel brooding over mankind, and I suppose is actually imitating similar effects in Handel; one might think it was like Bach, and that Handel would be too earth-bound, but we know Fielding admired Handel. I admit that the effect is sometimes forced, and strikes us as the theatrical rhetoric of the Age of Sentiment; but you do not assume he is insincere there if you recognize that at other times the effect is very real.

A moderate case of this high language comes early in the book when Squire Allworthy is discussing charity with Captain Blifil (11, 5). The captain is trying to ruin young Tom so as to get all the estate for himself, and has just remarked that Christian charity is an ideal, so ought not to be held to mean giving anything material; Allworthy falls into a glow at this, and readily agrees that there can be no merit in merely discharging a duty, especially such a pleasant one; but goes on:

To confess the truth, there is one degree of generosity (of charity I would have called it), which seems to have some show of merit, and that is where, from a principle of benevolence and Christian love, we bestow on another what we really want ourselves; where, in order to lessen the distresses of another, we condescend to share some part of them, by giving what even our necessities cannot well spare. This is, I think, meritorious; but to relieve our brethren only with our superfluities –

– to do one thing and another, go the balanced clauses, 'this seems to be only being rational creatures'. Another theme then crosses his mind for the same grand treatment:

As to the apprehension of bestowing bounty on such as may hereafter prove unworthy objects, merely because many have proved such, surely it can never deter a good man from generosity.

This too is argued with noble rhetoric, and then the captain inserts his poisoned barb. Now, the passage cannot be single irony, meant to show

Allworthy as a pompous fool; he is viewed with wonder as a kind of saint (e.g. he is twice said to smile like an angel, and he is introduced as the most glorious creature under the sun), also he stood for the real bene-factor Allen whom Fielding would be ashamed to laugh at. Fielding shows a Proust-like delicacy in regularly marking a reservation about Allworthy without ever letting us laugh at him (whereas critics usually complain he is an all-white character). Allworthy is something less than all-wise; the plot itself requires him to believe the villains and throw Tom out of Paradise Hall, and the plot is designed to carry larger meanings. The reason why he agrees so eagerly with the captain here, I take it, apart from his evidently not having experienced what he is talking about, is a point of spiritual delicacy or gentlemanly politeness – he cannot appear to claim credit for looking after his own cottagers, in talking to a guest who is poor; that was hardly more than looking after his own property, and the reflection distracts him from gauging the captain's motives. What is more important, he speaks as usual of doing good on principle, and here the central mystery is being touched upon.

One might think the answer is: 'Good actions come only from good impulses, that is, those of a good heart, not from good principles'; the two bad tutors of Jones make this idea obvious at the beginning (especially III, 5). Dr Johnson and Sir John Hawkins denounced the book as meaning this, and hence implying that morality is no use (by the way, in my *Complex Words*, p. 173, I ascribed a sentence of Hawkins to Johnson, but they make the same points). Fielding might well protest that he deserved to escape this reproach; he had twice stepped out of his frame in the novel to explain that he was not recommending Tom's imprudence, and that he did not mean to imply that religion and philosophy are bad because bad men can interpret them wrongly. But he seems to have started from this idea in his first revolt against the ethos of Richardson which made him write *Shamela* and *Joseph Andrews;* I think it was mixed with a class belief, that well-brought-up persons (with the natural ease of gentlemen) do not need to keep prying into their own motives as these hypocritical Nonconformist types do. As a novelist he never actually asserts this idea, which one can see is open to misuse, and in *Tom Jones* (1749) he has made it only part of a more interesting idea; but, after he had been attacked for using it there, he arranged an ingenious reply in the self-defensive *Amelia* (1751). He gave the opinion outright to the silly Booth, a free-thinker who disbelieves in free-will (III,5); you are rather encouraged to regard Booth as a confession of the errors of the author when young. When he is converted at the end of the novel (XII, 5) the good parson laughs at him for having thought this a heresy, saying it is why Christianity provides the motives of Heaven and Hell. This was all right as an escape into the recesses of theology; but it was the Calvinists who had really given up free will, and Fielding could hardly want to agree with them; at any rate Parson Adams, in *Joseph Andrews*, had passionately disapproved of Salvation by Faith. Fielding was a rather special kind of Christian, but evidently sincere in protesting that he was one. Adams is now usually regarded as sweetly Anglican, but his brother parson (in I, 17) suspects he is the Devil, after he has sternly rejected a series of such doctrines as give a magical importance to the clergy. I take it Fielding set himself up as a moral theorist, later than *Joseph Andrews*, because he decided he could refute the view of Hobbes, and of various thinkers prominent at the time who derived from Hobbes, that incessant Egotism is logically inevitable or a condition of our being. We lack the moral treatise in the form of answers to Bolingbroke which he set out to write when dying, but can gather an answer from *Tom Jones*, perhaps from the firm treatment of the reader in VI, i, which introduces the troubles of the lovers and tells him that no author can tell him what love means unless he is capable of experiencing it. The doctrine is thus: 'If good by nature, you can imagine other people's feelings so directly that you have an impulse to act on them as if they were your own; and this is the source of your greatest pleasures as well as of your only genuinely unselfish actions.' A modern philosopher might answer that this makes no logical difference, but it clearly brings a large practical difference into the suasive effect of the argument of Hobbes, which was what people had thought worth discussing in the first place. The most striking illustration is in the sexual behaviour of Jones, where he is most scandalous; one might, instead, find him holy, because he never makes love to a woman unless she first makes love to him. Later on (XIII, 7) we find he thinks it a point of honour to accept such a challenge from a woman, no less than a challenge to fight from a man (and that is the absolute of honour, the duel itself); but in his first two cases, Molly Seagrim and Sophia, he is unconscious that their advances have aroused him, and very grateful when they respond. Fielding reveres the moral beauty of this, but is quite hard-headed enough to see that such a man is too easily fooled by women; he regards Tom as dreadfully in need of good luck, and feels like a family lawyer when he makes the plot give it to him. He is thus entirely sincere in repeating that Tom needed to learn prudence; but how this relates to the chastity enjoined by religion he does not explain. We may however observe that nobody in the novel takes this prohibition quite seriously all the time; even Allworthy, when he is friends again, speaks only of the imprudence of Tom's relations with Lady Bellaston (XVIII, 10). In any case, the sexual affairs are only one of the many applications of the doctrine about mutuality of impulse; I think this was evidently the secret message which Fielding boasts of in *Tom Jones*, a book which at the time was believed to be so wicked that it had caused earthquakes.

We need not suppose he was well up in the long history of the question, but I would like to know more about his relations to Calvin; Profesor C. S. Lewis, in his *Survey of Sixteenth-Century Literature*, brings out what unexpected connections Calvin can have. He maintained that no action could deserve Heaven which was done in order to get to Heaven; hence we can only attain good, that is non-Egotist, motives by the sheer grace of God. In its early years the doctrine was by no means always regarded as grim; and it has an eerie likeness to the basic position of Fielding, that the well-born soul has good impulses of its own accord, which only need directing. At least, a humble adherent of either doctrine may feel baffled to know how to get into the condition recommended. However, I take it this likeness arises merely because both men had seriously puzzled their heads over the Gospel, and tried to give its paradoxes their full weight. Fielding never made a stronger direct copy of a Gospel Parable than in *Joseph Andrews*, when Joseph is dying naked in the snow and an entire coach-load finds worldly reasons for letting him die except for the post-boy freezing on the outside, who gives Joseph his overcoat and is soon after transported for robbing a hen-roost. But I think he felt the paradoxes of Jesus more as a direct challenge after he had trained and practised as a lawyer, and had come into line for a job as magistrate; that is, when he decided to write *Tom Jones*. He first wrote in favour of the Government on the 1745 Rebellion, in a stream of indignant pamphlets, and this was what made him possible as a magistrate; he was horrified at the public indifference at the prospect of a Catholic conquest, from which he expected rack and fire. He must then also be shocked at the indifference, or the moon-eyed preference for the invader, shown by all the characters in *Tom Jones*; nor can he approve the reaction of the Old Man of the Hill, who thanks God he has renounced so lunatic a world. To realize that Fielding himself is not indifferent here, I think, gives a further range to the vistas of the book, because all the characters are being as imprudent about it as Tom Jones about his own affairs; and this at least encourages one to suppose that there was a fair amount going on in Fielding's mind.

Tom Jones is a hero because he is born with good impulses; indeed, as the boy had no friend but the thieving gamekeeper Black George, among the lethal hatreds of Paradise Hall, he emerges as a kind of Noble Savage. This is first shown when, keen to shoot a bird, he follows it across the boundary and is caught on Squire Western's land; two guns were heard, but he insists he was alone. The keeper had yielded to his request and come too; if Tom says so, the keeper will be sacked, and his wife and children will starve, but Tom as a little gentleman at the great house can only be beaten. 'Tom passed a very melancholy night' because he was afraid the beating might make him lose his honour by confessing, says Fielding, who adds that it was as severe as the tortures used in some foreign countries to induce confessions. The reader first learns to suspect the wisdom of Allworthy by hearing him say (III, 2) that Tom acted here on a mistaken point of honour; though he only says it to defend Tom from further assaults by the bad tutors, who discuss the point with splendid absurdity. Whether it was 'true,' one would think, depended on whether the child thought Allworthy himself could be trusted not to behave unjustly. I have no respect for the critics who find the moralizing of the book too obvious; the child's honour really is all right after that; he is a fit judge of other ideas of honour elsewhere. Modern readers would perhaps like him better if they realized his basic likeness to Huck Finn; Mark Twain and Fielding were making much the same protest, even to the details about duelling. But Mark Twain somehow could not bear to have Huck grow up, whereas the chief idea about Tom Jones, though for various reasons it has not been recognized, is that he is planned to become awestrikingly better during his brief experience of the world. You are first meant to realize this happening halfway through the book, when the Old Man of the Hill is recounting his life, and Tom is found smiling quietly to himself at a slight error in the ethical position of that mystical recluse (VIII, 13). Old Man is a saint, and Fielding can provide him with some grand devotional prose, but he is too much of a stoic to be a real Gospel Christian, which is what Tom is turning into as we watch him.

All critics call the recital of Old Man irrelevant, though Saintsbury labours to excuse it; but Fielding meant to give a survey of all human experience (that is what he meant by calling the book an epic) and Old Man provides the extremes of degradation and divine ecstasy which Tom has no time for; as part of the structure of ethical thought he is essential to the book, the keystone at the middle of the arch. The critics could not have missed understanding this if they hadn't imagined themselves forbidden to have intellectual interests, as Fielding had. For that matter, the whole setting of the book in the 1745 Rebellion gets its point when it interlocks with the theory and practice of Old Man. So far from being 'episodic', the incident is meant to be such an obvious pulling together of the threads that it warns us to keep an eye on the subsequent moral development of Tom. As he approaches London unarmed, he is challenged by a highwayman; removing the man's pistol, and inquiring about the motives, he gives half of all he has to the starving family – rather more than half, to avoid calculation. Fielding of course knew very well that this was making him carry out one of the paradoxes of Jesus, though neither Fielding nor Tom must ever say so. The first time he earns money by selling his body to Lady Bellaston, a physically unpleasant duty which he enters upon believing at each step that his honour requires it (and without which, as the plot goes, he could probably not have won through to marrying Sophia), he tosses the whole fifty to his landlady, Mrs Miller, for a hard luck case who turns out to be the same highwayman, though she will only take ten; when the man turns up to thank him, with mutual recognition, Tom congratulates him for having enough honour to fight for the lives of his children, and proceeds to Lady Bellaston 'greatly exulting in the happiness he has procured', also reflecting on the evils that 'strict justice' would have caused here (XIII, 10). His next heroic action is to secure marriage for his landlady's daughter, pregnant by his fellow-lodger Nightingale thus 'saving the whole family from destruction'; it required a certain moral depth, because the basic difficulty was to convince Nightingale that this marriage, which he greatly desired, was not forbidden to him by his honour. We tend now to feel that Tom makes a grossly obvious moral harangue, but Nightingale feels it has pooh-poohed what he regards as the moral side of the matter, removing his 'foolish scruples of honour' so that he can do what he prefers (XVI, 7). Indeed the whole interest of the survey of ideas of honour is that different characters hold such different ones; no wonder critics who do not realize this find the repetition of the word tedious. These chapters in which the harangues of Tom are found obvious are interwoven with others in which his peculiar duty as regards Lady Bellaston has to be explained, and we pass on to the crimes which poor Lord Fellamar could be made to think his honour required. Critics would not grumble in the same way at Euclid, for being didactic in the propositions they have been taught already and immoral in the ones they refuse to learn. The threats of rape for Sophia and enslavement for Tom, as the plot works out, are simply further specimens of the code of honour; that danger for Tom is settled when Lord Fellamar gathers, still from hearsay, that the bastard is really a gentleman and therefore ought not to be treated as a kind of stray animal – he is 'much concerned' at having been misled (XVIII, 11.). There is a less familiar point about codes of honour, indeed it struck the Tory critic Saintsbury as a libel on squires, when we find that Squire Western regards duelling as a Whig townee corruption, and proposes wrestling or single-stick with Lord Fellamar's second (XVI, 2); but Fielding means Western to be right for once, not to prove that the old brute is a coward, and had said so in his picture of a country life (V, 12). When you consider what a tyrant Western is on his estate it really does seem rather impressive that he carries no weapon.

Fielding meant all this as part of something much larger than a picture of the ruling-class code of honour; having taken into his head that he is a moral theorist, he has enough intelligence to be interested by the variety of moral codes in the society around him. A tribe, unlike a man, can exist by itself, and when found has always a code of honour (though not police, prisons and so forth) without which it could not have survived till found; such is the basis upon which any further moral ideas must be built. That is why Fielding makes Tom meet the King of the Gypsies, who can rule with no other force but shame because his people have no false honours among them (XII, 12) – the incident is rather forced, because he is obviously not a gypsy but a Red Indian, just as Old Man, with his annuity and his housekeeper, has obviously no need to be dressed in skins like Robinson Crusoe; but they make you generalize the question. By contrast to this, the society which Fielding describes is one on which many different codes of honour, indeed almost different tribes, exist concurrently. The central governing class acts by only one of these codes and is too proud to look at the others (even Western's); but they would be better magistrates, and also happier and more sensible in their private lives, if they would recognize that these other codes surround them. It is to make this central point that Fielding needs the technique of double irony, without which one cannot express imaginative sympathy for two codes at once.

It strikes me that modern critics, whether as a result of the neo-Christian movement or not, have become oddly resistant to admitting that there is more than one code of morals in the world, whereas the central purpose of reading imaginative literature is to accustom yourself to this basic fact. I do not at all mean that a literary critic ought to avoid making moral judgements; that is useless as well as tiresome, because the reader has enough sense to start guessing round it at once. A critic had better say what his own opinions are, which can be done quite briefly, while recognizing that the person in view held different ones. (As for myself here, I agree with Fielding and wish I was as good.) The reason why Fielding could put a relativistic idea across on his first readers (though apparently not on modern critics) was that to them the word 'honour' chiefly suggested the problem whether a gentleman had to duel whenever he was huffed; one can presume they were already bothered by it, because it was stopped a generation or two later – in England, though not in the America of Huckleberry Finn. But Fielding used this, as he used the Nightingale marriage, merely as firm ground from which he could be allowed to generalize; and he does not find relativism alarming, because he feels that to understand codes other than your own is likely to make your judgements better. Surely a 'plot' of this magnitude is bound to seem tiresome unless it is frankly used as a means by which, while machining the happy ending, the author can present all sides of the question under consideration and show that his attitude to it is consistent. The professional Victorian novelists understood very well that Fielding had set a grand example there, and Dickens sometimes came near it, but it is a hard thing to plan for.

All the actions of Tom Jones are reported to Allworthy and Sophia, and that is why they reinstate him; they are his judges, like the reader. Some readers at the time said it was wilful nastiness of Fielding to make Tom a bastard, instead of discovering a secret marriage at the end; and indeed he does not explain (XVIII, 7) why Tom's mother indignantly refused to marry his father when her brother suggested it (Fielding probably knew a reason, liking to leave us problems which we can answer if we try, as Dr Dudden's book shows, but I cannot guess it). But there is a moral point in leaving him a bastard; he is to inherit Paradise Hall because he is held to deserve it, not because the plot has been dragged round to make him the legal heir. Lady Mary Wortley Montagu, a grand second cousin of Fielding who thought him low, said that *Amelia* seemed to her just as immoral as his previous books, and she could not understand why Dr Johnson forgave it, because it too encouraged young people to marry for love and expect a happy ending. She had enjoyed the books, and thought that Richardson's were just as immoral. I take it that, after a rather uncomfortable marriage for money, she found herself expected to give a lot of it away to her poor relations, so she thought they all ought to have married for money. Wrong though she may have been, the eighteenth-century assumption that a novel has a moral seems to me sensible; *Tom Jones* really was likely to make young people marry for love, not only because that is presented as almost a point of honour but because the plot does not make the gamble seem hopeless. The machinery of the happy ending derives from the fairy tale, as Fielding perhaps recognized, as well as wanting to sound like Bunyan, when he called the house Paradise Hall. The third son seeking his fortune gives his crust to the withered crone and thus becomes a prince because she is Queen of the Fairies; the moral is that this was the right thing to do, even if she hadn't been, but the tale also suggests to the child that maybe this isn't such a bad bet as you might think, either. The mind of Fielding, as he gets near in the actual writing to the end of a plot which he is clearly following from a complete dated skeleton, begins to play round what it means when an author, as it were, tosses up to see whether to give his characters joy or sorrow; he is the creator here, he remarks, but he will promise not to work miracles, and so forth. Rather earlier, he positively asserts that generous behaviour like Tom's is not rewarded with happiness on earth, indeed that it would probably be un-christian to suppose so. This is one of the introductory chapters of literary prattle (xv, 1); it is answered in xv, 8, after a joke about whether Tom has selfish motives for a good action (and the reader who remembers IV, 11 may well brace himself to hear a new scandal about Tom), by a firm assertion that the immediate results of such behaviour are among the greatest happinesses that earth can provide. However, this play of mind does not arrive at telling us what the happy ending means, and indeed could not, as its chief function is to make the suspense real even for a thoughtful reader. I take it that the childish magic of the fairy tale, and its elder brother, the belief that good actions ought to be done because they will be rewarded in Heaven, are reinforced in this novel by a practical idea which would not always apply; the outstanding moral of *Tom Jones*, if you look at it as Lady Mary did but less sourly, is that when a young man leaves home he is much more in a goldfish bowl than he thinks. The reader is to be influenced in favour of Tom's behaviour by seeing it through the eyes of Allworthy and Sophia, whom one might think sufficiently high-class and severe.But the end conveys something much more impressive than that these examiners give him a pass degree; he has become so much of a Gospel Christian that he cannot help but cast a shadow even on them. Against all reason and principle, and therefore to the consternation of Allworthy, he forgives Black George.

George robbed him, just after he was cast out, of the money Allworthy had given him to save him from degradation, for example, being pressed to sea as a vagabond, which nearly occurred. The gamekeeper was an old friend rather than a remote peasant, had become comfortable solely through the efforts of Tom to get him a job, and one would also think, as Tom's supposed natural-father-in-law, must have had an interest in letting him even now have a sporting chance. Fielding rated friendship specially highly, and always speaks of this betrayal in the tone of sad wonder he keeps for desperate cases. He says nothing himself about Tom forgiving George, but makes Allworthy give a harangue calling it wicked because harmful to society. We are accustomed in Fielding to hear characters wriggle out of the absolute command by Jesus to forgive, comically bad ones as a rule, and now the ideal landlord is saddled with it. The time must clearly come, if a man carries through a consistent programme about double irony, when he himself does not know the answer; and here, as it should do, it comes at the end of the novel. The practical lawyer and prospective magistrate would have to find the Gospel puzzling on this point; it is quite fair for Fielding still to refuse to admit that Allworthy is in the wrong, because he may well suspect that the command of Jesus would bring anarchy. To be sure, this is not one of the impressive tests of Tom; he is merely behaving nicely, just when every-thing is falling into his hands, and would lose our sympathy if he didn't; it comes to him naturally, which not all the previous cases did. But still, we have been moving through a landscape of the ethic of human impulses, and when Tom rises above Allworthy he is like a mountain.

There is already a mystery or weird pathos about George when he is first worked back into the plot (xv, 12). Partridge is overjoyed, after all their troubles in London, to meet someone who loves Tom so much:

Betray you indeed! why I question whether you have a better friend than George upon earth, except myself, or one that would go further to serve you.

The reader is bound to take this as single irony at first, but Fielding is soon cheerfully explaining that George really did wish Tom well, as much as a man could who loved money more than anything else; and then we get him offering money to Tom in prison. Though not allowed to be decisive for the plot, he is useful in smuggling a letter to Sophia and trustworthy in hiding it from his employer. As to his love of money, we should remember that we have seen his family starving (iii, 9) after a bad bit of eighteenth-century administration by Allworthy. I think Fielding means to play a trick, just after the theft, when he claims to put us fully inside the mind of George; acting as go-between, George wonders whether to steal also the bit of money sent by Sophia to the exile, and decides that would be unsafe (vi, 13). No doubt we are to believe the details, but Fielding still feels free, in his Proust-like way, to give a different picture of the man's character at the other end of the novel; I take it he refused to believe that the 'inside' of a person's mind (as given by Richardson in a letter, perhaps) is much use for telling you the real source of his motives. George of course has not reformed at the end; he has arranged to come to London with his new employer, Western, the more safely to cash the bill he stole, though, as he chooses the lawyer who is the father of Nightingale, the precaution happens to be fatal. I think the mind of Fielding held in reserve a partial justification for George, though he was careful with it and would only express it in the introductory prattle to Book xii, where both the case of George and its country setting are particularly far from our minds; indeed, I had to read the book again to find where this comment is put. While pretending to discuss literary plagiarism, Fielding lets drop that the villagers on these great estates consider it neither sin nor shame to rob their great neighbours, and a point of honour to protect any other villagers who have done so. George might assume, one can well imagine, that Tom

was going to remain grandee somehow whatever quarrels he had; in fact,
Tom at the time is so much wrapped up in his unhappy love affair that he
seems hardly to realize himself how much he will need money. On this
view, it would be shameful for George to miss a chance of robbing Tom;
for one thing, it would be robbing his own family, as the soldier reflects in
VII, 14. I agree that, so far from advancing this argument, Fielding never
weakens the tone of moral shock with which he regards the behaviour of
George (who was right to be so ashamed that he ran away); but I think he
means you to gather that the confusion between different moral codes
made it intelligible. This background I think adds to the rather thrilling
coolness with which Tom does not reply to the harangue of Allworthy
denouncing his forgiveness; it is in any case time for him to go and dress to
meet Sophia.

Sophia has the same kind of briefing as a modern appointments board;
thus she does not waste time over his offer of marriage to Lady Bellaston;
Sophia holds the document, but understands that this was merely the way
to get rid of Lady Bellaston, so it joins the list of points already cleared.
The decisive question in her mind is whether he has become a libertine,
that is, whether his impulses have become corrupted; if they have, she is
quite prepared again to refuse to unite by marriage the two largest estates
in Somersetshire. Fielding has been blamed for making the forgiveness of
Tom too easy, but I think his training as a bad playwright served him well
here, by teaching him what he could throw away. A reader does not need
to hear the case again, and Fielding disapproved of women who argue,
indeed makes Allworthy praise Sophia for never doing it; and he himself
has a certain shyness about expressing his doctrine, or perhaps thought it
dangerous to express clearly. Beastly old Western comes yelling in to say
for the average reader that we can't be bothered with further discussion of
the matter, and Sophia decides that she can allow it to have settled itself.
The fit reader, interested in the doctrine, is perhaps meant to feel rather
disappointed that it is not preached, but also that this is good taste in a
way, because after all the man's impulses have evidently not been
corrupted. Even so, it is nothing like the view of Flaubert, Conrad and so
forth, that a novelist is positively not allowed to discuss the point of his
novel.

I want now, though there is so much else to choose from in this rich
book, to say something about the thought of incest which terrifies Jones in

prison; both because it affects the judgement of Sophia and because it has been a major bond of contention among other critics. Dr F. H. Dudden, in his treatise *Henry Fielding* (1952), though concerned to do justice to an author whose morals have been maligned, admits that he had a rather nasty habit of dragging fear of incest into his plots (it also comes into *Joseph Andrews*); but decides that he means no harm by it, and that it was probably just an effect of having to write bad plays when he was young. On the other hand a *Times Literary Supplement* reviewer, quoted with indignation by Middleton Murry in *Unprofessional Essays*, had thought this frightening of Jones a specially moral part of the plot. When he goes to bed with Mrs Waters at Upton, says the reviewer, Fielding

seems to be making light of it, or even conniving at it. Yet it is the first step in a moral progress downhill. . . . And then, much later in the book, evidence comes to light which suggests [that she was his mother]. . . . Fielding's connivance was a pretence. He has sprung a trap on Tom and us; he has made us realize – as a serious novelist always makes us realize, and a frivolous novelist often makes us forget – that actions have their consequences. . . . It is this sense of the moral structure of life that makes Fielding important.

I could have quoted more sanctimonious bits, but this was the part which Middleton Murry found perverse:

What to a more normal sensibility constitutes the one doubtful moment in the book – the one moment at which we feel that Fielding *may* have sounded a wrong note, by suggesting an awful possibility outside the range of the experience he invites us to partake – becomes in this vision the one thing which makes the book considerable.

The reviewer of course was trying to speak up for Fielding, and make him something better than a flippant libertine; and it is in favour of his view that the Upton incident is the one place where Fielding says in person that casual sex is forbidden by Christianity as expressly as murder (IX, 3). Dr Dudden might be expected to agree with the reviewer; he maintains you have only to attend to the text to find that Fielding always not only denounces sin but arranges to have it punished 'inexorably and terribly'. This indeed is one half of what Fielding intended, though the adverbs hardly describe the purring tone of the eventual forgiveness of Tom, as when we are told that he has, 'by reflection on his past follies, acquired a discretion and prudence very uncommon in one of his lively parts'. Instead, we find that Dr Dudden agrees with Middleton Murry; they are more in sympathy with Fielding than the reviewer, but feel they have to confess that the incest trick is rather bad; chiefly, I think, because they like him for being healthy, and that seems clearly not.

I think the basic reason why Fielding twice uses this fear is that he had a philosophical cast of mind, and found it curious that those who laugh at ordinary illicit sex take incest very seriously. As to *Joseph Andrews*, the starting-point is that Fielding is to parody Richardson's Pamela, a servant who made her master marry her by refusing to be seduced. He had already done this briefly and fiercely in *Shamela*, where an ex-prostitute acts like Pamela out of conscious calculation – the moral is that Pamela is *un*consciously calculating, and that girls ought not to be encouraged to imitate this minx. He is now to do it by swapping the sexes; a footman would be cowardly, or have some other low motive, if he refused a lady, and a lady would be lacking in the delicacy of her caste if she even wanted a footman. Thus the snobbish Fielding, in opposition to the democratic Richardson, can prove that the class structure ought not to be disturbed. Or rather, he did not actually have to write this stuff, because he could rely on his readers to imagine he had, as they still do. It is false to say, as is regularly said, that Fielding started on his parody and then wrote something else because he found he was a novelist; he did not start on it at all. From the first words, he treats his story with an almost over-refined, a breathless delicacy; and by the time Lady Booby has offered marriage, and Joseph, though attracted by her, still refuses her because he wants to marry his humble sweetheart, most of the laughing readers should be pretty well outfaced. No doubt Fielding himself, if the story had been outlined at his club, would have laughed as heartily as the others; but he is concerned in this novel, where he is rather oddly safe from being thought a hypocrite, to show that his sympathy is so broad that he can see the question all round, like a judge. I think he did discover something in writing it, but not what is usually said; he discovered how much work he could leave the public to do for him. One type of reader would be jeering at Joseph, and another admiring him, and feeling indignant with the first type; and both of them would hardly notice what the author was writing down. You can understand that he might want to take some rather firm step, towards the end, to recover their attention. What he is really describing is the chastity of the innocent Joseph, adding of course the piercing simplicity of his criticisms of the great world; Parson Adams, whom Fielding certainly does not intend us to think contemptible, preaches to him a rather overstrained doctrine of chastity all along. Just as all seems ready for the happy ending with his humble sweetheart, a twist of the plot makes them apparently brother and sister; they decide to live together chastely, as Parson Adams had always said they should be able to do. Here the clubmen who form Type A of the intended readers no longer dare to jeer at Joseph for believing he has a duty of chastity; the opposed groups are forced to combine. I thus think that this turn of the plot is entirely justified; for that matter, I think that modern critics are rather too fond of the strategic device of claiming to be embarrassed.

In *Tom Jones*, I can't deny, the trick is chiefly used to heighten the excitement at the end of the plot – Tom must go either right up or right down. I agree with the *Times Literary Supplement* reviewer that it marks a change in the attitude of the hero, but it comes only as an extra at the end of a gradual development. Saintsbury defended Tom's relations with Lady Bellaston by saying that the rule against a gentleman taking money from a mistress had not yet been formulated; certainly it doesn't seem to have hampered the first Duke of Marlborough, but Tom comes to suspect of his own accord that some such rule has been formulated. He felt it when he first met Sophia in London (XIII, 11); 'the ignominious circumstance of his having been kept' rose in his mind when she began to scold him and stopped his mouth; the effect of this was good, because her actual accusations came as a relief and were the more easy to argue off convincingly. It is not till XV, 9 that Nightingale, as a fair return for the teaching of basic morals, warns him that he is liable to become despised by the world, and explains that the way to break with Lady Bellaston is to offer her marriage. Learning that he is one of a series makes Tom feel free to break with her, which he thought before would be ungrateful. By the way, I take it Fielding admired her firmness about marriage, as a protest against unjust laws on women's property; her criminal plot against the lovers is chiefly meant as a satire against the worldly code – she can be taken as sincere in telling Lord Fellamar that the intention is to save her ward Sophia from ruin, and Fielding only means to describe her Unconsciousness when he adds in XVI, 8 that women support this code out of jealousy. Tom refuses to marry a rich widow immediately afterwards (xv, 11); this is the sternest of his tests, and he is 'put into a violent flutter', because he suspects it is a duty of honour to accept this fortune, so as to release Sophia from misery. He seems like Galahad when he rejects the point of honour for love, and it does prove that in learning 'prudence', which is how Fielding and Allworthy describe his moral reform, he is not falling into the opposite error of becoming a calculating type. We next have him refusing to make love to Mrs Fitzpatrick, while easily rejecting her spiteful advice to make love to Sophia's aunt (xvi, 9). Both she and Lady Bellaston are affronted by his frank preference for Sophia and yet find their passions excited by its generosity – 'strange as it may seem, I have seen many instances.' The last of the series is his refusal to go to bed with Mrs Waters when she visits him in jail with the news that her supposed husband is not dying, so that he is safe from execution (xvii, 9); this might seem ungenerous rather than reformed, but he has just heard from Mrs. Miller that Sophia has become determined to refuse him because of his incontinency. The next and final book opens with the supposed discovery that Mrs Waters is his mother, so that he committed incest with her at Upton. This throws him into a state of shaking horror which serves to illustrate his courage; we realize how undisturbed he was before at the prospect of being hanged for an act of self-defence. It is thus not the case that Tom was shocked into disapproving of his previous looseness by the thought that it might cause accidental incest, because this fear came after he had become prudent; still less that the fear of death and horror of incest were needed together to crack such a hard nut as the conscience of Tom, because he has been freed from the fear of death just before the other alarm arrives. (I understand he was technically in danger under ecclesiastical law, but prosecution was very unlikely; in any case the question never occurs to him.) Fielding as a magistrate, surely, would think it contemptible to cheat a prisoner into reform by this trick, whereas the *Times Literary Supplement* reviewer seems to assume it would be moral. What one can say is the shock puts Tom into a grave frame of mind, suitable for meeting Sophia; and Sophia really does need winning over, with some extra moral solemnity however acquired, because she is quite pig-headed enough to fly in the face of the world all over again, and start refusing Tom just because he has become the heir.

My own objection to this bit about incest has long been something quite different, which I should think occurs oftener to a modern reader; and I think the book feels much better when it is cleared up. I thought the author was cheating in a way that whodunit authors often do, that is he put in a twist to make the end more exciting though the characters would not really have acted so. Those who dislike Fielding generally say that he makes his charcters so obvious, especially from making them so selfish, that they become tiresome like performing toys; but the reason why Mrs Waters gets misunderstood here is that here as always she is unusually generous-minded. A penniless but clever girl, she learned Latin under Partridge when he was a village schoolmaster and did so well that he kept her on as an assistant, but she learned too much Latin; a fatal day came (II, 3) when he jovially used Latin to ask her to pass a dish at dinner, and 'the poor girl smiled, perhaps at the badness of the Latin, and, when her mistress cast eyes upon her blushed, possibly with a consciousness of having laughed at her master.' This at once made Mrs Partridge certain not only that they were lovers but that they were jeering at her by using this code in her presence; and such is the way most of us fail to understand her final letter. A ruinous amount of fuss goes on, and it becomes convenient for her to work with Allworthy's sister in the secret birth of Jones, acting as her personal servant at the great house and paid extra to take the scandal of being his mother before leaving the district. The story is improbable, but as Fielding arranges it you can call it credible. Allworthy gives her a grand sermon against illicit love when she confesses to the bastard, but is impressed by the honour and generosity of her replies; he sends her an allowance, but stops it when he hears she has run off with a sergeant. We next see her when Jones saves her life (IX, 2); the villain Northerton is trying to murder her for what money she carries, and it is startling for the reader to be told, what Jones is too delicate to ask her (IX, 7), that she was only wandering about with this man to save him from being hanged, and only carrying the money to give it to him. She had expected to rejoin Captain Waters after his winter campaign against the rebels, but meanwhile Lieutenant Northerton was afraid of being hanged for murdering Jones (whereas it had been very lucky for Jones that the drunken assault removed him from the army), and needed to be led across hill country to a Welsh port. Fielding always admires women who can walk, instead of being tight-laced and townee, and though he tends to grumble at learned women he had evidently met a variety of them; he can forgive Mrs Waters her Latin. She need not be more than thirty-six when she meets Tom, and the struggle has exposed her breasts, which it appears have lasted better than her face. She stops Tom from hunting for Northerton,

earnestly entreating that he would accompany her to the town whither they had been directed. 'As to the fellow's escape,' said she, 'it gives me no uneasiness; for philosophy and Christianity both preach up forgiveness of injuries. But for you, Sir, I am concerned at the trouble I give you; nay, indeed, my nakedness may well make you ashamed to look me in the face, and if it were not for the sake of your protection, I would wish to go alone.'

Jones offered her his coat; but, I know not for what reason, she absolutely refused the most earnest solicitation to accept it. He then begged her to forget both the causes of her confusion.

He walks before her all the way so as not to see her breasts, but she frequently asks him to turn and help her. The seduction is entirely free from any further designs on him; she is as foot-loose as a character in the *Faerie Queene*, though perhaps her happening to fall in with Fitzpatrick next morning at the Upton Inn is what saves Jones from finding her even a momentary responsibility. Even so, her capacity to handle Fitzpatrick is rather impressive; the only occupation of this gentleman is to hunt for the woman he cheated into marriage in the hope of bullying her out of what little of her money is secured from him by the law, after wasting the rest; one would hardly think he was worth milking, let alone the unpleasantness of his company, so that she had better have gone back to her officer. Perhaps she wanted to get to London; the only story about her is that she is independent. We are told at the end that she eventually married Parson Shuffle.

When Fielding says he doesn't know the reason he always means it is too complicated to explain. Walking with her life-saver Jones she liked to appear pathetic, and she wanted to show her breasts, but also she really could not bear to let him take his coat off, not on such a cold night. The decision becomes a nuisance when they get to the inn because it makes her almost unacceptable, but this is got over; and she gathers from the landlady that Jones is in love with a younger woman.

The awkward behaviour of Mr Jones on this occasion convinced her of the truth, without his giving a direct answer to any of her questions; but she was not nice enough in her amours to be particularly concerned at the discovery. The beauty of Jones highly charmed her eye; but as she could not see his heart she gave herself no concern about it. She could feast heartily at the table of love, without reflecting that some other had been, or hereafter might be, feasted with the same repast. A sentiment which, if it deals but little in refinement, deals, however, much in substance; and is less capricious, and perhaps less ill-natured and selfish, than the desires of those females who can be contented enough to abstain from the possession of their lovers, provided that they are sufficiently satisfied that nobody else possesses them.

This seems to me a particularly massive bit of double irony, worthy to outlast the imperial eagle of the House of Austria, though I take it Fielding just believed what he said, and only knew at the back of his mind that the kind of man who would otherwise complain about it would presume it was irony.

Such is our main background information about Mrs Waters when she visits him in prison, assures him that her supposed husband is recovering fast so that there is no question of murder, and is rather cross with him for refusing to make love to her. Then her entirely unexpected letter arrives, which I must give in full (XVIII, 2):

Sir – Since I left you I have seen a gentleman, from whom I have learned something concerning you which greatly surprises and affects me; but as I have not at present leisure to communicate a matter of such high importance, you must suspend your curiosity till our next meeting, which shall be the first moment I am able to see you. Oh, Mr Jones, little did I think, when I passed that happy day at Upton, the reflection upon which is like to embitter all my future life, who it was to whom I owed such perfect happiness. – Believe me to be ever sincerely your unfortunate

J. Waters

P.S. – I would have you comfort yourself as much as possible, for Mr Fitzpatrick is in no manner of danger; so that, whatever other grievous crimes you may have to repent of, the guilt of blood is not among the number.

Partridge, who happened not to see Mrs Waters at Upton, has seen her visit the prison and eavesdropped on her talk with Jones, so he has just horrified Jones by telling him she is his mother; they think this letter confirms the belief, and certainly it is hard to invent any other meaning. We are not told who the gentleman was till XVIII, 8, when she tells Allworthy that the lawyer Dowling had visited her, and told her that

if Mr Jones had murdered my husband, I should be assisted with any money I wanted to carry on the prosecution, by a very worthy gentleman, who, he said, was

well apprised what a villain I had to deal with. It was by this man I discovered who
Mr Jones was. . . . I discovered his name by a very odd accident; for he himself
refused to tell it to me; but Partridge, who met him at my lodgings the second
time he came, knew him formerly at Salisbury.

She assumed it was Allworthy who was persecuting Jones in this
relentless manner, whereas Allworthy knows it must be Blifil, whom
Dowling hopes to blackmail; and since she greatly revered Allworthy,
though herself some kind of freethinker, she assumed that Jones had done
something to deserve it – this explains the postscript 'whatever other
grievous crimes'. 'The second time' is an important detail; the second
time Dowling came must have been after she wrote the letter, and was the
first time Partridge came. As soon as Partridge saw her he would tell her
Jones's fear of incest and she would dispel it; but Partridge has to come, to
meet Dowling and tell her his name (otherwise the plot of Blifil could not
be exposed). We have next to consider how she knew, when she wrote the
letter, about the anger of Sophia; but Jones would tell her this himself,
when she visited him in prison, because he would feel he had to offer a
decent reason for refusing to go to bed with her. A deep generosity, when
she has thought things over after the unpleasant talk with Dowling, is what
makes her write down that if Sophia refuses to marry Tom it will embitter
all the rest of her life. The delusion about incest is the kind of mistake
which is always likely if you interpret in selfish terms the remarks of a very
unselfish character. Certainly, the coincidences of the plot are rigged
almost to the point where we reject them unless we take them as ordained
by God; Fielding would be accustomed to hearing pious characters call
any bit of luck a wonderful proof of Providence, and might hope they
would feel so about his plot – as Partridge encourages them to do (e.g.
XII, 8). But the reaction of the character to the plot is not rigged; she
behaves as she always does.

I ought finally to say something about his attitude to the English class
system, because opinions about what he meant there seem often to be
decisive for the modern reader. What people found so entertaining at the
time, when Fielding attacked Richardson in a rather explosive class
situation (the eager readers of Richardson in French were presumably
heading toward the French Revolution), was that the classes seemed to
have swapped over. The printer's apprentice was the gentlemanly expert
on manners, indeed the first English writer to be accepted as one by the

polite French; whereas if you went to see Fielding, they liked to say at the time, you would find him drunk in bed with his cook and still boasting he was related to the Hapsburgs. His answer to Richardson was thus: 'It is useless to tell me what gentlemen do; I am one' The real difference was about the meaning of the term; Fielding thought it should mean a man fit to belong to the class which actually rules in his society, especially by being a just judge. His behaviour eventually made a lot of people feel he had won the argument, though not till some time after his death. To die poor and despised while attempting to build up the obviously needed London Police Force, with obvious courage and humanity, creating astonishment by his refusal to accept the usual bribes for such dirty work, and leaving the job in hands which continued it – this became too hard to laugh off; he had done in the heart of London what empire-builders were being revered for doing far away. He provided a new idea of the aristocrat, with the added claim that it was an older tradition; and he did seem to clear the subject up rather – you could hardly deny that he was a better idea than Lord Chesterfield. An impression continued that, if you are very rude and rough, that may mean you are particularly aristocratic, and good in an emergency; I doubt whether, without Fielding, the Victorian novelists (however much they forbade their daughters to read his books) would have retained their trust in the rather hidden virtues of the aristocracy.

Much of this wished onto Fielding later, but we have a series of jokes against the current idea of a gentleman during Tom's journey to London. The remarks in favour of the status are perhaps what need picking out. Tom leaves Old Man because he hears cries for help; he thus saves the life of Mrs Waters from the villain Northerton, who might seem to justify the contempt for mankind of Old Man. This is at the beginning of Book IX; at the very end of it, after the reader has learned how bad the case is, Fielding urges him not to think he means to blame army officers in general:

Thou wilt be pleased to consider that this fellow, as we have already informed thee, had neither the birth nor the education of a gentleman, nor was a proper person to be enrolled among the number of such. If, therefore, his baseness can justly reflect on any besides himself, it must be only on those who gave him his commission.

We learn incidentally, from this typical rounding on an administrator, that Fielding presumed men ought to be promoted to the ruling class, as a regular thing; the point is merely that the system of promotion should be adequate to save it from contempt. The exalted cynicism of Old Man (who by the way did not try to help Mrs Waters, though he and not Tom had a gun) might make one suspect that adequate members of such a class cannot be found, and Fielding has kept in mind the social question of how you should do it. I have known readers think Fielding wanted to abolish gentlemen, and indeed the jokes against them are pretty fierce; but he had planted another remark at the beginning of Book ix, in the chapter of introductory prattle, which is clearly meant to fit the last words of that Book. An author needs to have experienced both low life and high life, dull and absurd though it is, for

elegance, and a liberality of spirit; which last quality I have myself scarce ever seen in men of low birth and education.

The assertion seems moderate, perhaps hardly more than that most men don't feel free to look all round a question, unless their position is comfortable enough; but 'liberality of spirit' feels rather near to the basic virtue of having good impulses. Of course, he does not mean that all gentlemen have it; the total egotism of young Blifil, a theoretically interesting case, with a breakdown into sadism, which critics have chosen to call unlifelike, is chiefly meant to make clear that they do not. But it seems mere fact that Fielding's society needed a governing class, however things may work out under universal education; so it is reasonable of him to take a Reformist view, as the Communists would say, and merely recommended a better selection.

Indeed, it is perhaps flat to end this essay with an example which yields so placid a solution to a build-up of 'double irony'; nor is it a prominent example, because after we get to London the ironies are about honour rather than gentility. But I suspect that today both halves of the puzzle about gentlemen are liable to work against him; he gets regarded as a coarse snob, whose jovial humour is intended to relax the laws only in favour of the privileged. This at least is unjust; no one attacked the injustices of privilege more fiercely. His position was not found placid at the time, and there is one class paradox which he repeatedly laboured to drive home; though to judge from a survey of opinions on him (*Fielding*

The Novelist, F. H. Blanchard, 1926) this line of defence never gave him any protection in his lifetime. 'Only low people are afraid of having the low described to them, because only they are afraid of being exposed as themselves low'. The paradox gives him a lot of powerful jokes, but so far from being far-fetched it follows directly from his conception of a gentleman, which was if anything a literal-minded one. He means by it a person fit to sit on the bench as a magistrate, and naturally such a man needs to know all about the people he is to judge; indeed, the unusual thing about Fielding as a novelist is that he is always ready to consider what he would do if one of his characters came before him when he was on the bench. He is quite ready to hang a man, but also to reject the technical reasons for doing so if he decides that the man's impulses are not hopelessly corrupted. As to the reader of a novel, Fielding cannot be bothered with him unless he too is fit to sit on a magistrate's bench, prepared, in literature as in life, to handle and judge any situation. That is why the reader gets teased so frankly. The same kind of firmness, I think, is what makes the forgiveness by Tom at the end feel startling and yet sensible enough to stand up to Allworthy. I think the chief reason why recent critics have belittled Fielding is that they find him intimidating.

Rounding Off

I had written more about *Tom Jones*, and intended a longer essay, but then realised I was just making the same points about one chapter after another. So far as I remember, only one of the rejected details deserved to stay in; it is about Sophia. Late in the story, at Book xv, Chapter 11, Tom receives an offer of marriage from a rich, beautiful, young, devoted and unaggressive widow, and this 'throws him into a violent flutter', because it would supply all his needs, and, as regards Sophia, his love could only be a torment to her.

He had almost determined to be false to her from a high point of honour; but that refinement was not able to stand very long against the voice of nature, which cried in his heart that such friendship was treason to love.

This is proper for a high-minded young man, and no reader would be shocked, though some would feel that the rhetoric gives Nature too much credit. But it is a pale echo of what has already occurred to Sophia quite early in the story (vii, 9). She became tempted to obey her father because she had a very deep sense of religion, and this would be an act of extreme piety; indeed, as she became convinced upon further reflection, to marry Blifil would make her a martyr. This tickled her vanity; but then

Cupid, who lay hid in her muff, suddenly crept out, and, like Punchinello in a puppet-show, kicked all out before him. In truth, (for we scorn to deceive our reader, or to vindicate the character of our heroine, by ascribing her actions to supernatural impulse) the thought of her beloved Jones, and of some hopes (however distant) in which he was very particularly concerned, immediately destroyed all which filial love, piety and pride had, with their joint endeavours, been labouring to bring about.

This is artfully written, but what it amounts to saying is that bodily lust was the decisive factor, and that without it she would have incurred disaster. This was extremely challenging; that a lady just could not feel lust was a basic dogma of the period, and the half-joking reflections here were probably the chief thing Dr Johnson had in mind when he told a young lady that he scarcely knew of a more corrupt work. We do not easily realise the extreme violence of the prejudices that Fielding had chosen to combat, so we tend to regard the devices he used as a defence and for winning support as merely theatrical.

Not long after publication my piece got a strong though moderately expressed rebuttal (C. V. Rawson, *Notes and Queries*, 1959). It says that Fielding was a more direct writer than I make him, who after looking round a subject generally arrives at a forthright conclusion – as I confess about his treatment of class. This process should not be called 'irony'. Of course the great structure does now feel lumbering and preachy at many points; we cannot have the experience of being converted to views that are now commonly taken for granted; but the book feels much better if we recognize it as a struggle against established dogmas. There seems no reason why an eventual pronouncement on a subject (even within one book) should prevent the earlier jokes about it from being 'irony'; many of the readers who accepted the pronouncement, when it was new, would have resisted it if their convictions had not been shaken by the previous jokes. Also I still maintain that Fielding leaves us in doubt on many points; he will 'go too far', but in the rhetorical manner of his stage, which was close to that of the pulpit, and then present himself as 'moderate', but obviously saying less than he thinks.

Whether a daughter must obey her father, even in the choice of her husband, is crucial for the story. Western is always sure she must, though he learns some evasions to make the rule sound less harsh; Sophia too believes it at first, but finds a different evasion when faced with the grim result. Her father believes she has consented to marry Blifil when she says, 'You know, sir, I must not, nor can refuse to obey any absolute command of yours' (VII, 9) and the author implies that 'absolute' was an equivocation, though how any commands could be more absolute than Western's it is hard to see. She can thus escape on a visit to her cousin Lady Bellaston, in London, who teaches her that there is no such law. Lady Bellaston stands for the emancipated woman, and her advice is right so far; but when Jones rejects her she tries to have him enslaved by a press-gang, an action of massive wickedness. After her brief stay with this lady, Sophia says that a father can forbid a marriage but not impose one, though he may impose penalties for rejecting one. Surely it did not need the prophet Fielding to tell us this. The only time a woman speaks in the Prayer Book is to say 'I will', and the only possible reason for requiring her to speak is that she is entitled to say 'I won't'. Fielding makes Allworthy wish that the law 'could restrain' the claim of fathers to this power (XVII, 3), but assume that it cannot; and he positively blames the helpless parasite Parson Supple for not doing his priestly duty, which is to tell Western he has no such power (XVI, 2). However, all this permissiveness is only called out to defend a very extreme case, perhaps 'absolutely' extreme. Fielding tells us that Blifil is a sadist who expects pleasure from torturing his wife after he has acquired the legal sanction (VII, 6), and he assumes that Sophia can intuit this intention. It is only in such an extreme case, she says, where she can be certain that the results would be evil, that she would presume to disobey her father, and she ends up happily obeying him ever after (though he does remove himself a moderate distance to better hunting country). No father need be alarmed at being asked to allow such a very special case for exemption – unless foreseeing that it would let loose a good deal more. One might add that Sophia could not be made a consistent character, such as later novels lead us to expect, because the puppet had to fulfil various functions. She is praised for her beautiful peacefulness, her habitual refusal to show her wit by entering into arguments, and then she talks like a headmistress on an appointments board, or flies even higher (XVIII, 9):

At present there is no man on earth whom I would more resolutely reject than Mr Jones; nor would the addresses of Mr Blifil himself be less agreeable to me.

It would be tiresome, I think, to find subtleties of character here; the author is enjoying a theatrical effect, and perhaps the lady is too. Next day she marries Jones, obeying her father. Fielding has shown earlier that he can make her a bit ridiculous and yet still impressive, as in her famous tumble, and no more can be required.

His first wife, who had had the pluck to run away with him and must have found the life rather rough, he undoubtedly revered and deeply mourned; but one may suspect that he felt more at ease when he was writing *Tom Jones*, married to her servant. Like Marvell, he felt that ladies if treated with proper respect were a strain on a man, though being so vigorous and confident made Fielding able to carry it better – at the cost of some public ridicule. He seems to have been the first man to champion the wrongs of women in an outspoken bull-headed way, already in *Tom Jones*, and too much in *Amelia*.

YEATS

The Variants for the
Byzantium Poems

I had a short article on these two poems in *A Review of English Literature* for Summer 1960, arguing that they are not so transcendental as many critics have assumed. If Yeats had meant what these people say, the poems would be in bad taste, marking a low, not a high, spiritual condition. The argument was from internal evidence, and I thought no more was needed. I was taken aback when a friend said: 'Excellent; you have shown that Yeats was a pig unless he meant what you say, and obviously he didn't mean that; now we know he was a pig, as always seemed probable.' Justice then demanded that I should peer round for external evidence, though with little hope that it had survived. This was lucky for me, as I would not otherwise have read two studies of the rough drafts for these splendid poems; one by Curtis Bradford, 'Yeats's Byzantium Poems' (PMLA 1960, reprinted in *Twentieth Century Views* S–TC–23), the other by Jon Stallworthy (*Between the Lines*, 1963). I am rather against the collecting of rough drafts, but Yeats was right to let those ones pile up in a folder; in the main, they are not boss shots but extra material which his technique forced him to exclude. What was ripening in his mind would have made a good science fiction Long-Short, but he took for granted that he had to compress it into one or two Symbolist poems. The drafts, in letting us recover some of the rejected detail, make clear I think that his spiritual tone had remained decent, instead of becoming sanctimonious in the manner so often praised.

Perhaps it is not basically a matter of good taste. English and American critics interpret Yeats's poems as implying Christian doctrines whenever that is possible, and when they find it impossible they treat the passage with a tactful sigh as merely a lapse, because they cannot conceive of a good man, with a good heart, holding any other religious belief. He may often, they feel, be a sceptic, but he cannot really believe in Theosophy; at best, that would be a kind of play-acting. The compulsion is particularly striking in *The Unicorn* by Virginia Moore (1954), who starts out with a firm intellectual recognition that she must examine how Yeats's beliefs affect his poetry, and the book is a rich mine of attractive information, but she appears to end her penultimate chapter 'Was Yeats a Christian?' with the sentiment that he must have been pretty Christian if he could stay friends with Ezra Pound. What I print here had been drafted before I read Professor Stock's book on Yeats, but I am glad to offer it for her presentation volume, because she seems to me the only critic, among those who have covered the field of Yeats's work, who is not hampered in this way. I am inclined to disagree with her about one or two details of the Byzantium poems, but she is always world-minded, like Yeats himself; she is at home among his ideas.

Both these writers on the draft versions insist that Yeats meant Paradise by Byzantium, and therefore that 'the central correlative of Byzantium is not Justinian's sixth-century city'. Here is the main point where I disagree, but it would be foolish to quarrel merely over the term Paradise. They are wrong if they mean Heaven by it, as they presumably must when they assert the presence of God the Father, but on the right line if they mean a possible stage towards Heaven. Even so, it is a bad term to describe such a bustling and metropolitan stage, for the ghosts of many periods of history and many nations arrive there (it is Byzantium of the tenth century, not of the sixth) and purge themselves; much as an Edwardian gentleman, after the excesses of the season, would take the waters at Bath or Baden-Baden.

I must quote at once the few explanations given by Yeats himself. He wrote in a letter of October 1926:

I have just finished a poem in which a poet of the Middle Ages besought the saints 'in their holy fire' to send their ecstasy.

This would be an early draft of 'Sailing to Byzantium', and it seems clear that the poet asked for the ecstasy during his present life, not after death. Yeats wrote a prose outline for his own guidance before starting 'Byzantium' (30 April 1930) which says:

Describe Byzantium as it is in the system towards the end of the first Christian millennium

– that is, in his own system, which he had expounded in *A Vision* (1924), it treats the city as a type of the unity of aesthetic and religious experience. An addition to the outline says:

A walking mummy. Flames at the street corners where the soul is purified. Birds of hammered gold singing in the golden trees. In the harbour, [dolphins] offering their backs to the wailing dead that they may carry them to Paradise.

Another reference shows that the word 'dolphins' got left out here; to make the artificial birds carry the saints to Heaven would be too much strain. By the time he had finished, he had come to generalise the transport work of these dolphins; but from the start the city itself is obviously not Heaven. Also there are two comments planned for broadcast readings; in the first, for an Irish audience (1931), he said:

When Irishmen were illuminating the Book of Kells and making the jewelled croziers in the National Museum, Byzantium was the centre of European civilisation and the source of its spiritual philosophy, so I symbolise the search for the spiritual life by a journey to the city.

The patriot would easily reflect that Ireland in her great missionary period was a healthier place than Byzantium, though the capital had, so to speak, the *foie gras* of the spiritual life. He could revere its saints and its art and yet believe, as he occasionally suggests in *A Vision*, that the spiritual rarities were won at the cost of corrupting most of the population. He broadcast later, on a visit to America:

There is a record of a tree of gold with artificial birds which sang. The tree was somewhere in the Royal Palace of Byzantium. I use it as a symbol of the intellectual joy of eternity, as contrasted with the instinctive joy of human life.

This is rather misleading, but he certainly believed that some of the intellectual joy can be felt during life in this world. Some notes for lectures in America (1932) give a little more evidence:

Aristotle says that if you give a ball to a child, and if it was the best ball in the market, though it cost but sixpence, it is an example of magnificence; and style, whether in life or literature, comes, I think from excess, from that something over and above utility which wrings the heart. In my later poems I have called it Byzantium, that city where the saints showed their wasted forms upon a background of gold mosaic, and an artificial bird sang upon a tree of gold on the presence of the emperor; and in one poem I have pictured the ghosts swimming, mounted upon dolphins, through the sensual seas, that they may dance upon its pavements.

Surely it is important to realise that the magnificence of Aristotle is not a Christian virtue but the supreme secular one; there could be no occasion for it in Heaven. We find here that a dolphin can carry a ghost to the capital of this virtue also; and the ghosts give a more holiday impression than before, at least they are no longer wailing. Mr Stallworthy, the most recent critic to discuss the drafts, makes a pleasanter impression than the earlier ones because he has the nerve to blame the poet for the opinions with which he is saddled.

As several critics have noted, the Emperor in the two Byzantium poems is clearly a symbol of divinity ... That Yeats's symbol of divinity is in danger of falling asleep, but for the singing of Yeats's soul, is a revealing commentary on the poet's view of God and of himself.

What it reveals is that all these critics have been libelling Yeats, not on purpose but because they cannot grasp the spiritual points at which he differed from Mr Chadband.

In the summer of 1924 Yeats took boat to Stockholm for the ceremony of receiving the Nobel Prize; the Irish Civil War was over, and he had been made a Senator – an anxious duty, as he could not do enough to help either the arts or the Protestant ex-Ascendancy, and he was thankful for the Prize because he hoped it would give him more influence. In the autumn, bad health made him winter in the Mediterranean, and he saw some of the Byzantine mosaics of Sicily. He became sixty in 1925 and began 'Sailing to Byzantium' the year after. Thus he was faced very directly at the time with the problem of how to behave as a distingushed old father-figure without hypocrisy and this problem had thrust itself upon him quite suddenly; the final text of the poem already seemed to me frank about this, before I had read the earlier drafts. The first step towards the poem, Mr Stallworthy decides, was a page of personal reflections never used again:

> Now the day is come I will speak on of those
> Loves I have had in play ...
> That my soul loved
> That I loved in my first youth
> For many loves have I taken off my clothes
> For some I threw them off in haste, for some slowly and indifferently

and laid down on my bed that I might be ...
but now I will take off my body

That they might be enfolded in that for which they had longed
I live on love
That which is myself alone
O let me still be enfolded in my ...
and how shall we ever grow very ...

(The handwriting is hard to read, and more may perhaps be read in the future.) No one could accuse this of being spiritually pretentious. But one might find it too intimate, and Yeats next planned to express the basic idea in terms of another person's experience, using the symbols he had recently worked out in *A Vision*. He knew the city of formal magnificence, 'rigid, abstract and fanatical' as a draft calls it; he himself was a thousand years too late, but other Irish poets had actually made the trip, while Ireland was leading Western Europe out of the Dark Ages. He let a Danish merchant fulfil a vow by shipping such a man as a pilgrim. The dolphin keeps rearing its head in the drafts, but it does not fit a historically possible journey, and when the work was complete he had managed to hold it in reserve till the last verse of the second poem.

This Dark-Age poet however could not express why the twentieth century needed the Byzantine style, and soon began turning back into Yeats; a rather early draft makes him complain that his public, or maybe the mountain gnomes, 'cry that my tale is told, my story sung', and the saints in the mosaics are henceforth called 'sages' – which meant classical or Asian, not Christian, holy men. The voyage remains real, as it was in the line 'sail southeastward towards Byzantium'; but it now also involves time travel, because the spirit of Yeats must go back a thousand years. I suppose this is why so many critics have asserted that he went to Paradise instead, but the process that he calls 'dreaming back', in the chapter of *A Vision* called 'The Soul in Judgement', is just the same; he cites the book called *An Adventure* by two lady dons, who in the garden of the Petit Trianon found themselves contemporary with Marie Antoinette. He also covers the case of the Egyptian mummy in the poem, who has come at least as far forward in time as Yeats has gone back. In 'the sixth and final state' before rebirth, he says, the spirit can see the most remote consequences of the most trivial acts of the living, provided these consequences are part of its future life. In trying to prevent them it may become one of those frustrators dreaded by certain spirit mediums. One must suppose such spirits gathered into bands – for as yet they are without individuality – and with the consent of the Thirteenth Cone playing a part resembling that of the 'Censor' in modern psychology. (Section IX)

A spirit may delay its rebirth for centuries, becoming a guardian of a temple, or employed in taking care of the newly dead, if its nature requires unique circumstances for its rebirth (Section VIII). It cannot be reborn until 'it accepts its future life, declares it just', and making a good decision about one's next birth is of course a very important step. This mummy has delayed too long, a fusspot perhaps; but we need not doubt that it has important business at the watering-place, and would be a good steady type to give Yeats some tips.

People have naturally suspected blarney in such pronouncements of the poet, or in the whole scheme of *A Vision*. A believer in any form of life after death, one would think, is liable to have bouts of uncertainty, but Yeats did not consider the story he tells in the two poems at all an impossible one. A man is not suspected like this if he says he believes in Christian immortality, though it is inherently much less probable than rebirth, and also unjust, not allowing you another chance (though the circumstances of your life often warp your moral character). Geoffrey Gorer has conducted a questionnaire in England, finding that only half the population believe in any after-life, while a quarter of those believers do not expect to be eternal. A twentieth of the answerers directly said they believed in reincarnation. The belief is not recommended by any organised body they are likely to have met with, so this seems to prove that it is found natural. Also it is old and widespread, and Yeats was determined to accept such beliefs rather than those of current fashion. G. K. Chesterton's *Autobiography* gives a good picture of his practical attitude to the supernatural (and, of course, to understand his poems, I am trying to take the same attitude). As a young man he startled literary London by presenting himself as The Man who Knew the Fairies:

He staggered the materialists by attacking their abstract materialism with a completely concrete mysticism; 'Imagination!' he would say with withering contempt; 'There wasn't much imagination when Farmer Hogan was dragged out of bed and thrashed like a sack of potatoes – that they did, they had 'um out', the Irish accent warming with scorn; 'they had 'um out and thumped 'um, and that's not the sort of thing a man wants to imagine'. But the concrete examples were not only a comedy; he used one argument which was sound, and I have never forgotten it. It is the fact that it is not abnormal men like artists, but normal men like peasants, who have borne witness a thousand times to such things; it is the farmers who see the fairies.

This of course was long before he wrote 'Byzantium'; a few years after it when near his death, he wrote 'News for the Delphic Oracle', in which the dolphins are certainly not only used to carry spirits to Heaven. They are carrying Plotinus, of all people, as well as Pythagoras and some Irish worthies, to a classical orgy:

> And the brute dolphins plunge
> Until, in some cliff-sheltered bay
> Where wades the choir of love
> Proffering its sacred laurel crowns
> They pitch their burdens off ...

It is not directly said that the sages take part, but a later section of the poem labours to present bodily enjoyment:

> Foul goat-head, bestial arm appear,
> Belly, shoulder, bum,
> Flash fish-like; nymphs and satyrs
> Copulate in the foam.

A friend of Plotinus, after his death, asked the Delphic Oracle where his soul had gone, and it made a splendid reply (available to Yeats from 1917 in McKenna's translation of Plotinus). At death, it said, this friend of Apollo 'entered at once the heavenly consort', on the shores of a 'wave-washed coast':

where fragrant breezes play, where all is unison and tenderness and divine joy, and the place is lavish of the nectar-streams the unfailing Gods bestow, and with the blandishments of the Loves ... where dwell the just Aeacus, and Plato, consecrated power, and stately Pythagoras and all else that form the Choir of Immortal Love ...

Thus the sages themselves are the choir, and Yeats makes them wade, at least, in this foam. As Milton might have said of his own interpretation of the loves of the spirits, if the oracle did not mean something very like sexual pleasure its language was culpably misleading. Yeats had been suspicious of Plotinus's doctrine as late as *The Tower* (1926) but had come round to admiring it, and in 1931 he echoes this oracle in a poem of placid dignity; but in 1939, his final year, it had to be presented with comic realism. It seems clear that spirits may have all sorts of experiences while waiting to be reborn, and dolphins may carry them to the Isles of the Blessed as well as the Supreme Heaven; but Mr F. A. C. Wilson (*W. B. Yeats and Tradition*, p. 214), firmly calls the place Heaven, explaining that the satyrs are preparing to be reborn from it. He also quotes from a commentary on Plotinus by Henry More, deducing that the soul will not only enjoy Philosophy in the next life but also 'innocent Pastimes, in which the Musical and Amorous propension may be also recreated'; this it seems was 'favourite reading' for Yeats, and Milton is believed to have taken his doctrine of the angels from the same passage (first published in 1659 and the unfortunate More was soon struggling to explain it away).

It seems often to be thought that Yeats, towards the end, became iconoclastic about the high spiritual tone he had taken earlier; surely it is much more probable that he realized, with a shock, that his admirers had been reading him in a sickly manner, and tried to stop them. He was too stubborn-minded to change one of his major beliefs without telling people so; and the poem itself is not cross but gay. I suppose he would feel that Plotinus was 'served right', as well as rewarded, by being given in the next life what he had renounced in this, indeed all the 'codgers' look rather comical; but Plotinus of course was not a Christian – the Introduction of McKenna's text remarks how weak he is on Repentance and the Dark Night of the Soul – and I am not sure what reason he could have given for rejecting entertainment offered by Apollo. Yeats had now come to regard the dolphins as all-purpose transport animals, in an afterlife which offered many mansions of wide variety; and he would regard them in a practical way, as he had regarded supernatural beings all his life.

Many of the letters of Sturge Moore (now a separate book) discuss philosophy; this Moore, as well as drawing the very beautiful cover for *The Tower*, was brother to G. E. Moore, and could be used as a back door means of contact, as by a palace intrigue, with that intellectual royalty. Yeats flounders, and often deserves the scolding that is relayed to him from above; but in March 1926 (for example) the modern reader must feel, as Chesterton had done earlier, that there is a real argument behind the charming wilfulness:

Forty years ago the Society for Psychical Research succeeded in transferring mental images (numbers, geometrical forms, simple drawings) between two people (1) in the same room, (2) in different rooms (3) in different towns. From that moment all philosophy based upon the isolation of the individual mind became obsolete.

The ecclesiastics of the mechanical philosophy met this and all evidence of psychical research by the demand that no fact of this kind could be accepted until, as you put it, 'the conditions are known in which it will certainly recur'. This was an evasion, for psychical facts belong to mind which never does the same thing in exactly the same way twice because all moments of being are unique. They in fact demanded that the mind should become mechanism before they would consider its action.

Answering a reply, he says on the 31 March 1926:

My complaint about the claim to 'control' psychic experiment is that the men who make the claim want the living bird to behave like the bird in a Swiss clock. Of course there are always 'sequences', but those of mind are not those of mechanism.

He began 'Sailing to Byzantium' (says Professor Jeffares) in September of the same year. Five months would hardly be enough to forget that a mechanical song-bird was so ridiculous as to make a good weapon against his materialistic opponents. He must therefore, in saying he will choose to be reborn as one, imply a decent modesty about his spiritual condition; critics who labour to inflate this cuckoo till it sails to Heaven are exposing the poet to undeserved distaste.

Not much can be learned from the drafts here, except that the poem steadily improved.

> Or send the dolphins back and carry me
> Into the artifice of eternity.
> > The dolphin's journey done I shall not take ...
> It it must be the dolphin I shall take ...

seems to have been the version that came immediately before

> It knows not what it is; and carry me
> Into the artifice of eternity.
> > Once out of Nature I shall never take ...

These dolphins specifically carry the soul to death, as on Roman tombs. But he consistently removes them from this poem, where their effect would be limiting, and in 'Byzantium' he seems to give them the more general function which they evidently have in 'News for the Delphic Oracle'. It would be absurd to allow rejected variants to prevent a poet from improving on his first idea.

He had seen gilding on mosaics, and in both his sources the tree was made of gold, as well as the bird:

> That the Grecian goldsmiths make ...
> And set in golden leaves to sing
> Of present past & future & to come
> For the instruction of Byzantium.

He thus tumbled upon the Golden Bough, and Mr Stallworthy reports that the handwriting at this point 'quickens and runs boldly':

> Or hammered gold and gold enamelling
> At the emperor's order for his Lady's sake
> And set upon a golden bough to sing
> To lords and ladies of Byzantium
> Of what is past, or passing, or to come.

The talisman which allowed Aeneas to visit the underworld and return was just what Yeats wanted; and Aeneas when he is there hears plenty of talk about reincarnation, with a long-term political prophecy, so the whole background is very suitable. I think the accident felt like magic, or like having the gods on his side; only after that can the verse bring into focus its smooth gaiety and its lilting impudence. It is very far from fear of death; perhaps he achieves in this last verse the state of purity or detachment which he prayed so earnestly for in the second verse.

Both poems present the idea of burning people alive to purge them, which is appallingly strong and eminently Christian; but Yeats reduces it; he turns the saints into 'sages' halfway through the drafts, and the ghostly dancers on the emperor's pavement derive from the Noh play *Motomezuka*. The heroine's sufferings, as Yeats explained, are imposed by her own mind and are not said to be deserved: 'The priest tells her that if she can but cease to believe in her punishments they will cease to exist. She listens in gratitude, but she cannot cease to believe ...'; Mr F. A. C.

Wilson (I quote this from his *op. cit*, p. 241) goes on to say that such flames naturally do not need faggots:

they feed on their own dark energy, though they do so at the discretion of the emperor, whom I take therefore to be Yeats's symbol of God.

There is not a word to suggest that the emperor is torturing these ghosts, except that they choose to do their purging dance in the palace which he inherits. No doubt a tenth-century emperor was in fact wicked enough to torture anybody, but Yeats prefers to think of him as amiable and idle, and how *could* an emperor torture a ghost? Mr Wilson invents his ghastly insertion with easy confidence, because the only Heaven he can conceive is the Christian Heaven, where the God who was 'satisfied' by crucifying his son forces his chosen to gloat as he does eternally in a total realisation of the tortures of the damned. No wonder such critics make the poems feel incoherent. Yeats probably set off from the Christian horrors but drove them steadily into the background of his world-picture; and the Noh plays even when dreadful evoke a mood of cool tenderness.

The purgation is in any case not chiefly aimed at removing guilt or divine displeasure. We hear at one point in *A Vision* that passionate love is likely to call for purgation afterwards, but not because it is a sin or because the spirits are too pure for it. Indeed we hear of a man who was persecuted by his guardian angel because it fell in love with his sweetheart (maybe someone punished this angel, but clearly it was not sexless). Some spirits purge themselves for deeds which hurt their neighbours, but some for passions which were to their credit in this world; as when the ghostly hero of a Noh play repeatedly dances his final battle, though he no longer owes loyalty to his overlord. Yeats himself, to judge from his letters, felt he needed purging from hatred of his old political enemies; he would sooner have defeated them, but to be a liberated spirit one must be prepared to start afresh. Thus to desire release from 'complexity', the knotted cords of passion which tie us to one life – complexity is mentioned three times as an evil in 'Byzantium' – does not imply that Yeats wanted release from the Wheel, release from rebirth. When he felt the nuisance of being an old man, he could hardly wait to be reborn. He accepted the idea of ultimate release (not to have done that would have been unorthodox) and here, I think, we find what is so jarring and tasteless when critics insist that the Byzantium poems take place in the presence of God. Seeing God's face, in Christianity, would correspond for Yeats to Nirvana or release from the Wheel; it would mean not returning to this world; and he had decided, and given prominence to poems explaining that he had decided, that for the present he needed to continue, however painfully, his series of reincarnations around the phases of the moon.

And yet just before this decision, not a dozen years before he died, he had said in lines of delicious and haunting beauty that he had chosen never to be reborn as any live thing, only as a cuckoo-clock or thereabouts. This is a problem, and fortunately it was observed at the time (whereas modern critics are content to show by learned parallels that the built-in tweet-tweet is the voice of God and so forth). Yeats wrote 'Byzantium' because Sturge Moore had told him that 'Sailing to Byzantium' ended badly; at least, that is what he told Sturge Moore, glad perhaps to have found a way to make him a generous answer. Moore wrote to Yeats on 16 April 1930 (two years after the poem had been printed) that the final verse 'let him down' because

such a goldsmith's bird is as much nature as a man's body, especially if it only sings like Homer and Shakespeare of what is past or passing or to come to Lords and Ladies.

Homer had said it of the soothsayer Calchas (*Iliad* 1, 70), and somehow this makes the mild comment more appreciative; there was no great need for a defence. Yeats only recalls it when writing to Moore about the bookplate on 4 October:

Yes, I have decided to call the book Byzantium. I enclose the poem from which the name is taken, hoping that it may suggest symbolism for the cover. The poem originates from a criticism of yours. You objected to the last verse of 'Sailing to Byzantium' because a bird made by a goldsmith was just as natural as anything else. That showed me that the idea needed exposition.

The book was finally called *The Winding Stair*, and the cover has a pinched-looking stair up the centre with ineffective obscurities in the four corners. The cover of *The Tower* even when battered still makes the tower look brave and the river wet, just as the 'Wild Swans at Coole' continue to fly; if Moore had been allowed the outline of St Sophia and a dolphin or two in the Bosphorus he would have brought off his splendid trick again. It was a sacrifice, and the reason for it was that the title of the collection had to draw attention to its central theme, a quasi-evolutionary struggle, and Yeats chose to put near the start a dialogue in which, as has been well said, 'he chooses for his soul reincarnation rather than a resting-place in the artifice of eternity'. Reincarnation thus became increasingly important to him as basic to the interpretation of 'Byzantium'.

It is hard to say just what 'exposition' Yeats had given to the idea of the bird by writing the poem; perhaps he would answer that his treatment had brought out more of the inherent beauty of the 'image', and that anything so beautiful must adumbrate a truth. He was quite capable of teasing his correspondent with a mystery, in a grand manner; and it seems plain that he could have chosen a more impressive example of the good which may be done by exalted works of art, if that was all he had required.

An article by Mr T. L. Dunne in *Modern Language Notes* (1952) settled the question of the sources for Yeats's bird. The Nobel Prize money (1923) let him do various useful things, among them buying himself a small working library which included *The Cambridge Medieval History* and Gibbon's *Decline and Fall* – 'in a good edition' he wrote to Lady Gregory (13 January 1924), so presumably she had told him to get one. I was pleased to find this in the *Letters* because I had argued beforehand that his advisers would regard Gibbon as more than a history, a major weapon of the Enlightenment against the priests. Yeats became prone to boast, falsely no doubt but with a sad kind of truth, that he had remained ignorant till he could educate himself out of his Nobel Prize money. Each of these large books allows a brief passage of somewhat rhetorical contempt to the mechanical toys of the Emperor Theophilus; they are plainly the immediate source of the bird of Yeats, which gave its first tweet in a poem written about two years after the massy volumes had reached his home. That is, he may have heard of it before, but this reading was what made him use it. Yet it is hard to see how even so contrary a man as Yeats could choose to be reborn as such a bird, in the face of the black scorn of the two surveys.

One reason, of course, was the then recent discovery of the merits of Byzantine art, a major tributary of the river in which the mind of Yeats swam. But this does not go far enough. Exclusively religious, the art was interrupted for a century by the Iconoclast Movement, and was different when it re-emerged. Theophilus, reigning 829–842, was a fanatical iconoclast, and rebuilt the palace in imitation of the Moslem splendours of Haroun al-Raschid. Even worse, he was the last iconoclast emperor;

when the bird was made, the art-works admired by Yeats and his friends had been suppressed or fought over, for a clear century, with the habitual vile cruelty of the masters of the holy city. The Moslems of course were iconoclasts too, and I have not been able to learn about the Baghdad style of animal sculpture. The *Cambridge Modern History* says that:

On audience days, when a foreign ambassador entered the hall, the birds in the plane-trees fluttered and sang, the griffins sat up on their pedestals, the lions arose, lashed the air with their tails, and gave forth metallic roars.

Gibbon is less funny (Chapter 53 at note 35), but remarks what a barbarian the man would have appeared to the Athenians. The taste of Yeats in visual art has become hard to sympathise with, but at least his social judgement was alert; as the toy outraged his whole theoretical position, and both his books told him it was vulgar, he might naturally have left it alone.

Indeed, I see only one explanation. He must have loved such a toy when he was about ten years old, in 1875, before he had developed any crotchets against the Machine Age. At the time there were very fine specimens on sale. Maybe he only flattened his nose against a shop window admiring them, as he wrote about Keats, but his father was indulgent at the time about a model yacht for the Round Pond. It does not seem a painful memory, but the child, not any ghost, may have been wondering whether it was worth while to let oneself grow up in the world, and this makes more understandable what the poem tells us, that the answer of the touchy pet would vary with its moods. When I was small (born 1906) I was sometimes taken to visit a venerable great-aunt, and after tea she would bring out exquisitely preserved toys of an antiquity rivalling her own. Chief among them was the bird of Yeats in its great cage, wound up to sing by a massive key; a darkish green tree, as I remember, occupied most of the cage, and a quite small shimmering bird, whose beak would open and shut while the musical box in the basement was playing, perched carelessly upon a branch at one side. The whole affair glittered, but I cannot claim to have seen the Golden Bough; it was prettier than a gilt tree would have been; and of course the bird was not plumb on top of it, like Satan in Paradise. I remember being struck to hear my mother say, by way of praising the great age of the toy, that she remembered being shown it herself when she was a child after such a tea;

and she and Yeats were born in the same year, 1865. I can raise no visual memory of the ones Queen Victoria presented to the Empress Dowager of China, which were on view in the Summer Palace (the Communists preferred to show other treasures after a bit), but I remember thinking they were just like Aunt Lizzie's, only plastered with semi-precious stones. Considering the date (1873), when the Empress first sent an envoy to London, hers and Aunt Lizzie's and Yeats's were probably all made by the same firm. Such toys were undoubtedly made earlier (Lord Macartney, in the *Journal* of his Embassy to China in 1793–4, reports embarrassment at finding in the park at Jehol 'orreries, clocks, and musical automations' much better than what he had brought – both lots had been made by the English firm of Ellicott, explains a footnote to the 1962 edition); but they had acquired a special prestige around 1870. They had come to be felt somehow edifying, or at least poetical in a high-minded way; many people nowadays, while regarding this sentiment as quaint and remote, would yet feel that the doll in *Petrouchka* is telling some mysterious truth which half comforts you and half makes you cry. (Whereas nobody would be tempted in this way by the mechanical griffins.) Yeats would be familiar with the idea that a child viewing such a toy is already in Paradise (perhaps from gaining a sense of magical power also needed by emperors), though he would not want the idea in his poem; and I agree that to that extent his Byzantium represents Paradise.

As to the date of the Byzantium of the poems, we should realise that after he had bought his history books he went on mulling over them to fit in the phases of the moon. In *A Vision* (1924, first edition) he says he would like to visit the Byzantium of Justinian, say AD 500, but the directive for writing 'Byzantium' (1930) envisages AD 1000. The singing bird erected by the last Inconoclast would no doubt keep its place indefinitely, so that if the spirit of Yeats came at about the turn of the century it could see both the bird and the new mosaics. This would be convenient, as AD 1000 in Yeats's system was a particularly eerie time. He expected AD 2000 to end Christianity with a new dispensation, probably a very unpleasant one; the date halfway through Christianity would thus be a central rendezvous for spirits past and to come – the poem might well include a nostalgic and despairing visitor from AD 2000, as well as an indignant hot-gospelling Early Christian; but this completeness would seem trivial to Yeats, whose mind was always on the needs of the next step ahead. In *A Vision* V.iv. (1925) he speaks of the later Byzantine

mosaics as inferior, mentioning the churches in Sicily he had seen the
year before (later than his writing for the first edition). I think he means
that the mosaics made after the Iconoclastic break at first recovered the
old stern majesty, but that later ones became humanistic:

The return of the images may, as I see things, have been the failure of synthesis
(Phase 22) and the first sinking-in and dying-down of Christendom into the
heterogeneous loam ... Full moon over, that last Embodiment shall grow more
like ourselves, putting off that stern majesty, borrowed, it may be, from the
Phidian Zeus – if we can trust Cefalu and Monreale; and his Mother – putting off
her harsh Byzantine image – stand at his side.

He goes to report tales of Popes appointed by ruling courtesans, and
hearing their sighs in the confessional after exciting their cries of love;
'outside a few courts and monasteries, another book tells me of an Asiatic
and anarchic Europe'. By 1000, if I follow his mind, the city was still
keeping anarchy at bay but had become oppressively autumnal, and
already the ghosts were more distinguished than the living. It was the best
time to choose, if you wanted to meet the ghosts.

I am not sure how to interpret the assumption that naturalism is bad,
and that ill-nature is good because unnatural; the formula confuses at
least two different factors. The Ravenna mosaics (say AD 500) often
combine much human or natural charm with their religious earnestness,
whereas the Sicilian ones (say AD 1000) are very formal or unnatural in
line except for the faces, always of elderly and severe characters, which are
often strikingly lifelike and convincing; they are not spiritual but ruling-
class. Technically, the Ravenna ones are made of quite large bits of
unshaped stone, often with the mortar or concrete showing between
them; and this unnaturalistic texture gives a shimmer of intense though
eternally fixed vitality – you feel the artist relied on his luck, so it is not
really very different from the effect of a snapshot. The Sicilian ones give
the contours of robe and cheek a perfect smooth curve, evidently the pride
of the technicians but slimy in effect, with pursy sagging curves. Boris
Anrep, who recovered the Ravenna technique and used it for example on
the floor of the National Gallery, lectured on it at Cambridge while I was a
student; he needed only to hint his distaste for the Sicilian curves and
follow them on the magic-lantern screen with his pointer to make the
audience roar as at an obscene farce. This would be in the year that

'Sailing to Byzantium' was written, and Yeats was 'in the movement' about Byzantine art, so the distinction was probably clear to him. The passage I have quoted is tiresomely obscure, but probably because he felt uncertain about history, not about art. The Sicilian characters are strong enough to control a mob, however plainly the 'abstract forms' of their drapery are elderly bellies and testicles; and control of a mob is admittedly one of the themes of 'Byzantium'.

The spiritual tourist is shocked by the holy city as soon as he arrives there; his moral taste has not sunk so low as that of his critics, who mistake it for Paradise. I claim some credit for recognising this from the first three lines of the finished poem:

> The unpurged images of day recede;
> The Emperor's drunken soldiery are abed.
> Night's resonance recedes; night-walker's song ...

I was not found convincing there, but it turns out that the earlier drafts made the point much more strongly: 'all that roaring rout of rascals', 'the emperor's brawling soldiers', 'the last benighted robber or assassin fled', 'the drunken harlot's song'. Critics who still insist that this town is Paradise must be struggling to hush up a scandal. But Yeats wanted to show that an other-worldly art had power to handle the harsh forces of the world, so his picture of the city is wanted, as well as true; and I suppose he cut it down merely because he needed severe compression all along.

'Byzantium' has only five verses. In the first, night falls after the visitor's first day in the city; in the second, he meets what we learn from his private directive to be the ghost of a mummy; the third is given up to the bird and what it can do; in the fourth, still on the emperor's pavement, the spirits dance their purgation; and the mysterous fifth celebrates the triumph of the smithies of the emperor over the flood. Mr Bradford, in his final paragraph, says; 'Death the summoner, disguised as a walking mummy, calls the souls of the departed to Paradise'; in his view, the throne of the Emperor, who is God, is the end of the pilgrimage of these wailing dead. Hence the bird cannot influence their behaviour, because they are past being influenced when they first see it. At least, this is so if I am right in believing that Yeats would regard actually seeing the face of God (an experience he does not write about) as equivalent to Nirvana, the end of the process of rebirth. The mummy would be 'Death the summoner' all right, but there would no longer be any point in the bird.

I used even to disbelieve the idea that the mummy is meant to act as a guide to Yeats, but here the variants have convinced me. Mr Stallworthy says that, by the third draft of the poem, Yeats

> would seem to have conceived the idea of a single guide, who would lead him through Byzantium as the Sibyl led Aeneas, and Virgil led Dante. This, presumably, is the 'walking mummy' of the first draft.

The third draft has the line 'His breathless body moves and summons me', and a later draft puts 'beckons' for *summons*; then we have:

> A mouth that has no moisture and no breath
> (May better summon me) Can merrily summon me
> To adore ...

'Merrily' carries a strong suggestion that we have not heard the whole story. Even without this unnerving detail, it would be probable that if we had the science fiction Long-Short we would find the mummy at least giving some gruff directions to the poet. But, even so, it would be quite unsuitable, and extremely unlike what happens to Virgil, if this mummy led Yeats into the presence of God.

Also the interest of Yeats seems to be not in deciding where the guide would take him to but in considering the nature of such a guide. Other variants say:

> (Harsh) Death in Life, or that dear Life in Death

> Limbs that have been bound in mummy-cloth
> Are more content with a winding path

> It knows the winding of the path

Mr Stallworthy says that the stanza 'grows round the nucleus of a Coleridgean image', but Mr Wilson probably did better by deriving 'death-in-life' from a fragment of Heraclitus: 'Men and gods die each other's life, live each other's death'. Neither reference is much help here. This mummy has presumably refused rebirth for at least a thousand years, and Yeats would think of its existence as like the sordid old age of a man who has refused to risk a life at the call of duty. Such a state is readily

called 'death in life', and the desirable 'life in death' would be becoming
an immortal poet, or a toy which is a reliable entertainer of children, or
something decent like that. But no such distinction is made in the poem;
the visitor 'hails' the cynical old mummy with relief, and addresses him
both ways round; anyhow, he is better worth meeting than those beastly
live people were, during the day.

A final version, after many variants, says:

> A mouth that no moisture and no breath
> Breathless mouth may summon.

Here I have the unusual satisfaction, after saying that the merit of a line is
inherently to be ambiguous, of reading evidence that the poet had drafted
the meanings separately and struggled till they were combined. We get

> A mouth that has no moisture and no breath
> Cries out the summons / Can stoutly summon
> can merrily summon me /Can all blood summon

but also

> A mouth that has no moisture and no breath
> Breathing mouths may summon.

The ambiguity marks an astute observation of Yeats, of a problem often
quarrelled over. Human mouths, breathless with terror, have raised
Mephistopheles, but Mephistopheles said he hadn't been fetched at all,
he had merely chosen to come and fetch Faustus. The poetical effect of
the ambiguity is a kind of tender mystery and awe; but still, 'hailing' the
vision is hardly the way Yeats would have received a call to death without
rebirth, whatever the variant 'merrily' means; and no variant says that
Yeats obeyed the beckoning of the mummy, any more than Pope obeyed
the beckoning of the Unfortunate Lady.

Still, though I need to deflate the mummy, I recognise that is is viewed
with awe as a way-finder; not only in a number of splendid lines which
were rejected but in a grand mystery of the final version:

> For Hades' bobbin bound in mummy-cloth
> May unwind the winding path.

The struggle of Yeats for compactness has led him here to a startling
conceit, and as I have had a long disagreement with my colleagues about

Imagery I enjoy insisting that they ought to make a picture of this too. Egyptian mummies were wrapped in a continuous narrow bandage of great length, so they actually could be used as the ball of thread was used by Theseus in the labyrinth and by Curdie in George MacDonald's *The Princess and the Goblins* (1872). If Yeats picked this mummy up and twirled it round, he could leave a line of bandage behind him, and after completing his adventures wind up his way back to daylight. It seems clear at least that he is not eager for extinction. But the mummy could be allowed a more active part. Curdie, when he followed the thread into unknown depths of the mine to the haunts of the goblins, was (however magically) being guided; and perhaps this mummy is a guide who will lay a trail of bandage for his remote posterity by dancing round as he advances. I hope I will not be told of some aesthetic reason why I should close my mind to these Images, as not sufficiently in the mode; they occupy the only bit of the poem which is about *The Winding Stair* a conception so important to the poet that the volume could not be called 'Byzantium' and the cover design had to be spoilt. The mummy showed a truth by being bound up, because to liberate oneself is necessarily a circuitous process; and he did it to live for ever. A man so very entangled, the drafts imply through their excellent poetry, will probably be an expert in the pedantries of the next world, good at showing the way.

I expect that this is another case of relying upon childhood memories, though they are not so badly needed here as for justifying the clockwork bird. Theseus and Ariadne, though well known, are not I think a usual game for children. *The Princess and the Goblins* was published when Yeats was seven years old, and became part of the equipment of every respectable Victorian nursery. One of my earliest memories is of clutching a candle in my shaking hand and climbing over heaps of coal as I wound up the thread left by my sister across the vasty and labyrinthine cellars of Yokefleet Hall. If the child Yeats had not played this game too, it is hard to see why the grotesque conceit rang a bell in him. One would like to have more story in the poem here. The poet says: 'A ghost has appeared, and I see it is a mummy; not surprisingly, because all these artificial products of hieratic skills, like the sages in the mosaics, are artful at finding their way out of the underworld.' Anybody may need to get out of the underworld, but Yeats in doing this piece of time-travel while yet alive finds it specially urgent.

When he says that the vision is 'more image than a shade' he perhaps means a little that it is a Symbol, being a Symbolist himself; but this would get in the way of the narrative, and the main meaning has to be 'statue' – indeed, a mummy actually is a statue superimposed upon the shell of a human body. A draft of 'Sailing to Byzantium' says that he hoped to meet there a statue by Phidias, and probably the idea was still knocking about in his mind. It would be aesthetically a bit unnerving to see these two entities stalking past one another on the magic pavement, and I daresay that Yeats, when he talked about an 'image' but gave only abstract paradoxes, was trying to avoid being too visual here. All the same, we would expect to meet both of them in the film of the poem.

The next verse is the mechanical bird, and the drafts do not give much help; Mr Stallworthy is evidently right about a 'literary influence', but the poet succeeded in driving it out, When he wrote

> What mind decreed or hammer shaped the metal

he must have been comparing the poor toy to Blake's tiger, thus making it hard for me to argue that he viewed the bird with self-deprecating humour. But he would think of it as like Swift or Joyce, harsh wits who made cauterizing jokes and were both feared and revered; to regard a wit as a tiger is typical of the Dublin of the nineties. Also I do not deny that the bird is allowed a dignified entry in the last verse, as one of the products of the Byzantine smithies.

Because reincarnation decided the name of *The Winding Stair*, when 'the cocks of Hades crow' they must be inciting the spirits to choose to be reborn. But this bird is said to crow 'like' them, therefore is not presented as one of them; naturally not, because it is in tenth-century Byzantium. One draft says it

> Mutters night long out of a golden bough
> What the birds of Hades know.

This adds to its moodiness, which Yeats would regard as an unmechanical feature, though it is familiar in many an old car. The final version says it

> Can like the cocks of Hades crow,
> Or, by the moon embittered, scorn aloud
> In glory of changeless metal
> Common bird or petal ...

That is, it sometimes encourages the ghosts who visit the city to accept the arduous duty of rebirth; but, in its blacker and more Swift-like moods, it tells them that life on earth is not worth returning to. This might answer the question of Sturge Moore; although the art-work itself was material, its beauty allowed it to influence the spirits.

Mr Bradford says that the poems present rather different towns; in the town of the second poem:

Unity of Being is threatened, though it is miraculously restored when the symbolic dolphins carry the souls of the dead to a Yeatsian paradise of art, art which is at once sensual and spiritual.

It seems to have become a rule that the effect of saying 'symbolic' is to throw away the story; no poet must any longer write an allegory – he had already been forbidden to write a literal story, like Chaucer. At first, I think, the symbolists despised a story for being exciting; but here is a case where refusal to attend to the facts presented makes a poem too much of a thriller. This miraculous restoration was the permanent state of being of the holy city, not a trick which a crack corps of dolphin-riders brought off once. The actual spirits, arriving by regular dolphin service for a bit of purging at Byzantium, dancing on a magic pavement and what not, were in pretty bad shape and had no idea of rescuing or destroying the city.

> Astraddle on the dolphin's mire and blood
> Come the thin shades
>
> The crowds approach; the marble breaks the flood
>
> Shadowy feet upon the floor
> Innumerable feet, passion-heavy feet
> Intricacy of the dancing floor ...
> Simplicity of the dancing floor
> A crowd of spirits

Not exactly Biggle's crowd, swooping in for a rescue, surely. A reader may well ask 'Why then *are* they supposed to have come?' and Yeats I think would answer 'Well, around 1000 it actually was a very haunted city'. So many vehement generations had expressed themselves in such numinous art-works that the place attracted spirits as a corpse does flies. But he also believed that the city did many of the visiting spirits good, and felt confident that he would himself win some good there if he could arrange the trip. We would like to know many more things about it, for example, what proportion of these ghosts had living bodies like Yeats, to which they would return?

Some critic said that when the poet wrote

> That dolphin-torn, that gong-tormented sea

he meant that 'the cathedral bells terrify the population by foretelling death'. I thought this farcically low-minded, but who would care, if it explained anything about the magical line. The drafts are not much help but as before they show the poet labouring to say two incompatible things, until at last he can say both at once:

> The dolphin-tortured flood breaks into spray
> That gong-tormented current breaks in spray in foam

The moral of the dolphin was that it could jump through the surface of the sea for play, and in the course of play it had saved the lives of men; it could thus adventure from one element to another, or even from an animal to a spiritual world, and yet safely return. Yeats too wanted to get back, and felt the charm of the dolphins on the Roman tombstones. The truth is that the classical authors were talking in a confusion between two creatures called dolphin, a small whale and a fish, and could not be bothered to distinguish them (no symbolism I hope need be attached to this merely sordid mental condition). The breaking of the surface between two media really is, however, a major theme of 'Byzantium', and it is in key with this to have the verses presented each as a separate rough diamond. The gong makes everything shake, even the surface of the sea; the holy noise shakes it from above as the dolphin does from below. The cathedral bells continually recall to the population that they ought to engage in more spiritual activity, but this does not mean exciting terror by threatening immediate death. The wonderful line is rather weak on symbolism, but at least it does little to encourage holy terror.

Finally, I have to admit that the symbolist method prevents one from interpreting the poem fully as a science fiction narrative; but I maintain that the effort is still worth pushing as far as it will go, because the symbolic resistance is only met at a fairly deep level. The ghosts are the same as the sea on which they ride, liable to 'flood' the city unless coped with by breakwaters, and therefore the same as the disruptive passions of the living inhabitants of the city, which would also overwhelm it if not countered by its supreme art-works. The doctrine of rebirth gave ghosts a status rather inferior to that of men, so the ambition of Yeats in choosing to be reborn as an art-works could not be satisfied by merely having a good influence on ghosts. The smithies too must also keep at bay the evil of the human inhabitants of the city, but the poem does not say so, and indeed would have no time to, because of the magical compression of its technique. The mysterious triumph of the last verse, holding disaster for ever at bay as by the routine of a juggler, may well seem an answer to the objection of Sturge Moore, even if only shouted by an unknown authority down a corridor in a dream. 'In the mediumistic condition', said Yeats (*A Vision* III, 8), 'it sometimes seems as if dreams awoke and yet remained dreams.' On some such ground, I suppose, one might even admit the presence of the Christian God the Father, though he must not expect to start indulging himself in his unpleasing personal habits as soon as he gets through the door. In any case, I think, the poem feels much better if one takes a waking interest in its story; there is no need to say that its merit resides in the confusion at a deep level which seems to be inherent in symbolist technique.

ELIOT

My God, man, there's bears on it

The facsimile of the original drafts of *The Waste Land*, edited by Valerie Eliot, is a sumptuous edition, making a great contrast to the unbuttoned casualness of the comments and variants which it reports; but the occasion really deserved one. The poem is inherently a mystery; I would never have believed that the Symbolist programme could be made to work at all, if it had not scored a few resounding triumphs, such as this. Many people, when the poem was new, felt greatly affected by it without understanding why; and even if you decide that the effect was an accident you cannot help wanting to know how it happened.

Being thus dubious about symbolism, I was one of the mugs who hoped that the story of the poem would be unveiled when the lost bits were restored; and I do find that the Introduction to this first edition of the bits lets the story peep out. That is debatable, but another surprising result is quite plain; Eliot was imitating Dickens. 'He do the Police in different Voices' had been his temporary name for the growing rag-bag of character-sketches, and all the longer bits cut out from the final poem are cases where he had failed to catch the character's voice. He had not known well the Boston roisterers or the Cape Cod fishermen, who bumped into an iceberg so big that it had bears on it, and had hardly even decided whether or not his English debutante Fresca was 'literary'. But (in the 'Game of Chess') the neurotic lady is his first wife, and we now learn that the tireless pub narrator is their housemaid; he had listened to both for hours. The most surprising case comes at the start, the lady who went tobogganing with the Arch-Duke. I never felt sure about the discovery of Mr Morris, that this bit is taken from the memoirs of Countess Marie Larisch, *My Past* (1913), because not one phrase from the book is echoed in the poem; but now Mrs Eliot explains that the poet had met her, and was using her conversation. Her book was a belated act of self-defence, demonstrating that she had not in any way helped to cause the death of the heir to the throne of Austria, though intimate with the persons concerned. Presumably, when the book was newly out, she would be in a sense thrown open to the public; the young Eliot was

probably presented to her at a grand reception, before the war, when he
was a student in France or Germany. She would be twice Eliot's age, and
the death of the Crown Prince which ended her life at Court had
happened in the year Eliot was born. She had been a great deal more of an
athlete than he ever was (the Empress had a private circus with trick
horses) and she would mention tobogganing because she thought he must
at least have done that much. Never again had she been so happy, it
appeared, as tobogganing had made her in her childhood, and Eliot ought
to have answered that he had been happiest when boating, as a college
boy, off Boston. Very likely he did give this answer, as he evidently heard
her talking for some time; but the poem says:

> What are the roots that clutch, what branches grow
> Out of this stony rubbish?

There is an excellent book *The Substantial Ghost* by Violet Powell, with
a whole chapter about the Countess. The ghost was an English journalist
who specialised in writing or re-writing the memoirs of ex-royalties,
coaxing out of them bits that were likely to sell. For her the Countess was a
rather a minor figure, but high scandal might be expected. Very unusually,
the Countess had already written her book, and did not want to have it
altered, but did not mind adding suggestively tactful sentences about the
Empress's corsets and suchlike. Her mother had been an actress with
some Jewish blood, and the marriage had only been accepted on condition
of signing away some titles which her children might otherwise inherit.
But she was a strong beautiful blonde, and the Empress liked to appear
'unconventional', so she made this cousin her personal attendant. The
Countess became indignant after a time, and her book does leave the
impression she wanted – that there was something the matter with the
Hapsburgs; but not with her. After the First War they were all in disarray
but could at least have fed her; she chose to be general servant to a
struggling Jewish family in Berlin. The Ghost discovered her there, and
said that, considering how she cooked, this family were the ones who
really deserved pity. But she took out the Countess to a smart lunch, with
champagne to recover her nerve, and after some further publicity the
Countess received a cable offering marriage from the Middle West. A
fluttering inquiry was sent to the Ghost, who sternly telegraphed 'accept',

and into the Middle West she disappeared. 'Substantial' in the book-title means that the Ghost, as also the Countess, had become fat. Violet Powell has a sympathy for these comic characters, but she despises the Countess almost as much as the young Eliot did. A son of the Countess had killed himself because a gossip had told him untruly that his real father was the Crown Prince; it was to clear up such points that she decided to write her book. I find her an impressive character, definitely not stony rubbish.

Anyway, a touch of the craving to scold may be observed in the poem here, with its assumption that the poet is nobler and purer than anything he contemplates. The French writers who invented Symbolism seem never to have thought of turning it to the uses of a cats' tea-party; but then, if Eliot was imitating Dickens, he was bound to scold, and Dickens would have shown no mercy to a Hapsburg courtier. The difference is that Dickens had a plot, which allowed him to show adequate reasons for his scolding; it is true that the plot is often perfunctory – no admirer of *Oliver Twist* would try to detail the itinerary of the villain; but to scold without even a residual plot, as a Symbolist, is bound to feel self-regarding. Even so, it felt a good deal more human than Mallarmé or Valéry.

The poem is of course much more than a collection of sketches, but he seems to have let the sketches pile up in the hope of finding a theme for them. Thus he would not be startled when advised by Pound (nearly always rightly, I agree) to leave half of them out. But what was this theme which Pound intuitively recognized and eagerly admired? Given his main interests, as they were to develop later, it seems likely he would be most struck by an aspect that English readers tend to regard as incidental. 'London has just escaped, from the First World War, but it is certain to be destroyed by the next one, because it is in the hands of international financiers. The very place of it will be sown with salt, as Carthage was, and forgotten by men; or it will be sunk under water.' This approaching doom, whether desired or feared, comes into every section of the surviving poem, and the semitic Carthage appears in sections I, III, and IV; the fifth and last needs only the hooded hordes swarming from Eastern Europe, the commies you need not doubt, and 'London Bridge is falling down'. London is regarded all through with fascination, astonishment or horror, a weird place of exile, shot through with occasional memories of a splendid past, and now insolently rotting away.

This edition, on the other hand, is keen to insist that the theme of the poem was a private one. A sheer page near the start is given to a reported assertion by the poet, of unknown date and uncertain accuracy (surely, Eliot would never *talk* this kind of formal irony to Ted Spencer):

Various critics have done me the honour to interpret the poem in terms of criticism of the contemporary world, have considered it, indeed, as an important bit of social criticism. To me it was only the relief of a personal and wholly insignificant grouse against life; it is just a piece of rhythmical grumbling.

The placing of this remark gives it too much importance, but I am sure he did at some time say such things and believe them. What then was the grouse about? One might expect it was about his first wife, already chronically ill and perhaps starting to go mad. But the edition refutes that. Just before writing *The Waste Land*, Eliot was feeling so ill that his wife arranged for him to see a specialist and the bank gave him three months' sick leave (September 1921):

I really feel very shaky, and seem to have gone down rapidly since my family left. ... I am going to Margate tomorrow, and expect to stay at least a month. I am supposed to be alone, but I could not bear the idea of starting this treatment quite alone in a strange place, and I have asked my wife to come with me and stay as long as she is willing.

He is still regarding her company as an indulgence. He had a stern code of lying for loyalty, but would not invent this detail merely to deceive Richard Aldington. They both had nervous illnesses, but were if anything drawn together by them. She admired the 'Game of Chess' very much, and composed one of the lines for it. In fact, she makes a very good impression; the marriage did not go wrong till at least five years later. The grouse, as this edition makes plain for the first time, was about something quite different.

In January 1919, Eliot wrote to his patron Quinn that he needed to bring out some kind of book in America, 'for private reasons':

I am coming to America to visit my family some time within the summer or autumn, and I should particularly like to have it appear first. You see, I settled here in the face of strong family opposition, on the ground that I found the environment more favourable to the production of literature.

Other letters have expressed a thorough-going distaste for the environment (he 'did not think he would ever come to like England'), so the stiff formula leaves one rather puzzled. His parents, it is clear, were inclined to believe that he had made a mess of his life (had he been wanted to join his father's firm?), but a book would 'go toward' appeasing them. Three weeks later, he wrote again saying that his father was dead, but that made it all the more necessary to bring out a book in America, however unsatisfactory to himself, as his mother was still alive. Probably he knew about the will already, as it would be considered fair to warn him of the proposed change before he married; but he does not mention it to Quinn till five years later, when he has to explain why he is unwilling to leave the bank – otherwise he may appear grasping or cowardly. If he dies at his post his wife will receive a pension, and she is too ill to be left destitute (April 1923); but

owing to the terms of my father's will any property coming to me is in trust, and reverts to my family on my death – instead of being left outright, as to my brother and sisters. Thus my wife can get no benefit from my inheritance in the event of my death. My father disapproved of my residence in England.

The last sentence is penetratingly mild; Father's objection seems to have been racial rather than national. Probably he would not have done this if his son had married a Frenchwoman, at least, not without meeting her or knowing anything to her discredit; but he would have done it, with the approval of St Louis behind him, if his son had married an American Negress. Eliot was rather prone to conceive that his honour had been smirched and to react fiercely, partly as a result of his Southern upbringing no doubt, and here is a case where any man might feel that he ought to stand up for his wife. Besides, he kept on believing that Vivienne would recover if only she had a respite from the pressure of struggle and anxiety; so he would feel that his father's prejudice was driving his wife mad. Such was the grouse; and it is enough to explain a good deal.

We can deduce too, I think, that Mother was a disappointment, though she is not blamed. He wrote to her that his New Year resolution for 1920 was to write 'a long poem I have had on my mind for a long time'; this was nearly a year after his father's death. In February he wrote to his brother that he was thinking of his desire to see Mother all the time, and would never be happy unless he could really *see* her again, but that she felt she ought not to leave America till her husband's affairs were in order. Apparently she could not finish settling Father's will till the summer of

1921, when she was seventy-seven; then she stayed in Eliot's flat for the summer, and was 'terrifyingly energetic' at sight-seeing. The Eliot couple had to leave Clarence Gate Gardens and took a flat in Wigmore Street, getting on to a mile away; at least, Vivienne stayed there at first, but 'as she was under medical orders to be in the country at that time of year Eliot insisted on her getting away whenever possible' (p. xxi). I have looked round one of the flats at Clarence Gate Gardens, which were considered advanced when Mrs Eliot came, and it had two large bedrooms with double beds in them, also there was a recess or alcove on the other side of the passage, which could be curtained over as a sleeping-place for a nurse or personal servant. Presumably one could telephone down for room service as required. The old lady was attended by a daughter, who would probably sleep on another bed in her room; we do not hear of any extra attendant, but she could be fitted in if she came. Mrs Eliot was quite rich enough to go to a hotel, but she would regard living in her son's flat for a week or two as rather fun, like camping out. If she had wanted to meet the young couple, there would be no real inconvenience in telling them to stay. I grant that Eliot's brother and another sister were sometimes around too, but it would not occur to *them* to drive their host out of his own flat. It seems clear that the mother had refused to sleep under the same roof as the wife. Eliot wrote to Aldington, in June, 'these new yet old relationships involve immense tact and innumerable adjustments. One sees a lot of things one never saw before, etc.'; but in October he wrote (as already quoted): 'I really feel very shaky, and seem to have gone down rapidly since my family left'; and then completed *The Waste Land* on sick leave. It seems clear that Mother, though she had some latitude under Father's will, had refused to budge an inch.

The central theme of *The Waste Land*, or symbol as one might say, is about a father; it is evoked by the variations upon 'Of his bones are coral made', which come into all five sections of the poem (ll. 48, 125, 192, 316, 423). The play by Shakespeare, of course, gets its chief dramatic tension from the doubt whether the all-powerful father will choose to revenge himself, while he makes arrangements about the marriage of his child; but young Ferdinand is wandering about a strange island believing everyone else to be drowned, including his father, when he hears this line sung to him from the empty air; the voices of the island are telling him lies, and yet they are benignant and aim at the happy ending. In Eliot's poem (according to his Notes at any rate) an heir to the fisher kingdom has come to an island engaged on some kind of cultural quest, 'musing upon the king his father's death' (the death of the king his brother as well was presumably added merely for camouflage). 'Those are pearls that were his eyes. Look!' does manage to convey that you might be shown something rather eerie by the fortune-teller, if your card was the Drowned Phoenician Sailor: Shakespeare or the lying Ariel have done their best to turn the idea to favour and to prettiness, but the natural man might view it otherwise. Many critics have explained that the poem adumbrates an eventual rebirth after a sacrifice, and probably it does, but the new edition tells us how the sacrifice was conceived.

It is done by exultantly rancorous parodies, describing the rich London Jews rotting under water; they seem to me better poetry than the few bits which have been quoted from his youthful sex-fun poems, but they have the same confident bounce, and they were plainly among the major impulses behind writing *The Waste Land*:

> Full fathom five your Bleistein lies
> Under the flatfish and the squids ...
>
> That is lace that was his nose
> See upon his back he lies
> (Bones peep through the ragged toes)
> With a stare of dull surprise
> Flood tide and ebb tide
> Roll him gently side to side
> See the lips unfold unfold
>
> From the teeth, gold in gold.
>   Lobsters hourly keep close watch
> Hark now I hear them
>   scratch scratch scratch

Full fathom five is of course another quotation from the same scene of *The Tempest* – I thought it occurred in the final poem, and had to look through several times to make sure that it doesn't. The quotation mosaicked into the speech of the fortune-teller had at first a grander setting:

> Those are pearls that were his eyes. See!
> And the crab clambers through his stomach, the eel
>   grows big

> And the torn algae drift above him,
> And the sea colander.
> Still and quiet brother are you still and quiet

In the final poem the only echo of this joke, at the enemy being eaten under water, comes in the graceful regret for Phlebas the Phoenician which is all that survived of Section IV:

> A current under sea
> Picked his bones in whispers.

Almost the whole passage had been thriftily saved from *Dans le Restaurant*, a rather nasty poem in French, but this bit was added and supplies the poetry. The enemy is no longer jeered at if his body is eaten by inanimate natural forces, instead of by crabs, and yet the comparison is only just ignored. Eliot came to feel that the calm of this point of turn-over (after Pound had insisted on his retaining it) was so effective that each of the *Four Quartets* has a similar lyrical penultimate section. The rejected passages of Jew-baiting are still deeply involved in the final poetry.

I am not inclined to pull a long face about this. A writer had better rise above the ideas of his time, but one should not take offence if he doesn't, and the surprising thing is that Eliot and Pound were so careful to take the Jew-baiting passages out. Hilaire Belloc's pot-boiling comic novels, attacking the new governing class of high finance, are useful evidence here because they presume a ready public acceptance. Belloc is soiled by hatred perhaps, but his associate G. K. Chesterton was a most saintly character, and he wrote about Jews in the same way. It would be charitable to think what they meant by Jews was simply capitalists, or international financiers: and this indeed was the moral or economic point of their line of talk, but they tricked it out with a very specific picture of their Jew. I should guess that there actually has been a successful absorption of Jews in England, within living memory, so that these antisemites were describing something real; of course, there would have been no absorption if the antisemites had got their way. Then again, the young Eliot had a good deal of simple old St Louis brashness; half the time, when the impressionable English were saying how wonderfully courageous and original he was to come out with some crashingly reactionary remark, he was just saying what any decent man would say back home in St Louis – if he was well heeled and had a bit of culture. (For example, such a man would think the

English policy towards the lower races dangerously permissive.) But maybe this general reflection hardly applies to the present case: the young Eliot, who confined himself to comic verse about Jews, cannot be called more illiberal about them than Belloc. Eliot in later life, reports Mr Bergonzi in his recent biography, was affronted at the accusation of antisemitism:

a terrible slander. . . . And they do not know, as you and I do, that, in the eyes of the Church, to be antisemitic is a sin.

Surely this is a good deal more alarming for a Jew than the horror joke poems, which might fairly be called Dickensian.

Indeed, a reader may feel I am giving these bits too much importance; Eliot wanted to grouse about his father, and lambasted some imaginary Jews instead (as a backroom boy at Lloyd's, doing rather technical work, and living very quietly, he was not of course regularly meeting the millionaires). But we have also to reckon with the very odd habits of Symbolist poetry. What is happening to the Jews is what was happening in *The Tempest* to the prince's father; have they then something in common? Eliot's grandfather went to St Louis as a missionary preaching Unitarianism, and incidentally founded a university there; Eliot's father continued to be a staunch Unitarian while going into business. Eliot himself at Harvard read Sanskrit, a thoroughly Boston-Brahmin thing to do, and remarked soon after that it was almost impossible to be a Christian after studying the Far Eastern religions. Unitarians describe themselves as Christians but deny that Jesus was God, whereas Eliot was beginning to feel a strong drag towards a return to the worship of the tortured victim. Now if you are hating a purse-proud business man who denies that Jesus is God, into what stereotype does he best fit? He is a Jew, of course; and yet this would be a terrible blasphemy against his family and its racial pride, so much so that I doubt whether Eliot ever allowed himself to realise what he was doing. But he knows, in the poem, that everything has gone wrong with the eerie world to which the son is condemned.

Several odd judgements in his later work are explained by this. In September 1919 Eliot wrote his essay on *Hamlet*, saying that Shakespeare had experienced 'the inexpressibly horrible', and seeming to presume it was about his parents (as usual, Eliot has foresuffered all), but the play is a failure because Shakespeare thought he could express this feeling

through an old plot, about murder, incest and suchlike trivialities, so that
we feel Hamlet is making a fuss about nothing. An author needs to find an
'objective correlative' for his emotion – this phrase assumes that the
outside of his writing can never simply belong with the inside, because he
must never write about the things that really matter to him. One ought to
have realized at the time that only some great personal distraction could
account for so bizarre a judgement. A third of a century later, in *The
Confidential Clerk* (1954), the trouble is more deeply hidden. It is a
twittering drawing-room comedy about bastards who need to know who
their father was, because they won't feel comfortable till they take up
father's profession. The chief one is being quite good at business, till he
hears that his father was a village organist, too incompetent for promotion,
and then he thankfully determines to do only that. I remember telephon-
ing John Hayward, who was still sharing a flat with Eliot, to warn him that
I. A. Richards had walked out of the first night. 'Funny old thing. Did he
say why?' drawled Hayward with his invincible loyalty, and I hope I got so
far as to hint that I agreed with Richards. A man may have no son, but
surely he has had a father, I said to myself; surely he must know that this is
simpering gross falsity, Henry James at his worst? I had still no idea that he
had abandoned his father's religion, as well as nationality. Maybe this
complex also explains the phrase 'In my beginning is my end', repeated in
the *Quartets*. Granting that Eliot did not begin at St Louis, one felt at the
time, why should he begin in the English Midlands? Surely his Bible
would tell him, let alone any later authority, that these rustics had come
from somewhere else. Yes, but they became Christian in the Midlands; all
infidel ancestors of Eliot, whether before or after this event, did not count.

    What the Unitarians had chiefly revolted against, though they seem to
have lost their battle by being too tactful about it, was the nightmare belief
that the Father was given a unique 'satisfaction' by the Crucifixion of his
Son. It was to this that Eliot returned, with glum eagerness; whether or
not with some confusion between his own father and the Heavenly one.
Around 1930 I was sometimes allowed into Eliot's office to find books for
review, and into the weekly At Home of Harold Monro in the Poetry
Bookshop or nearby, which Eliot attended. I was much impressed by the
chalk-white face with the swollen purple lips, and felt confident that he
had been brooding over the Crucifixion all night, or some other holy
torture. But I never spoke to him about his religion, and might be asked

now whether I have any evidence for this interpretation of his appearance. Well, it all seemed consistent. Literary gatherings talk a good deal about the sexual lives of other writers, and Eliot always welcomed any report of a crackup in these affairs, as a mercy in disguise; I thought at first it was a kind of joke, but it came out firmly and steadily. 'The greater torment/Of love satisfied' was a quite practical doctrine to him. Later on, John Hayward would make mild fun of how the tactful producers of his plays had to coax him into taking out his casual hair-raising descriptions of martyrdoms, which in those days would have put the audiences off. I too thought it rather fun to have a friend in such a medieval frame of mind, besides, it was interesting historically – in short, it seemed to be generally known. Not till I got back to England in 1952, and realized how the influence of Eliot had worked out, did I feel I had been given a direct peep into the monstrosity of the religion.

In his last years, after his second marriage, he would have accepted a good deal of this accusation against his previous frame of mind, though not of course against Christianity. I only met him a few times, but he was saying it, in a general way, at every opportunity. He spoke about his poetry, indeed, as if his father or his son had written it; sturdy in defence, but with no authority to expound. Not so with his prose: 'I was very sick in soul when I wrote that passage,' the deep voice would begin, 'and I wish now that I could rewrite such material entirely. But there won't be time.' It seems to me that remarkably little attention has been paid to these reflections of his final years.

The edition is full of entertaining discoveries, which I have had to neglect, but perhaps there can be brief mention of a few. It was of course Count Dracula, and not a bat, who crawled head downward down a blackened wall. After poor old Tiresias had been forced to watch the seduction of the typist he ran away like mad, as fast as he could stump, through the now finally doomed City:

> 'This music crept by me upon the waters'
> And along the Strand, and up the ghastly hill of
>   Cannon St.,
> Fading at last, behind my flying feet,
> There ...

where he got to a City Church. Originally, the poem said that Eliot (or

Tiresias) did not know whether the young man carbuncular was a small house-agent's clerk or a culture-snob who claimed to have spent the day with Nevinson in the Café Royal; it was hard to tell the difference. But Pound had swallowed the nonsense of T. E. Hulme, who said that poetry must be concrete and definite, so this bit had to go. I daresay the young man was T. E. Hulme in person, really.

JOYCE

Ulysses: Joyce's Intentions[*]

When I was young, literary critics often rejoiced that the hypocrisy of the Victorians had been discredited, or expressed confidence that the operation would soon be complete. So far from that, it has returned in a peculiarly stifling form to take possession of critics of Eng. Lit.; Mr Pecksniff has become the patron saint of many of my colleagues. As so often, the deformity is the result of severe pressure between forces in themselves good. The study of English authors of the past is now centred in the universities, where the teachers have a responsibility to the students, and yet there must be no censorship – no work of admitted literary merit may be hidden from the learners. Somehow we must save poor Teacher's face, and protect him from the indignant or jeering students, local authorities or parents. It thus came to be tacitly agreed that a dead author usually hated what he described, hated it as much as we do, even, and wanted his book to shame everybody out of being so nasty ever again. This is often called fearless or unflinching criticism, and one of its ill effects is to make the young people regard all literature as a terrific nag or scold. Independently of this, a strong drive has been going on to recover the children for orthodox or traditional religious beliefs; well, showing them how these beliefs operated in standard authors of their own tradition is of course a good way to do it, providing an actual use for the Eng. Lit. with which the schools have been saddled. The material is processed with confident firmness to suit this intelligible policy; and when you understand all that, you may just be able to understand how they manage to present James Joyce as a man devoted to the God who was satisfied by the crucifixion.

The concordat was reached over his dead body. When *Ulysses* first leaked through the censorship, it was almost universally denounced for its

---

*I have written other pieces about this great riddle, but they record a gradual approach to a solution of it, so they contain statements in which I no longer believe. However, this essay, first published in 1970, had better be printed, because it deals with a question that needs to be taken as settled in the main argument which follows ('The Ultimate Novel'). I have shortened it a bit, and added one or two more anecdotes from Ellmann.

cold jeering, its lack of joviality or human sympathy, its unnatural contempt for the world – exactly the qualities which are now praised. It has not got any of these qualities, whether they are good or bad. Clearly, such an extravagant degree of misunderstanding could not happen unless Joyce had laid himself open to it. He was a disciple of Ibsen, who believed that an author should dramatise 'problems' and refuse to tell his public the answers; not because he would be in any doubt, but because this was the way to influence his public most strongly. The answers would be sociological and political as well as aesthetic, and the public must hammer them out for itself by debate and turmoil. Joyce would have suffered very much if he had foreseen that his adroit opponents were going to turn the tables on him, taking advantage of the manoeuvre taught him by his Master. I therefore think it important to realise that the massive biography of Richard Ellmann (*James Joyce*, 1959), together with the volumes of letters and occasional criticism, contain enough ammunition to blow sky-high the whole dungeon into which he has been kidnapped.

I am not sure how far Hugh Kenner (*Dublin's Joyce*, 1955) invented the now established image of Joyce and his work; probably he was riding the crest of an American wave which had already travelled some distance. But no one else has presented it in such a lively, resourceful and energetic manner, so the best name one can find for it is the Kenner Smear. The chief claim of this theory is that Stephen Dedalus is presented not as the author when young (though the book-title pretends he is) but as a possible fatal alternative, a young man who has taken some wrong turning or slipped over the edge of some vast drop, so that he can never grow into the wise old author (intensely Christian, though in a mystically paradoxical way) who writes the book. The author nearly fell but did not quite. I agree that the Stephen of *Ulysses*, though he makes some good jokes, is in a terrible condition, near the edge of madness or of crime; but the title of the earlier book ('the artist when young') should at least encourage us to expect that he will emerge from his throttling situation. On the Kenner view, Stephen is simply deluded when he boasts that he will write a novel ten years later, giving the date when the book actually appeared. Now, Joyce was an extremely self-centred man, fiercely determined to become a great novelist; he is wildly unlikely to have presented himself, without any warning or explanation, as incapable of becoming one.

People arguing this case, I noticed, always make use of the same detail –

Joyce in *Finnegans Wake* wrote a parody of a claim made by Stephen in the *Portrait*. Jim the penman, says the joke, was always studying copying:

so as one day to utter an epical forged cheque on the public for his own private profit

whereas Stephen's diary, in the last-but-one sentence of the *Portrait*, says:

Welcome, O life! I go to encounter for the millionth time the reality of experience and to forge in the smithy of my soul the uncreated conscience of my race.

No wonder they use this example, because there is no other where Joyce can be supposed to be giving us a direct hint at the great secret. It is a rather forced joke or pun, likely to have been invented for the second occasion rather than intended to lurk behind the exaltation of the first one, because 'to forge in the smithy' is quite another process from forging a cheque. Also, Joyce can be found making this ethical claim in his own person, without using the dubious word. In 1912 he wrote to Nora asking her to join him for Horse Show Week in Dublin (Ellmann, p. 344):

The Abbey Theatre will be open and they will give plays of Yeats and Synge. You have a right to be there because you are my bride; and I am one of the writers of this generation who are perhaps at last creating a conscience in the soul of this wretched race.

He had recently failed to get *Dubliners* published there, after a long struggle, and no doubt felt particularly keenly that they needed improvement. He had plainly no suspicion that there was anything odd about the claim that his books would help to do it. (He did not mean, of course, that he had recommended Christian virtues such as chastity, which he considered bad). That he echoed it in a much later book with a jolly bit of self-mockery gives no reason to believe that the title *Portrait of the Artist* was an elaborate lie.

Ellmann, who is not impressed by the moral claim, suggests that Joyce first thought of it in this letter to his wife, and used it soon afterwards in a rewriting of the *Portrait* (p. 365):

Joyce also emphasized, partly as a result of his experiences in 1912, the patriotism of Stephen's effort to hit the conscience of his race and cast his shadow over its imagination.

But the moral claim was deeply built in to Joyce's theoretical position; that (in a way) was the use he was trying to make of Aquinas. To say that he invented it merely as a boast to satisfy his wife is just a way of belittling it. However, I need not quarrel with Ellmann for thinking the claim ridiculous; we agree on a more crucial matter, that Joyce himself did not think the claim ridiculous when he wrote the book. A draft of the *Portrait* certainly existed in 1912, whether or not it already carried this claim; he had thrown it into the fire in 1911, but his sister Eileen had fished it out (p. 325).

If we consider why he thought of a smithy, for the fine sentence at the end of the book, we find ourselves in another world. At the crisis of *Ulysses*, Stephen bangs his ashplant at the gaslight in the brothel, crying 'Nothung', so there is a row, and Bloom helps him away. This was the name of the sword forged by Siegfried in *The Ring* of Wagner, a work recalled fairly often in the course of the book; and surely it is obvious that the reference is meant to be important. We find it being prepared for in the previous novel. Stephen in the last chapter of the *Portrait* leaves a group of students with his friend Cranly, saying 'we can't speak here. Come away', and their conversation is grim and searching, but first:

> They crossed the quadrangle together without speaking. The bird call from Siegfried whistled softly followed them from the steps of the porch.

Dixon is merely arranging to play billiards with Cranly afterwards, but we are reminded that all these young men sing and that Wagner is immensely revered. The birds talked to Siegfried as soon as he entered the forest with the ancestral sword which he had re-forged, but he could not understand them till he had killed the dragon; then they told him he had already won a treasure and need only walk through the fire to win Brünnhilde. The self-importance of Joyce, as many people have felt, is rather unattractive, but at least he is not presenting Stephen as worthless and certain to fall.

Also this part of Wagner was forward-looking and progressive; it meant Socialism. Joyce in a letter to his brother of February 1907, which Ellmann quotes, does indeed say: 'The interest I took in socialism and the rest has left me.' But this is only to prove that he has been reduced to the hoggish mental condition of his fellow clerks – he has even been left cold by a procession in favour of the Nolan, so he had obviously better leave Rome at once. A critic is free to say that the advanced ideals entertained by authors around the turn of the century were silly; but if he won't even admit that they held such beliefs, what he says about them is sure to be wrong. He might also object that the ideals came in a standard mixed bag and were hard to combine; but, there again, the resulting difficulties are no proof of insincerity. Americans, as is well known, tend to disapprove of socialism unless it is called by some other name; and when Ellmann jeers at the politics of Joyce he feels he is protecting an innocent (because Joyce didn't *know* that a socialist is practically a cannibal). Still, Ellmann gives us an important bit of information here; that Joyce owned Bernard Shaw's book *The Quintessence of Ibsenism* (1891). The book explains that Ibsen is progressive and a liberator, and the article *Ibsen's New Drama* by the young Joyce seems clearly affected by it (recent critics have of course debunked Ibsen, arguing that his final years were anti-democratic; but this, even if true, was not known to Ibsenites at the turn of the century; and it cannot have been oppressively clear to Ibsen himself, when he wrote to Joyce approving his youthful article). Joyce wrote:

But the naked drama, either the perception of a great truth, or the opening up of a great question, or a great conflict which is almost independent of the conflicting actors, and has been and is of far-reaching importance – this is what primarily rivets our attention.

Such was the generous-minded way to talk about the matter, extremely remote from recent Joyce criticism, and the young man was sure also to have read Shaw's *Perfect Wagnerite* (1898). This description of the theme of *The Ring* as a socialist pamphlet is one of the most splendid pieces of writing by Shaw, so lucid, so penetrating, so bare, so full of decisive detail, so rewarding to the imagination. He said in the second edition that he had merely reported what all his friends were saying, and Joyce could not have thought him a 'mountebank' here, though it was a fair enough comment on the later plays. The penniless young Joyce was living in a much more expansive world for the imagination than we can afford, and we only look dirty when we try to cut him down to our own mean size. So of course 'forging' meant to him the forging by Siegfried, for which even Bernard Shaw could penetrate to such unexpected depths of feeling.

It becomes clear that I must defend every clause of the penultimate sentence of the *Portrait*, as it has been nagged at by a series of critics. We now reach the clause 'for the millionth time'. Obviously this can't be true, they say, the young man's vanity makes him use inflated language. No, it is a kind of humility; he recognises that the process has happened a million times before, because he knows he is only an avatar of the needed culture-hero, as it might be of Vishnu or the Buddha. This indeed is the main place where the Victorian 'Wisdom of the East' (and for that matter of the Radical Reformers of the sixteenth century, who appear to have held precisely the same opinions), parts company with Christianity, which claims there is no basis for goodness except as derived from the one Atonement. I have to try to put the matter sharply, because for a majority of Eng. Lit. critics, especially in America, it seems to have become a convention to pretend that one has never heard of the opinions of the Enlightenment, and this little elegance of course entails that one's opinions about many past authors are bound to be wrong. The very technique of Joyce in such a case, releasing as it were into the atmosphere an awareness of the status of Stephen as an avatar by little reminders of the socialism of Ibsen, Wagner, Shakespeare and so on, is one which his modern American critics have been 'carefully brought up' to be uncon-scious of, exactly like the rich young ladies in the plays of Oscar Wilde: 'Mama, whose ideas on education are remarkably strict, has brought me up to be extremely short-sighted, so ...' ... and so too the unfortunate young man, who went into the English Literature business with honest enough intentions, finds that his grant will not be renewed unless he co-operates with the current trend. He is thus forbidden to understand the young Joyce, who is feeling here that to be yet another liberator, another incarnation of the culture-hero, is as high as the artist can hope to go.

Of course, his author might still intend him as a parody-hero, a totally unworking model of Siegfried; I only say that this would be very unlike Joyce, and that all the arguments for thinking so collapse as soon as they are examined.

The beginning of the sentence, 'Welcome, O life!', needs also to be considered, as Kenner allots a tremendous scolding to Stephen's ecstasy at the end of the previous chapter; here he has a vision of earthly beauty, and I suspect of progress too (the angel seems to be flying one of the new aeroplanes), so he dedicates himself to the labour of literary creation. Kenner says he is 'irresponsible' and not 'mature', and that the meaning-less word *life* 'recurs and recurs'. Stephen here is just leaving school; only the final chapter shows him at university. If mature he would be incredible.

He considers his present condition as a living death, and he is determined to break out of it; naturally he does not know what life will be, only that he has powers within him which demand to be unchained. I find I can believe in this child all right, though he is almost too impressive. To maintain that the author intended to jeer at the whole sequence, and dropped hints so that the reader could join him in this activity, seems to me to betray a degree of mean-mindedness positively incapacitating for a literary critic.

I don't deny, of course, that Joyce is often laughing at Stephen, and at times does it fairly severely ('I haven't let off this young man lightly, have I?' he appealed to Budgen); but to say this is quite different from saying what Kenner does, that the fit reader is intended to enjoy the hopeless fatuity of the thoughts of Bloom and Stephen just as the Blessed in the Christian Heaven (according to Aquinas) enjoy their eternal ringside view of the torments of Hell. Kenner brings out this quaint old bit of tradition with tender amusement; it is just the kind of thing, he feels sure, that Joyce, with his Irish humour, would find particularly attractive. Joyce would have listened with sickened horror, only gradually realising that his readers are being told to enjoy his book like this *all the way along*. Maybe he would have vomited again. But, later, he would have become keen to explain to Kenner that this smart idea is typical of what is hopelessly wrong with established Christianity, and indeed that, ever since Aquinas proved that this is what really goes on in the Christian Heaven, no decent man has ever been willing to go there. I must say, I find it astonishing that misinterpretation could reach this wild peak.

Still, I can't deny that, as Joyce deliberately refused to express his reaction to what he described, his reaction is often hard to gauge. Joyce can make a character ridiculous without any loss of sympathy for him, and a modern critic finds this hard to imagine, because he has been taught to be a brass-faced scold; though surely it was familiar to the public of Dickens. Bloom's vision of his dead son at the end of the brothel chapter is intended to make us both laugh and cry, and I gather that the battle over this example has been more or less won. But Ellmann in the biography points out another case, which I do not think anyone could have guessed (p. 254). Joyce disliked working in Rome so much that he decided he had not given Dublin its due, and he added his best short story, 'The Dead', to redress the balance. The book had not so far reproduced, he wrote to his brother, the ingenuous insularity of Dublin and its hospitality; the latter 'virtue' so far as I can see does not exist elsewhere in Europe.

Conroy in his conventional speech at the dismal Christmas party says almost exactly the same, and it would be quite reasonable to suppose that the author meant this as a satire on Irish complacency. I must admit then that it is easy to go wrong over what he means. Also, though he was pleased with his skill at the famous Irish bitterness, he felt that he needed to get away from it – whether he 'really meant it' might become a question. Bernard Shaw used the admissions of Joyce on this point as the only way he could sincerely praise *Ulysses*; the book exposed, he said, what was fundamentally the matter with Dublin, 'the fatal habit of low jeering'. And indeed the idea is presented quite firmly in the first pages of the book (the part that Shaw read); for example, Mulligan upbraids Stephen for spoiling a chance to borrow money from the English visitor:

I blow him up about you, and then you come along with your lousy leer and your gloomy Jesuit gibes ...

After his escape from Dublin, Joyce succeeded in rising above this fault, even if sometimes at the cost of reckless sentimentality. He does not deserve to be forced back, his ghostly protests inaudible behind a barrage of praise, so that everything he wrote must be interpreted as lousy Jesuit jeering.

One or two minor points need fitting in here. It is part of Kenner's argument, to prove that Stephen is already damned, that he is made to expound the wrong aesthetic philosophy. Joyce was letting him get the theory right in *Stephen Hero*, but when he rewrote and concentrated the material as the *Portrait* Stephen was turned into a sentimental neo-Platonist; that is, he considered the artist superior to earthly details, instead of letting the artist deduce realism from Aquinas. If we actually did find this alteration, I agree that the argument would carry some weight, though the evidence would need to be very strong. But, so far as I can see, there is only one definite bit of evidence offered, that Joyce in rewriting left out the technical term 'epiphany', invented by himself to describe the moment of insight which sums up a whole situation. I can tell you why he left it out; because he was not always too egotistical to write well. Even he, during revision, could observe that it was tiresome to have Stephen spouting to his young friends about this invented term. But I find no change in doctrine; he still firmly rejects

Idealism, the supreme quality of beauty being a light from some other world, the idea of which the matter was but the shadow,

and explains that the 'claritas' of Aquinas comes when the image

is apprehended luminously by the mind which has been arrested by its wholeness and fascinated by its harmony.

This is surely the doctrine which Kenner approves, and we next have as clear a pointer from the novelist as he ever allows us:

Stephen paused and, though his companion did not speak, felt that his words had called up around them a thought enchanted silence.

A critic who can believe that Joyce wrote this whole passage in order to jeer at it has, I submit, himself taken some fatal turning, or slipped unawares over the edge of some vast drop.

It is also argued that the spelling of the legendary name 'Daedalus' was changed to *Dedalus* in the Portrait so as to warn us that Stephen is now 'dead', and that the first syllable should henceforth be so pronounced. One must grant that this would be a romantic name for a doppelgänger; but in the same book 'esthetic' is so spelt, and later (for instance) we get 'Eschylus' in 'The Holy Office'. Joyce had merely adopted the Italian way of transliterating Greek, and it involved no change of pronunciation.

[I can now say a bit more about the pronunciation of 'Dedalus'. I asked Professor Ellmann, who kindly wrote and asked Samuel Beckett. He answered that he could not remember any particular incident when Joyce said the word, but if Joyce had said 'deddalus' he would remember, because his ear would have been shocked. One might doubt whether he and Joyce were brought up to say 'deed' or 'dayd' (a new pronunciation of Latin was gradually coming in), but either would count as a long vowel, and this was of great importance for writing Latin verse; the schoolboy would be beaten for a 'false quantity', so no wonder the ear of Beckett would be shocked. This short vowel has become universal in America for the work, and was used by Kenner to argue that Stephen was already 'dead'.

One might think it is the only natural way for an English speaker to pronounce the word so spelled, but the effect is uncertain (compare 'lethal', 'penal'), only 'dedd' would be decisive. The young Stephen in the *Portrait* is well aware that his family name comes from 'the fabulous artificer', and draws encouragement from it, though Joyce had already established his new spelling for the name. Maybe the unfortunate tradesmen who dealt with the house often pronounced the name wrong, and old Dedalus gladly snubbed them for it. It does not appear that Kenner believes young Stephen to have gone fatally wrong till he has started drinking. Also, for anyone fairly well-read, this spelling would not be unfamiliar. During the seventeenth century the English sometimes accepted the Italian way of spelling Latin names (*NED*); and at all other times would pay respect to it by printing 'AE' in its curious combined form. Various derivatives were made from 'Daedalus', for example 'dedale' which is listed as having no other pronunciation that 'deedal'. This would be irrelevant if Joyce had not insisted upon it himself. He introduces the word among the imitations of period styles in the Hospital chapter, and actually in verse, as if to make sure of the intonation. The medical student Costello is sardonic and appears to be malignant, as was expected of hunchbacks, but when Stephen expresses a resentful despair he tells him to rejoice in the wonder and richness of the world; then the thunder comes, terrifying Stephen but ending the drought.

> Behold the mansion reared by dedale Jack,
> See the malt stored in many a refluent sack,
> In the proud cirque of Jackjohn's bivouac.

Stresses are heaped up at the end of each line, and I do not understand how anybody could want to pronounce the word as 'deddle' here. After I had realised that the young man has missed catching his Nora, I was forced to admit that Kenner was right on an essential point; Stephen will never get round to writing the novel. But Stephen as we see him on Bloomsday has only just started to go wrong; he is not less than archangel ruined, or else, indeed, his author could not describe him from within. To say that he is already dead, even as a sectarian dig, is off the target; a dreadful wriggling life as a Dublin bar-fly, all acrackle with scandal and artistic pretension, just enough by his concert-singing to scrape by, extends far before him. In the novel, he is a disagreeable young man, but not more so than the young Joyce, judging from the few records, actually was. Except in his refusal to wash; someone reports that, during that summer, he was greatly enjoying the swimming. But Joyce might easily have talked so, to annoy an English patron.

One can see how the idea arose, of a change in Stephen; Joyce does narrow the portrait as he concentrates it, though probably by degrees and not on any principle. Actually, when at college, his mind had been greedily accepting the latest thoughts and news, but he came to present himself as an underprivileged recluse, a kind of rock-plant, nurturing his aestheticism upon the stones of Aquinas only. It was to show himself in this prickly aspect, refusing service on yet another front, that he is made to reject a socialist manifesto which all the other students were signing – a great help to his later admirers in America. He must have been converted to Socialism a year or two later, so the incident can hardly be made a central pillar of the belief that Joyce intends to denounce and bemoan every development of human culture since the start of the Renaissance. And besides, if this is what the young man is up to, he cannot also be gloated over as the invincibly fatuous modern man. I suppose that Kenner, quite early in his study of this author, glimpsed a truth which would be painful to him – that the mind of Joyce was at a number of points very like that of H. G. Wells. A brilliant recovery was made, and he found two routes of escape from the oppressive conclusion; but the trouble is, he tries to use both at once.

The basic purpose of all the 'interpreting' (I take it no one would be eager to deny this) has been to prove that Joyce was not really opposed to Christianity – for example, we are often told that he attacks bad priests but not the priesthood. This is just credible about his published works, where he is struggling to be 'detached', though one ought to be able to see through it fairly easily. From the evidence of the letters and the Ellmann biography, his critics would be more sensible to blame him for an obsessional hatred of the religion, strong as ever when he died. I will report a brief sequence, enough to be representative; a full list would be tiresome. One should first realise that he did not quarrel with his Christian friends about religion, as his brother Stanislaus did; sometimes he would talk rather insincerely about it, to avoid ill feeling – as when he told some visitor that the only reason why he didn't become a priest was that he couldn't stand celibacy. And the effect of the anti-intellectual aesthetic movement is that the novels never give any reason why Stephen abandons his religion; the change appears as a kind of wasting mental disease, though really of course the young Aloysius and Stanislaus were arguing about Christianity all the time. But there is very little to be discounted.

In 1908, when he was twenty-six, Nora and Stanislaus became active because he was drinking more than his health or his family could afford, and on one occasion Nora cried out: 'Yes, go now and get drunk.... Faith, I tell you I'll have the children baptised tomorrow.' This threat was so appalling to him that he took the pledge; he kept it till the British Fleet paid a visit to Trieste, a time when he became unconscious on a battleship (p. 277). His immense capacity for making friends, indeed, is one of the surprises of the biography. In 1909, he wrote to Nora from Dublin upset by doubts of her loyalty – she had done a suspicious thing shortly before he left Trieste (p. 314):

A priest passed us and I said to you 'Do you not feel a kind of repulsion or disgust at the sight of one of those men?' You answered a little shortly and drily 'No, I don't.'.... Your reply hurt and silenced me.... Are you with me, Nora, or are you secretly against me?

He sometimes told his South-European friends that the religion was only harmful in Ireland, not elsewhere, but this letter proves he only said it to spare their feelings. (And he was sometimes patriotic enough to assume that Catholics are better than Protestants, but this did not interfere with his conviction that both are very bad.) In 1913, a young woman he was flirting with, Amelia Popper, had appendicitis, and he wrote: 'The surgeon's knife has probed in her entrails and withdrawn, leaving the raw, ragged gash of its passage on her belly ... Libidinous God!' (p. 356). The operation had been successful, but any reminder that God has a sexual craving to inflict torture on all his creatures is enough to set Joyce off, never mind whether God has been frustrated on this occasion. Realising this settled frame of mind, one can see the force in the novel *Ulysses* of calling God 'chewer of corpses' whenever Stephen remembers the slow death of his mother and more elegantly *'dio boia*, hangman god' while sympathising with the troubles of Shakespeare. A superstitious horror, one might also deduce, and not any residual attachment to the religion, was what made the lad Stephen in the *Portrait* say that he dare not go to mass unbelieving, because:

I imagine there is a malevolent reality behind these things I say I fear.

The Christian God cannot be the supreme God – one may feel safe so far; but his doctrines are quite wicked enough to do black magic.

The later references are much less highly strung, but do not mark any softening in theory. In 1917 Joyce is writing gay limericks, with the *Portrait* at last coming out and *Ulysses* nearly finished; one of them describes the bounce of Lloyd George, laughing at it but praising him for it – the populist side of Lloyd George was what Joyce liked in a politician, and it ends: 'Bully God made this world, but I'll save it' (p. 433). A bad line, likely to make one guess that *bully* is some kind of jovial American slang; but no, it is just our familiar schoolboy word. The Creator is a cad, but L. G. can outwit him. Joyce sent another one to Pound about himself, the 'lounging Stephen' (p. 428):

> 'Whose youth was most odd and uneven.
> He throve on the smell
> Of a horible Hell
> Which a Hottentot wouldn't believe in.'

I have often had essays written for me by students who believed, as they had been brought up to do, that the author Joyce entirely approved of the terrorist sermon, and felt glad it had made young Stephen vomit as he deserved.

Between the wars, he may be found complaining mildly that he is supposed to be in the same political and literary movement as Pound, Eliot and Wyndham Lewis (almost the last friends left for poor Hitler in Europe, p. 687), but he did not have to complain of being thought a Christian, which nobody dared pretend till he was dead. He seems, in a grim tacit way, to have arrived at a working arrangement about the matter which remained firm for the rest of his life. For example, the elaborate bit of prose which he wrote around 1930 to help the tenor Sullivan (*Critical Writings*, p. 258) only comes to life in the evocation of the bells of the churches of Paris gloating over their hopes of murder on the Eve of St Bartholomew:

> Have you got your knife handy? asks the
> bellman St Andy. Here he is and brand new,
> answers Bartholomew. Get ready, get ready,
> scream the bells of Our lady. And make sure

they're quite killed, adds the gentle Clotilde.

Your attention, sirs, please, bawls Big Brother Supplice ...

The church is St Sulpice, but the tortures were what secured public attention. In 1932 we find him at a party in Zurich where a priest praises the Creation while exhibiting the stars from a terrace, and Joyce grumbles (in German): 'the whole thing depends on mutual destruction'. Animals eat each other, but hardly stars; it seems an automatic reaction to any thought of the Father. By this time he was fairly advanced upon *Finnegans Wake*, which uses a good deal of Christian symbolism, but it had not affected his basic resistance. His grandson was born in 1932, and 'a year or two later' his old friend Byrne paid a visit. During chat about the grandchild he said something implying that it had been baptised. Joyce was appalled, and Byrne managed to pass his remark off as some flat joke about the child, its leakiness presumably. The baptism would have counted as a personal betrayal. In 1938 he was still inscribing a text of *Ulysses* for a young admirer: 'Veille de la fête de Madame Bloom', and this, reports Ellmann, still perturbed Nora, because the day was also the eve of the nativity of the Virgin Mary. This seems to have been the last spurt of lava from the old volcano, but there is good authority for thinking that he did not change at the end. After his death in 1941:

A Catholic priest approached Nora and George to offer a religious service, but Nora said, 'I couldn't do that to him'.

She would say it with humour but he really would have considered it a betrayal, and he regarded betrayal with great horror. He would regard it as an enormous betrayal that, since his death, everything he wrote has been twisted into propaganda for the worship of the torture-monster. It is pitiful to think of his ghost for ever dancing in fury.

The Ultimate Novel

I

It is wonderful how Professor Kenner can keep on about *Ulysses*, always interesting and relevant and hardly repeating himself at all. He acts as a clearing-house, reporting promising new ideas and weeding out un-successful ones; but he had plenty more of his own for the centenary volume (*A Starchamber Quiry*, 1982), even though he had just brought out his own book (*Ulysses*, 1980). In both he propounds what I think is a new idea, and anyhow needs refuting. Stephen, he maintains (Kenner's *Ulysses*, p. 152), is practically blind all through the book; his eyes without his glasses focus eight inches in front of his nose, and he broke them 'yesterday'. This proves that whenever he claims to see anything he is only remembering what he usually sees. He is thus merely a windbag.

This disability in Stephen would soon become obvious in the book: but, for instance, he can catch the glint of the dusty jewels through the shop window. The strongest refutation comes at the start, when he and Malachi look out from the Martello tower at the morning sea. Malachi tells him to revere our great sweet mother, and Stephen looks at the mail-boat clearing the harbour mouth. Kenner is right to insist elsewhere that the 'stream of consciousness' method reports what the subject thought at the moment: Stephen must have recognised the mail-boat. Malachi then says his aunt believes that Stephen killed Stephen's own mother by refusing to pray for her. Stephen regards the sea as green bile which her vomiting had torn up from her rotting liver (she died of cancer). Kenner, with very bad taste, I think, calls this 'a brilliant example of Joyce's scrupulous care for the limits of a character's perceptions'. Next they quarrel over a phrase which had been used by Malachi as soon as Stephen's mother was dead. Malachi goes, but Stephen 'stood at his post, gazing over the calm sea towards the headland. Sea and headland now grew dim. Pulses were beating in his eyes, veiling their sight ...' When Malachi has gone he becomes calm, and can look again: 'Woodshadows floated silently by through the morning peace from the stairhead seaward where he gazed. Inshore and farther out the mirror of water whitened, spurned by lightshod hurrying feet. White breast of the dim sea ...'

Kenner says that Stephen is merely 'trying out phrases, outdoing Yeats', or perhaps imitating Homer (*Starchamber Quiry*, p. 26): but Kenner is the one who has no eyes here. Joyce often expresses fascination at the incessant slight movements of water around the tidal estuary of the Liffey: consider the reappearances of the throwaway pamphlet in the Wandering Rocks chapter, consider the end of *Finnegans Wake*. The brief description here is as vivid as it is beautiful.

The explanation is simple. Kenner's evidence is that Stephen fails to light a cigarette in Nighttown and says: 'Must get glasses. Broke them yesterday. Sixteen years ago.' It was an hour ago, or a little more, but he is amused by the technicality that a new day begins at midnight – as when he tells Bloom he hasn't dined since the day before yesterday, 'improving on himself'. Also he remembers being unjustly beaten over breaking his glasses when he was a new boy at school; in a blurry way, he is reflecting about time. The glasses were broken in a scuffle at Westland Road station, where Malachi was taking the last train back to the tower. It left at 11.10 p. m., and Stephen had arrived there in time to quarrel with him; Bloom was following Stephen, thinking he might need help, and is our only source of information about what happened. Kenner does well to draw attention to this part of the story, and it is a pity that he missed the further point. Stephen feels triumphant when he arrives at the brothel, led by Lynch, but about two-thirds of the way through the chapter he begins to say that his hand is hurting. It would be numb at first, but he would feel it 'after an hour or two', says Kenner (p. 116), and he feels it just after he has mentioned the broken glasses. The girls have just said that it is 'long after eleven'. Probably Stephen merely shouted insults at Malachi, who knocked him down and left him on the platform, but the bruised hand seems to represent an honourable wound. If the glasses had really been broken on the day before, the incident would have nothing to do with the novel.

This is not quite the end of it. One might ask why the glasses were not mentioned in the first chapter, when other needments were being assembled. Well, there are larger questions to answer there. Stephen's mother has been dead for a year, all but ten days, and he is still in strict mourning for her, though it is hard for him to get clothes: but why does no one mention the eccentricity of this prolonged mourning? Why has Stephen waited a year before quarrelling with Malachi over a phrase used just after the death? They have been in close contact for most of the time. And why does he not shave when Malachi does? Malachi had coaxed him into giving up his Paris beard (Ellmann's *Joyce*, p. 136), and this was to have been a gala day for Stephen, standing treat with his earnings. Kenner himself gives the answer (p. 31): that the first page of *Ulysses* is like 'the first page of a novel', meaning a short story for a magazine. It must be smart and 'gripping', with stock sentiments (Wyndham Lewis jeered at them heartily, not realising that they were intentional). This is enough reason for it to leave out the detail of the spectacles. Ellmann also reports that he disliked having to wear them, leaving them off at parties apparently, but surely he would wear them when taking a class, at which he notices a boy using a crib.

Kenner has long been inclined to take the mickey out of Stephen, and still maintains here that he was incapable of becoming the great novelist. This theory is a step towards the right answer, but taken alone it is absurd. Joyce was a self-important man, as he needed to be, and he had described Stephen in a book title as a portrait of himself when young: he would not trivialise the character without warning, in a continuation. Actually, the book confronts Stephen with a grim necessity: for a time at least, he must commit himself to becoming a concert-singer, a companionable life, but one from which the novelist would be unlikely to emerge. Joyce himself had escaped it , because he saw Nora walking along a street and at once stopped her and took her name and address. With Nora behind him, he could leave Ireland and teach English abroad (with his BA), but without her he would sink. Bloomsday, as Ellmann discovered, was the day she first consented to walk out with him, and he expected his friends to celebrate it as a sort of private Christmas. The story of the book is sad, but it can be treated with satirical gaiety because it did not happen: instead, a goddess had descended, and Joyce had reacted with instant vigour. But it would be foul to drag Nora into his autobiograpy; impossible, too; the only way to demonstrate her importance was to tell what would have happened without her. Molly Bloom, of course, is not a doctored version of Nora; as Nora remarked when asked the question, with her usual command of brevity: 'She was much fatter'. Because Nora enabled Joyce to leave Dublin, he can survey it as from a pinnacle. All this should have been obvious since Ellmann published his great biography, in 1959.

The many experts summarised by Kenner are keen to make the book as

prosy and flat as possible. American higher education allows much
freedom of choice, and English students may practically major in *Ulysses*,
but Teacher has the duty of keeping it from doing them harm. No weaker
hypothesis, I submit, can explain the glee with which Kenner reports a
total agreement of modern experts that Molly has been pure during the
ten years without normal sex which have been imposed by her husband;
though a few envisage one contact with the tenor d'Arcy. The evidence
comes from one Answer in the Question-and-Answer chapter, and
ignores the rest of the book. Bloom in his sleepy final reflections recalls a
number of men who have been charmed by Molly; none of them has been
to bed with her, so far as he knows, except the final one, Boylan. Bloom
has been avoiding the name of Boylan all day but feels he has to face it, as
he gets into his wife's bed; but he does not want to think about any earlier
lover. He is thinking about men who admire her more slightly; they feel an
attraction mixed with alarm, then they understand her, then they become
tired of her; and Boylan is 'impressionable', so he is likely to do the same.
She is more dependent upon her husband than she realises – that is what
he is getting at here, and her own monologue in the final chapter bears it
out. She does not, indeed, name a lover from this long interval in her
reflections, and one may deduce that none of them has meant much to
her, but anyway her pronouns treat all men as identical. On the other
hand, we have brief comic acts put on by Lenehan and old Dedalus,
implying that she is promiscuous – not impressive witnesses, but they are
sure that all hearers will accept it. Molly is a well-known public figure in
Dublin, very expansive, and her husband is rather despised for giving her
so much rope. But no one is surprised. The talk carries no animus against
her; in a way the gossips are heartless, but they would gladly repeat instead
the story told by Kenner, because it is much more surprising, if there were
any hope of getting it believed. If she had had no lover for ten years, they
would feel a certain awe of Bloom, which they do not. Their sources of
information are vastly larger than ours, as we can only read the book. Still,
even a reader can get an impression from her casual remarks, such as 'its
all very well a husband but you cant fool a lover' or 'I dont like a man you
have to climb up to get at'.

Early in her chapter, Molly remembers that d'Arcy did something
unnamed to her on the choir stairs after they had give an recital in a
church, and afterwards he said it was terrible to do it there (the vigorous

kiss proposed in Kenner, p. 144, would not have been sacrilege), but Molly is unabashed and thinks of showing her husband the place 'some day not now'. So Bloom doesn't know about this event, though she sometimes does tell him such things. The author is following a consistent plan in this curious list: and I don't deny that, wanting a wide range of readers to like Molly, he may have been deliberately obscure. But the immense hidden fret of Bloom about Boylan all day is clearly not usual: bringing the lover to the house, so that the husband stays out late, is new. The real trouble about Boylan, I submit, is that he is 'organising' the new tour, a phrase Bloom dislikes having to repeat; it means he will take the share of the profit which usually goes to Bloom. Bloom is afraid of him:

Making for the museum gate with long windy strides he lifted his eyes. Handsome building. Sir Thomas Deane designed. Not following me?

Didn't see me perhaps. Light in his eyes.

The flutter of his breath came forth in short sighs. Quick. Cold statues: quiet there.

Safe in a minute.

No, didn't see me. After two. Just at the gate.

My heart!

His eyes beating looked steadfastly at cream curves of stone. Sir Thomas Deane was the Greek architecture.

This cannot be mere embarrassment; he is afraid – unreasonably, perhaps – that Boylan will beat him up. He must make some firm plan (fearless of the risk to Stephen).

Some may feel that Stephen would refuse to take her on, if she is as bad as all this – or rather, so much despised even by creatures like Lenehan. This is one of the scars left by the reactionary movement of T. S. Eliot: modern critics cannot realise that an author around 1900 was usually trying to be advanced. Stephen was not a decadent but an Ibsenite: he would consider Madam Bloom an unusually satisfactory specimen of the New Woman. She earns enough money to be independent, by her art, without sacrificing either her sexual or her domestic life. The contempt of fools only makes her a bit of a martyr. In effect, Bloom is offering Stephen a smart appointment; and another advantage of it is that it will annoy his father.

The brooding presence of Mrs Bandman Palmer, who acted Hamlet in person on the previous evening, no longer carries its due weight because she has been so completely forgotten. She managed an acting company as a rule on the Northern Circuit, which took in Bradford and Huddersfield as well as the larger towns; it could pop over to Dublin via Liverpool, and Bloom has seen her Hamlet on an earlier visit. The owner of the grocery and off-licence in my street when I worked at Sheffield was proud to have been in her troupe when young, and shocked to find I had never heard of her. Her rendition of Hamlet, I gathered, had been tempestuous: 'The farting Hamlet they called her. But when she left £40,000, they felt a respect for the old girl.' Ellmann reports Joyce as trying to get more information about her visits to Dublin, while he was writing *Ulysses*, but without success on that occasion. The English actresses who worked in the South are much better remembered; they needed to be ladies and to have at least some contacts in Society; but Mrs Bandman Palmer was free to be populist, like Lloyd George. For Joyce, she would be the New Woman at the top of her form: very unlike Molly, of course, but he needed a contrasting specimen. (*The Hey-Day* by Bamber Gascoigne (1976) gives an entertaining caricature of life in the troupe of Mrs Bandman Palmer, and probably contains much truth. The play *Leah*, which Bloom tells his wife he saw that evening, turns out to be a melodrama denouncing anti-semitism, and the audience is expected to concur. The name of the author is not mentioned.)

However, these social observations would not have disturbed him. One might think that a man so deeply (though not legally) married as Joyce would regard the sexual problems of the Bloom household chiefly as farce. But around that time Free Love was considered a very important idea, very advanced, and Bloom suffers as a result of accepting it. Someone in the period, Havelock Ellis probably, said that sexual jealousy was the next great obstacle before mankind, demanding a heroic culture-conquest. (It is a bit pathetic that they thought nothing worse would crop up.) Joyce insisted at one point, when the book was newly out, that it had no moral 'and not one serious line in it', but this was a claim to be an artist, usual among Ibsenites: he could not have meant to deny that he was fully abreast of modern thought. He would have wanted to present a real modern marriage, with the problems that were usually ignored in other novels, and leave his reader to draw the deductions. Four years before Bloomsday, in the *Fortnightly Review*, Joyce had praised Ibsen for doing what other authors neglect: 'but the naked drama, either the perception of a great truth, . . . or of a great conflict which is almost independent of the conflicting actors and has been and is of far-reaching importance – this is what primarily rivets our attention.' At that rate, his first two books hardly do more than present his credentials; after *Dubliners* and the *Portrait*, works of basic reportage, he is prepared to advance upon a work of true greatness. Stephen raises the question of what calling he should follow, but for Bloom and the mature Joyce a more universal question looms up behind him: 'What to do with our wives?' Maybe Ibsen would not have been pleased by the result, but Joyce was not straying far here from his master.

II

All the same, one would expect him to need direct experience of a triangle, before he could write about it in depth. He arranged one, and the Ellmann biography, by a remarkable coup, catches him at it (Ellmann, p. 327). Roberto Prezioso, editor of the inflammatory sheet *Piccolo* in Trieste, was a pupil of Joyce and became his warm admirer. Joyce 'rather encouraged' his admiration for Nora, who 'went so far as to have her hair done'. This was about 1911, when Joyce was 28 and Nora rather younger. Eventually the editor made some advance to her, and she told her husband. Joyce upbraided him in the Piazza Dante, and the painter Silvestri 'saw tears running down Prezioso's humiliated face'. Ellmann shows that the results were used effectively in the play *Exiles*. He seems to assume that Joyce laid the trap deliberately, as a devoted aesthete collecting material for his play: I do not believe he was cool enough about it to do that. Much more likely, he thought the happy triangle a noble ideal, and tried to arrange one; and then he found, at the first approach to it, that his feelings resisted violently. In 1916, after finishing *Exiles* and starting on *Ulysses*, he kept a notebook in which he recorded Nora's dreams with his own interpretations. One entry says:

Prezioso weeping.
I have passed him in the street.
My book 'Dubliners' in his hand.
. . . The point with which he tried to wound me has been turned against him – by her; the motive from which I liberated myself in art he is unable to liberate himself from in life.
His complaint . . . is a secret disappointment that for her it is impossible to unite

the friendship of two men through the gift of herself differently to both for that which seemed possible in the first case is almost impossible in the second case.

'Differently' must be a fig-leaf only; if the sexual act itself is not in prospect, the whole thing is trivial. Nothing seems to be known about the earlier 'case', but he had taken the ideal of the happy triangle pretty seriously if it took two such disasters to convince him it was no good. Five years after the second one, he is still pretending to himself that his friend had tried to betray him, whereas the friend was only trying to carry out Joyce's scheme, and that Joyce's wife secretly regretted its failure, though the story is that she told Joyce of the friend's advances at once, rightly presuming that Joyce would stop them. One would suspect that Joyce's intimates had made the whole story up, in their gossip, if he did not admit it himself in these absurd private efforts at self-justification. He admits that he had wanted a happy triangle, because he claims to have liberated himself from it by his art. He never realised that *Exiles* is a bad play, boiling with self-righteous excuses and irrelevant claims to have been wronged, in which the author uses the hero frankly as a mouthpiece, with the sadism and masochism quite raw: but given a certain moral depth, however unpleasantly, by a craving to incur and enjoy shame. No doubt he felt peaceful after writing it, as after a good cry or a good scold.

So Joyce when planning *Ulysses* would not aim at propaganda for the happy triangle; he might even regard it as another pretentious ideal which he had exploded, though, in fact, he had only found it to be incompatible with his own temperament. But he would believe the practice to be quite usual, though treated with absurd secrecy; the offer was a likely thing to intrude upon young Stephen (if he had not found Nora). The triangle proposed is almost grotesque, but still has its magic; it may well give Bloom the crucial bit of help that he needs, the 'disintegration of the obsession' of Molly for Blazes Boylan. (In the same way, Joyce's published work always ridicules spiritualism, though he had listened earnestly to AE when young; but he still feels that it is charming, and a normal kind of thing for people to believe.) To make Stephen bolt from it as if he were Bertie Wooster, 'howling for Jeeves', would seem very out of character: and yet, the author wants the average reader to treat his question at the end, 'Will Stephen return?', as a real and challenging one.

At present there is a thick fog blanketing all such questions, a general movement among American critics towards formalism or unrealism. Its most startling tenet is the Wimsatt Law, which lays down that no reader can grasp the intention of any author. As that is just what the reader ought to be trying to do, the Law is a powerful means of destroying all literary appreciation. Here it takes the form of believing that an Arranger adds into the text all the parodies and comments that accompany the main narrative. The Arranger is not the author, but in effect one of the characters, or presumably several. It has a shockingly trivialising effect: one needs to realise instead that Joyce is always present in the book – rather oppressively so, like a judge in court.

This is not to deny that he is sometimes hard to interpret. In the Wandering Rocks chapter, which appears to give a typical sample of the streets of Dublin, Stephen meets an Italian called Artifoni who tells him he is sacrificing his voice by trying to become an author, not a singer, and he promises to think again. This seems a crude bit of boosting for Stephen: he is torn between two splendours, and foreigners plead for him in the streets. The presence of Artifoni is never explained: in fact, the device is so bare that he might have strayed out of the Circe chapter, where he makes a brief token reappearance. For years I thought it justified as satire, debunking the high claims for Stephen's voice: 'arty-phoney' – what could be plainer? At last I noticed in the Ellmann biography that this was the name of a senior in Joyce's teaching organisation, who had given him help and advice. (He had welcomed Joyce as a brother Socialist, so not everyone regarded the political ideals of the young Joyce with the same contempt as Ellmann.) Maybe Joyce wanted the long-suffering official to read the apparently complimentary passage before he died, imagining that he had received an immortal reward, whereas English-speaking readers could take it otherwise; or perhaps he was merely sure that an Ellmann would come along some time. One could not recommend this as a way to write a novel, but at least it is better than inventing an Arranger who is not the author.

The question how the author intended the reader to react to his way of ending the story has been important in the gradual acceptance of the book. The reader is made to take an increasing interest in Bloom and Stephen; then they meet and are found to need each other; then they are alone together for two long chapters, but they seem to get duller and duller, as well as less and less able to communicate. Can it mean that they were never worth bothering about at all? This was presumably what caused E. M. Forster's first reaction to the book: he said it insulted the universe, meaning that it insulted the heart of man. Kenner thought they both deserved all they got, for being heretics, so he was pleased by the ending, though he made the same error. Budgen reported Joyce as saying they become like stars, eternal and remote, and plainly that is the effect: but does it imply that Stephen will not return? Stars usually drift apart, but sometimes collide, causing turmoil; and for the author to turn on a chill by technique does not even pretend to alter the characters. The process of bargaining is often felt as a chill. Our sympathies have been so much aroused that any theory allowing the events of the day to do them some kind of good comes as a relief, in keeping with the book's realistic good-humoured tone. Even Kenner now lets drop (Kenner's *Ulysses*, p. 118) that their nightmares will probably help them to shake off their phobias later, but this seems merely a sop for a common demand. The book is 'not a psychological treatise,' he says, implying that all novels are forbidden to suggest any means by which such an improvement could be made. It seems plain that each of these men, left to himself, would continue to get worse: that is a major reason for wanting to know what happened next.

A Christian interpretation would be less bleak, but the Ellmann biography made that much less probable, as was widely recognised. However, such attempts are still being made. Robert Boyle SJ, in the *Quiry* points out the liturgical grandeur of the language at the parting of Bloom and Stephen, as they purge themselves by pissing together in the garden with eyes in the lighted blind which shows that Molly (the Holy Ghost) is not yet asleep. Boyle finds various echoes from Dante which probably were in the mind of the author, and he did mean them to praise Molly and not laugh at her, but this is not enough. Boyle concludes with an enhancing modesty: 'I believe that the omens indicate ... that it is at least equally likely that Stephen may drown this time.' Joyce might answer that he had renounced the authority of an autobiographer over that stage of the night, so he could not tell. However, it might be asked: 'What else would he leave the house for?'

If he wants to get anywhere with Molly, it would be fatal to meet her first as a homeless derelict brought in by Bloom out of charity – his ever uneasy pride would be enough to tell him that. Also, as we heard in the first chapter, he usually feels unable to face life in the morning, before he has got a pint in him; tomorrow morning will be particularly bad. And all the more because he is practically blind (the broken spectacles fit in well with the plot here). Nowadays he would have to wait for weeks, but I can remember a graduated tray of spectacles in Marks and Spencer's, all for sixpence, and you could choose for yourself the pair that felt comfortable. Bloom has just repaid him thirty shillings, when he presumably thought he had thrown all his earnings away, so he feels no longer a suicide, and able to make small arrangements. Even he might reflect that a clean shirt would be a help, but he would probably first think of bringing Molly a bouquet – not too expensive in June. It does seem suicidal, one can't deny, when he sings to Bloom the insulting ballad; it is like firing on the rescue ship. But when Bloom refuses to be insulted he becomes accepted by Stephen, all the more readily because Stephen has no anti-Jewish feelings and merely used the insult that was available. It does seem odd that he should continue to make jokes against Jews, even though much milder ones, but he feels that he has established a joking relationship (as defined by anthropologists). Bloom is made to reflect, before Stephen has even drunk the cocoa, that Stephen has 'an equal and opposite power of abandonment and recuperation'. If there was any doubt, it becomes plain that he is not going to drown himself when he imitates a jew's harp as he walks off down the back lane. As to where he spent the rest of the night, the previous chapter told both Stephen and the reader the whereabouts of two dosshouses, one rather low for sixpence, but in the other 'you got a decent enough do... for a bob'. The derelict Corley told Stephen this, and Stephen gave him half-a-crown. The details seem to need fitting into the action: when Stephen felt ready for a dosshouse, he probably chose the one for a bob.

However, the possible suicide is not central to Boyle's argument. He offers evidence that Joyce gradually became reconciled to Christianity, and his attendance at Church services will probably seem the stronger part. But he had always admired the liturgies of some particular days of the Church year, and heard them when he could; there is no evidence that he did it more often when he was older. One need not deny that his feelings would be religious as well as aesthetic: he could react very fully to the Good Friday services without ascribing any virtue to the Father. Boyle says that Joyce came to recognise the importance of the Church, as if he did not know that from the start, as if he would automatically worship any big enough evil. Also he 'publicly consented to act as a believing Catholic' when he 'signed his name as sponsor' for a daughter of Ford Madox Ford; but he could regard this merely as a promise to help the child in case of need, and he would go quite a long way for a legal convenience, even marrying his wife, eventually, to secure her rights. One might say that he became more indulgent about such matters in later life, but that is not a conversion.

Papist critics have a strong argument, though perhaps an accidental one, when they infer from the Hospital chapter that Joyce disapproved of contraception. Sure enough, Joyce called this chapter the Oxen of the Sun; it corresponds in the *Odyssey* to the fatal murder of some sacred cattle by the crew of Ulysses, and the divine vengeance pursues the innocent Ulysses throughout, thus causing the story. In Joyce's chapter, cattle are paraded through the streets for export to England, Stephen has got into the evening paper the letter by Mr Deasy about a cure for foot-and-mouth disease, and a thunderstorm terrifying to Stephen has broken a long drought, restoring fertility. The raffish medical students presumably do use condoms, and cheap ones would be made from cows, but they never say so. In what I should call the 'real' story of the novel the intention is quite different. The visit is a test of Bloom's determination to overcome his phobia against having another child. The appalling experience of Mrs Purefoy is what he will risk putting Molly through, and the gay jokes of the students are particularly unpleasant here. He seems to be the only person in the room who thinks it wrong of her husband (who is a Protestant, so the balance is held fairly) to force her into producing a ninth child by three days of agony. But he is cautious about saying so, and other things are going on in the chapter; the reader is expected to know his attitude from previous remarks. They come in an unexpected place. Walking out for his lunch, he sees one of the Dedalus daughters:

Home always breaks up when the mother goes. Fifteen children he had. Birth every year almost. That's in their theology or the priest won't give the poor woman the confession, the absolution. Increase and multiply. Did you ever hear such an idea? Eat you out of house and home. No families themselves to feed. Living on the fat of the land ...

When Bloom has found a decent place for lunch, with one glass of burgundy, he hears across the bar, in another room, old Dedalus still singing beautifully to please his friends; so presumably he could still have earned money in a concert-room; and his children are starving in the street. The combination, of having children because he is orthodox and refusing to feed them because he is a gentleman, makes it particularly bad. The boy who inherits the voice ought to be looked after.

Both Bloom and Stephen receive insults at the hospital party, so that they are geared up to have nightmares of self-reproach in the next chapter; Malachi presumes Bloom to be impotent, and Stephen is given some insult about his mother by the nastier Lenehan, which though obscure almost drives him from the room. I do not deny that the vaunted parallel with Homer is overstrained here. Ulysses had a curse on him because his crew had killed the Oxen of the Sun: but Bloom has not been using any contraceptive with Molly, and the medical students are in no way the crew of Bloom. Surely the parallels are often just whimsical displays of ingenuity, as in his superstitions. I suggest that he had never taken these parallels to the *Odyssey* with any moral earnestness; killing the Oxen of the Sun had not been a real crime even to Homer. T. S. Eliot attached an importance to the technique of parallels which it will hardly bear, and he never gave any reasons for it. I suspect Joyce regarded it chiefly as a Distraction Procedure, allowing the real story to continue its stealthy movement forward. Before publication, he removed the Greek titles to the chapters, as if they had only been scaffolding, and I have tried to avoid using them in this essay.

Wiping off the accumulated piety, I submit, makes it more likely that Stephen did come back, as he had promised, and at least have a shot at winning Molly. Kenner has always been eager to maintain that he didn't, and his chief apparent argument (in both these books) is that the question is childish, because nothing happens after the end of a novel. I agree that there was a fashion for this attitude around 1904: the decadents admired frank artificiality, whereas the Russian short story often ended with a situation of quiet despair, to imply that Czardom was imposing paralysis. Joyce himself could use the Russian manner very sincerely in *Dubliners*, because he believed that the Church was causing paralysis in Ireland. But in *Ulysses* the end is a great question-mark, and if you are not interested in the answer you have no real interest in the book. As for the supposed logical rule, Trollope and Thackeray and suchlike took for granted that a novel should have a final chapter promising the reader that things went on all right after the book stopped. Forster said that the peculiar merit of the novel form, and also the reason why it needs so much detail, is that it can work up to making a reader feel: 'That's true. I know it now, though I would never have guessed it. That is just what the charater *would* have done.' The end of *Ulysses* does the same, but it takes the final step of refusing to tell the answer.

Kenner quotes a passage that makes the character of Bloom vividly clear, his sturdy good judgement and good will and his mysterious absurdity, and says: 'There is no Bloom. There is language' (*Quiry*, p. 28). He does the same in the other book (p. 56): 'On nothing is *Ulysses* more insistent than that there is no Dublin there, no Stephen there ... simply language.' But come now, this book is a continuation of a novel about Stephen called *Portrait of the Artist as a Young Man*. Are the first readers to regret that they have no book in their hands, because the author drowned himself ten years ago? And when was there no Dublin, anyway? There is just a bit of truth behind the sophistry, one need not deny: this author is rather more ready than most to generalise a situation. Burns does it splendidly in 'Cutty Sark' whenever he drops the dialect and gives a couplet in standard English: the experience is recognised as universal. This does not entail not caring what happened next.

The other argument of Kenner is more powerful, but has to be insinuated by winks and nudges: he finds it obvious that refined educated Stephen could not endure coarse ignorant Bloom. Next day, Stephen will be saying to some of the other aesthetes: 'My dear, it was *too* embarrassing. I had to tell any lie I could think of, just so that I could crawl out of the house, *flapping* my bright red ears.' But Stephen despised young men like that intensely, partly from envy perhaps; if his compulsive rudeness had no other merit, it did at least save him from behaving as they did.

III

So far I may have given more expression of preference than solid argument. I need now to list the main details throughout the book which prepare the reader for Stephen to accept the Bloom Offer. There is at once a rather quaint obstacle. Most readers of *Ulysses* do not believe in omens, but Joyce eagerly did; in this he is genuinely like Homer. Four of the characters receive omens, and Joyce would regard these as an assurance that some great event would occur. Stephen on the previous night had a disturbing dream which he increasingly recalls; and the absurd Haines, who was also sleeping in the Martello tower, had a nightmare. He thought himself attacked by a black panther, which he tried to shoot, and Malachi fired some shots to reassure him. Probably Haines had fired real shots too: both young men were accustomed to the use of sporting guns, which Stephen was not. The incident really occurred, and Joyce walked out of the tower for ever, in a drizzle, before dawn. In the novel there is no immediate break, because the author needs to keep the other two characters available. Haines makes occasional reappearances during the day, chiefly as a figure of farce, but usually with a recall of his black panther. Stephen twice very dimly thinks of Bloom as the black panther.

Stephen first recalls his own dream while walking along the beach, at leisure to reflect after being paid off from his teaching job. He has nowhere to go, and nowhere to sleep that night, except possibly the brothel ('Are you staying the night?'); but he will keep his promise, and try to get the schoolmaster's letter about foot-and-mouth disease printed in the Dublin papers. He recalls contemptuously his past literary ambitions, and surely this implies an impulse to become a singer instead. The reader is not told why he throws up his job, which has not been presented as hard or disagreeable for him: we only know that he tells lies about it to the medical students, pretending he got the money for their drinks by selling his poems. It seems another hint that he is inclined to become a concert singer. He is rather annoyed to find himself making a poem, another of his drawing-room ballads with doom and the sea in it, but he thinks, 'Here. Put a pin in that chap', and tears off the end of the schoolmaster's letter to write the lines down. After all, he might get paid for it. When he thinks, 'Better get this job over quick', he means finishing the poem, but he becomes interested instead in how to transcribe the sound of the waves. However, the poem goes on working in him, and the one verse is better when he recalls it in the Press chapter. The dog which has come with the cockle-pickers, scrabbling in the sand, as if to vulture the dead, now reminds him of Haines's panther:

After he woke me up last night same dream or was it? Wait. Open hallway. Street of harlots. Remember. Haroun al Raschid. I am almosting it. That man led me, spoke. I was not afraid. The melon he had held against my face. Smiled: creamfruit smell. That was the rule, said. In. Come. Red carpet spread. You will see who.

Later in the day, after his talk in the library, at about three o'clock, he is walking away with Malachi, and they pass Bloom. Malachi speaks to him, and then warns Stephen that Bloom lusts after him; Stephen reflects that this is the Oxford Manner: which means that he is contemptuous of Malachi's opinion. Immediately before, he has been noticing the birds in the portico of the library:

Aengus of the birds. They go, they come. Last night I flew. Easily flew. Men wondered. Street of harlots after. A creamfruit melon he held to me. In. You will see.

Then Malachi inserts his bit of poison, and so Stephen watches Bloom.

A dark back went before them. Step of a pard, down, out the gateway, under portcullis barbs.

Bloom has been moving unobtrusively, so as to get his business done without interrupting the conversation, and he is habitually conscious of his tact. I cannot feel that this end to the chapter goes with such a bang as the author intended: but it is the point where the reader should first realise that Bloom is Stephen's doom, or his saviour. Stephen does not realise it till quite late, not till after he has agreed to come home with Bloom. To feel himself generally doomed, while throwing away his only source of money, with nowhere to sleep that night, is of course only rational.

Molly laid out the cards in bed that morning, after Bloom had brought her breakfast, and learned that she would soon meet a poet, a young man, neither dark nor fair. She is not specially devoted to Boylan, we learn from her chapter, and would readily take Stephen instead, though probably not till after the concert tour with Boylan: anyhow Stephen will not have to fight Boylan, which he would certainly refuse to do. So what Bloom reports when he gets back to her bed is what she had been expecting from the cards; her firm assurance about it should convince the reader.

Bloom is not a man to brood over his dreams, and we hear nothing about them till he is reflecting gently on the beach after being stirred by Gerty MacDowell. His dream was merely a promise of oriental luxury, of being invited into a harem; and his memory of it is confused by a conviction that he only wants his own wife:

That's what they enjoy. Taking a man from another woman. Or even hear of it. Different with me. Glad to get away from other chap's wife. Eating off his cold plate. Chap in the Burton today spitting back gumchewed gristle. French letter still in my pocketbook. Cause of half the trouble. But might happen sometime, I don't think. Come in. All is prepared. I dreamt. What? Worst is beginning ...

Probably the last phrase means 'only breaking the ice is really embarrassing', but even so it is a grudging memory; he refuses to be deluded by the omen. Yet in his shopping before breakfast his mind expands at every hint of oriental luxury, and when he arrives at the Hospital chapter a Pepys-like narrator assures us, among his thumb-nail sketches of those present, that Bloom 'had a strange fancy of his dame Mrs Moll with red slippers on in a pair of Turkey trunks which is thought by those in ken to be for a change ...' They do seem to be nearing a crisis.

Joyce (I think) planned a dramatic moment for the omens in Nighttown but then felt it would not do, and left only a trace. First, before Bloom finds Stephen in Mrs Cohen's, he has a vision of his wife, 'in Turkish costume', as expected. His delight and eagerness to tell her things are heart-felt, but she snubs him. Later on, he imagines her enjoying Boylan, and is thrown into a kind of fit, visible to the others for once; they laugh at him. This seems to cheer up Stephen, who begins mocking the varieties of sex, and the madame says, 'None of that here', but his friend Lynch explains he is back from Paris, and the girls ask for some parleyvoo. He imitates a Paris pimp, and even the madame is delighted. He becomes exalted, and remembers bits of his dream: 'Mark me. I dreamt of a watermelon.'

STEPHEN

(*Extending his arms*) It was here. Street of harlots ... Where's the red carpet spread?

BLOOM

(*Approaching Stephen*) Look ...

STEPHEN

No, I flew. My foes beneath me. And ever shall be. World without end. (*He cries.*) *Pater!* Free!

BLOOM

I say, look ...

STEPHEN

Break my spirit, will he? *O merde alors!*

He has a vision of his father, a hunting scene follows, and then a race meeting, where 'a dark horse, riderless, bolts like a phantom past the

winning-post, his mane moonfoaming, his eyeballs stars'. It is hard to
know what the others see or hear, but Zoe hears singing in the street
outside, and cries 'Stop!' and demands twopence for the pianola. They all
dance; it seems their only cheerful moment; then Stephen dances alone,
an ecstatic affair which he calls a dance of death (but the words describing
his thoughts convey very little). He stops dead, and the corpse of his
mother rises stark through the floor. After a brief terrible conversation, he
smashes the chandelier and flees from the room.

It has been explained that what Bloom is prevented from saying, in this
crucial sequence, is simply 'Look out', perhaps meaning 'don't do
anything dangerous'. This is not impossible, because their minds are
mysteriously in touch, but no one else could tell that Stephen's mind was
going to change so rapidly from euphoria to convulsive horror. Telling the
girls about his good-luck dream is a bit tipsy perhaps, but not a bad
symptom otherwise. There is a much more direct thing for Bloom to have
in mind: 'We have had the same dream, and it has more or less come true.
An interesting coincidence.' Probably no one at Mrs Cohen's would have
paid attention even if he had managed to say it. But the reader would
notice it, if he had remembered any of the things mentioned earlier, red
carpets or flying or a water-melon. Probably Joyce had given some such
detail to start with but then became shy of it. Yeats had a theory about
dreams, as a proof of his brand of spiritualism; he was especially pleased at
finding a dream which had drifted across country, occupying one person
after another. (One must agree that such a dream could not be produced
by the unconsciousness of each person separately.) So the superstitions
about dreams were no longer universal and of the people: they had
become a part of a movement, and Joyce would not care to be identified
with it.

However, he still makes Stephen believe that he is doomed, pretty
clearly in the Hospital chapter, and specifically when Bloom has taken
him home. Before the hospital party, for which he buys the drinks, but
not, presumably, the food – so that a mild party must have been planned –
he has been out of the reader's sight for six or seven hours. He was
mooning about the streets in the Wandering Rocks chapter, after his talk
in the Library, at about 3.30, and he is with the party of medical students
by about 10.00. Kenner thinks he has been boozing and standing drinks
all the time, which proves he has gone rotten, and he does seem to have

lost thirteen shillings – but surely this includes the outlay for the student party itself. He notices, earlier in the day, that he needs to buy a handkerchief, and that standing drinks to the journalists has set him back a bit. After being penniless for so long, he probably needs other things – socks, for instance. It seems wonderful now that his money can go so far. He needs drink to make him shine in company, and would stoke up a bit before arriving at the hospital with his gifts: but for most of this gap of time, I suggest, he drifted about, glowering, and deciding that his apparently favourable dream had meant doom. Keener well points out that he claims to be presiding at a Last Supper during the party: he has only called himself the Eternal Son in answer to a challenge, but it is a fairly grim joke when his refusals have left him with nowhere to lay his head. Soon after comes the thunder, and he is terrified: but again Joyce may be consistent in his superstition – Stephen need not think that the True God is rebuking him, but merely expect a doom. When the Bloom Offer percolates into his exhausted mind, during the Cabman and Eccles Street chapters, he begins to think that the doom might have been worse: he will only lose his immortal fame, as he had already become rather inclined to do.

But he is still very tense about it, and his pride makes him bite any hand that feeds him. Bloom and Stephen have been intoning to one another 'fragments of verse from the ancient Hebrew and ancient Irish languages' – packed with error, as Kenner explains. Each of them tacitly recognises that the other's nation is offering stubborn resistance to ancient wrong. Bloom sees in Stephen 'the predestination of a future' and hears 'the traditional accent of the ecstasy of catastrophe'. He encourages Stephen to sing a 'legend on an allied theme', and the catastrophe comes, with the effect of a practical joke. It is fair to remember that Stephen is in revolt against Irish nationalism, and there was a good deal of talk in the Dublin of that time against Jews, without actual persecution: he may have felt that a disagreeable side of nationalism should also be recalled. The ballad is about a Jewish girl who attracts and then murders a Christian boy. Stephen is at his worst here, but he recovers. Bloom remains silent for three pages, chiefly remembering things about his own daughter, no doubt with an air of humane calm. It is his usual resistance to such talk, and he does not foresee that it will disarm Stephen. Stephen knows he has gone too far; he has no serious opinions against Jews, merely, in a schoolboyish way, thinking them funny and Bloom really is rather mysteriously funny, perhaps from being kept at arm's length by Dublin; even the newsboys caper behind him, imitating his walk. He is only half a Jew by birth, none by religion, and very little by family training, so one might think the matter could be treated as a joke. But Stephen realises that will not do here. He stammers out a lengthy explanation of the ballad, remote from it but fitting his own situation; he is afraid he has a doom on him; and the odd style of the chapter allows us to receive this jumble in a brief paragraph of great beauty, perhaps the most haunting that Joyce ever achieved:

Condense Stephen's commentary.

One of all, the least of all, is the victim predestined. Once by inadvertence, twice by design, he challenges his destiny. It comes when he is abandoned and challenges him reluctant and, as an apparition of hope and youth, holds him unresisting. It leads him to a strange habitation, to a secret infidel apartment, and there, implacable, immolates him, consenting.

Kenner finds the occasion to need a wild degree of special pleading. He explains that the style of the chapter does not let us know the actual tone of the conversation, but that poor Stephen must have been embarrassed. Therefore (Kenner's *Ulysses*, p. 139): 'we can understand why Stephen sings the ballad about the imperilled Christian boy in the Jewish habitation, and departs within minutes of singing it.' These 'minutes' occupy 12 severely compressed pages, and report a successful negotiation, after which Stephen promises to return. The commentary on the ballad is followed by a long silence; then Bloom abruptly asks Stephen to stay the night. Stephen refuses, in a polite and friendly manner, but Bloom in his turn now becomes anxious. He returns the money he was guarding for Stephen. The text goes on:

What counterproposals were alternately advanced, accepted, modified, declined, restated in other terms, reaccepted, ratified, reconfirmed?

To inaugurate a prearranged course of Italian instruction, place the residence of the instructed. To inaugurate a course of vocal instruction, place the residence of the instructress. To inaugurate a series of static, semistatic and peripatetic intellectual dialogues, places the residence of both speakers (if both speakers were resident in the same place), the Ship hotel and tavern ...

And so on through an absurd list of public places. The next question-and-answer tells us that Bloom is afraid Stephen will never return.

What ever the meaning of the word 'counterproposal', it is clear that Stephen promised to return earnestly and repeatedly, while realising that the promise was important to Bloom: this follows from the sequence 'advanced ... reconfirmed'. But he might have felt himself badgered into it, and therefore free to break his promise, if all the counterproposals came from Bloom: this would be out of character for Stephen, but many readers have evidently presumed it. And the absurd style is a sort of parody of legal or pedantic language, in which many authors would feel free to use the words wrongly: but Joyce would try to get them right. In the *NED*, this word is listed only under 'COUNTER-3',with many other such nouns, as '... against, in opposition to, as a rejoinder or reply to ...' Thus it would not apply if Bloom begged Stephen to return, and he refused, and then Bloom said: 'Well, meet me in a pub, anyway'. Stephen must have made the first counterproposal, and probably the first two, as the word is in the plural; and these are all he could sensibly have made. But how could he have known that Bloom suspected Molly of pronouncing wrongly the Italian of her songs? I submit that there is a slight change of convention, beginning late in the previous chapter, which is usually accepted unnoticed because it feels natural. Bloom is now talking very openheartedly to Stephen, and anything reported as a thought by Bloom is actually said to Stephen, except when we are told that he checks himself – better not explain why he didn't go to the mother's funeral. The new rule is already well established at the end of the Cabman chapter, when Bloom after extravagant praise for Stephen's voice lets drop that it had better be properly trained: this bit of tact is plainly meant to be spoken, and the passage is a struggle to win Stephen over.

Joyce in later life was rather prone to say that he had been too poor to have his voice trained (maybe he thought he sang better without), so Stephen would not mind letting Molly as a professional give him a few tips. He may remember the idea of lessons for himself, but the idea of lessons for Molly he must pick up at once. Several times during the day Bloom has expressed his doubts about Molly's Italian (he will have observed a few people in her audience makes faces) but he has not betrayed this to Stephen. He does now, immediately after asking Stephen to stay the night, because it may help him to accept.

What various advantages would or might have resulted from a prolongation of such extemporisation?

For guest: security of domicile and seclusion of study. For the host: rejuvenation of intelligence, vicarious satisfaction. For the hostess: disintegration of obsession, acquisition of correct Italian pronunciation.

The teasing style does not tell us, but it does not deny, that Bloom spoke to Stephen, making these points somehow. Surely we need not suppose that he sat in agonised silence, awaiting the refusal? He is confident that his offer is a good one, and these words would be a tactfully moderate way of saying it, if translated into spoken language. Breaking the silence afterwards to ask a pointless question (had Stephen known Mrs Sinico?) shows that he was not totally overawed. So far, then, the conversation can be reconstructed. Stephen picks up at once the point about Molly, and says that, though he has to go away just now, he will come back and exchange education with her on these specific points. They are decently limited, and he must at least be curious to meet Molly. It was foolish of poor Bloom (making counterproposals against these new proposals of Stephen, which excluded Bloom) to beg for further intellectual conversations, and one can hear the voice of Stephen offering to fit them in while he walked from one pub to another. But that will settle itself. What Stephen would not consider trivial is his promise to return to the house, 'reaccepted, ratified, reconfirmed'.

This makes a coherent story, consistent with the text as a whole, but the author seems to have tried to make us feel doubtful about Stephen's return. Bloom thinks that Stephen is nearly off his head, so he is patient with him, but cannot think him reliable. There is an answer: Stephen did have a craving to destroy the chance which is being offered him, but afterwards he feels that Bloom has passed a test by taking the insult so calmly. He mumbles excuses and feels on more intimate terms; he is now even less likely to tell polite lies. There is a worse obstacle in the question-and-answer beginning 'Why might these several'; the previous one, already considered, was moderate and sensible, presenting the advantages for all three if Stephen moves in; there is every reason to suppose he said it to Stephen. The one after describes a merely social query, evidently meant to relax the tension while Stephen decides. But in the middle one Bloom apparently offers Stephen his daughter as well as his wife, which could only impress Stephen as threatening an appalling amount of bother.

Bloom cannot have said it. And yet the mention of 'a Jew's daughter' does suggest that he said something, referring in an oblique way to the ballad, and telling Stephen that he actually has a daughter; the further suggestions were really there, but only in Bloom's own busy mind. This is the only point at which Bloom sounds positively appalling, as Kenner assumes him to be all along; and though it can be explained, I do not think it can be justified. Probably it was a late addition, made when Joyce was being harassed by the law and needed obscurity.

Joyce has made Stephen strongly in favour of telling truth and keeping promises (consider the telegram to Malachi) – rather more so than Joyce himself, perhaps; also, just before he leaves the house, he makes a solemn affirmation to relieve the dejection of Bloom, whose fear that Stephen will break his promise is suddenly expressed as fear for the whole future of mankind.

Did Stephen participate in his dejection?
He reaffirmed his significance as ... a conscious rational reagent between a micro- and a macrocosm ...

Empty rant, one might feel: but he would not intend to be facetious while asserting his dignity, and Bloom is said to 'apprehend the affirmation substantially', though his anxiety soon returns. Probably Stephen still believes that he is doomed, as well as vowed, to return.

Only a few pages from the end of the book, Molly re-interprets what the cards had meant when she laid them out in bed that morning, and decides they had meant that Stephen would become her lover. She can remember the lay-out eighteen hours before with astonishing detail, and is clearly an old hand at such work; but matters are so arranged that the reader feels better able to interpret them than Molly herself. Just for a moment, wearing a knowing grin, the innocent reader is tricked into believing in them as much as she does. Or such was the intention of the innocent author. He thought perhaps that his cultured readers would find a dream more convincing than these cards, so Molly does mention having a dream, though she finds the cards more decisive:

didnt I dream something too yes there was something about poetry in it I hope he hasnt long greasy hair ...

All this, I submit, has plainly been arranged by the author as part of the basic structure, and to intend all the omens to be false would be very unlike either Joyce or Homer. The important aspect of the prophecy is that Bloom will conceive a son, who will live to grow up this time; we need not doubt that the side effects will be uncomfortable.

It seems unlikely that Molly would have no thoughts about Stephen till the end of her chapter, though her husband had told her just before it began that this new lover was coming. The author has planted some excuses, but chiefly for this dramatic or structural purpose. Kenner, debunking the story wherever he can, says that Bloom had never asked for breakfast in bed next day, but that Molly misunderstood his mumbles about the primeval egg. Kenner says this because someone else long ago said that Bloom has begun to assert his manhood, and the couple are breasting their way into the light. But it is a convention of the book that remarks do not have to be quoted twice, as when Bloom shows Stephen a photo of his wife, and later thinks 'he said it was handsome'. To say less than that would be positively rude, and Stephen would say it almost without noticing, but Bloom would not have deceived himself if Stephen had stayed mum. In bed with his wife, Bloom feels he has had a hard day, mainly in her interest, catching Stephen for her, and deserves a lie-in; her private grumbles do not suggest that she has never brought him breakfast before. He boasts that he has made friends with Stephen partly to cover up where they have been together, and he feels sure she would scold if she knew the truth; but it is not a strong fear, and he always considers the future. Presumably he now feels sure that Stepehen will return, because otherwise he would be risking a disappointment for his wife which would have unpleasant consequences for himself. She, on her side, is certain of it. The discovery sounds like a revelation:

... he liked me too I remember they all do wait by God yes wait yes hold on he was on the cards this morning when I laid out the deck union with a young stranger neither dark nor fair you met before I thought it meant him but hes no chicken nor a stranger either besides my face was turned the other way what was the 7th card ... then there was a letter on its way and scandals too the 3 queens and the 8 of diamonds for a rise in society yes wait it all came out ...

Then she begins calculating his age: 'I'm not too old for him if hes 23 or 24' (he is twenty-two, the previous chapter has revealed). It is sad but unflinching, and the affair between them could not last very long; all the same, it may last long enough to do what Bloom is working for.

The last twist about the omen from the cards arrives in a complaint against Bloom for sleeping noisily:

> O move over your big carcass out of that for the love of Mike listen to him the winds that waft my sighs to thee ... if he knew how he came out on the cards this morning hed have something to sigh for a dark man in some perplexity between 2 7s too in prison for Lord knows what he does that I don't know ...

It is a pleasure to know better than she does. The cards were speaking allegorically here; Bloom will not be held between two policemen but between two lovers of his wife, Stephen nagging and needling, Blazes badgering and blustering. This is probable, and yet Bloom may succeed in his main purpose, as has been amply foretold.

IV

After destiny we must consider choice. What does the novel present as the most deep-lying desire in each of the three characters? With Bloom the answer is simple: he wants a son begotten by himself upon his wife, and fears that he may already have lost the opportunity. He likes having a daughter, but she does not really count: or the renewed desire for a son may be the result of the daughter becoming grown-up. The clearest example comes among his thoughts after hearing 'The Croppy Boy' sung in the Lunch chapter:

> I too, last my race. Milly young student. Well, my fault perhaps. No son. Rudy. Too late now. Or if not? If not? If still?
> He bore no hate.
> Hate. Love. Those are names. Rudy. Soon I am old.

There is no need for a joke here because the singing excuses the sentiment, but in another case he might be thought to turn sardonic. He is listening to old Dedalus, in the cab taking them to the funeral:

> Noisy selfwilled man. Full of his son. He is right. Something to hand on. If little Rudy had lived. See him grow up. Hear his voice in the house. Walking beside Molly in an Eton suit.My son. Me in his eyes. Strange feeling it would be. From me. Just a chance. Must have been that morning in Raymond terrace she was at the window, watching the two dogs at it ... Give us a touch, Poldy. God, I'm dying for it. How life begins.

No doubt Joyce feared this passage would be considered mawkish unless the two dogs were brought in at the end, and Bloom may be supposed to feel the same. The reflection that a passing impulse of lust may have this momentous consequence is an obvious one, but why 'Just a chance'? Maybe they were using a contraceptive when in bed, but on this spontaneous occasion it was not handy. They were already being too cautious: that is the point of the two dogs in Bloom's mind, though to a reader they may seem mere debunking. The death of Rudy gave him a horror of the whole business of childbirth (or gave it to his wife – it is never clear whether she was partly responsible), so that even while using a contraceptive he could no longer perform the normal act with her. This phobia is what he hopes to overcome before they are both too old, but by now there is only a chance.

Bloom also has a kink: he is a voyeur. Maybe every man is, or every jealous man, but it is insisted upon here for a reason, part of the plot. Besides, not every man would be satisfied by a good look at Gerty MacDowell's knickers. 'Goodbye, dear. Thanks. Made me feel so young', he reflects after she has limped away. Perhaps as an extension of this, he enjoys seeing another man enjoy a woman who attracts him; even the thought of the hated Boylan at work with Molly has a guilty fascination for him, and in the nightmare he says:

Thank you, sir, I will, sir. May I bring two men chums to witness the deed and take a snapshot? (*He holds an ointment jar.*) Vaseline, sir?

He is afraid that being a pacifist makes him unmanly, and this is the bite in the self-accusation, but he is also ashamed at feeling the direct pleasure. He takes no interest in the men chums, who remain quite unpictured; even when he imagines himself as wholly female, he is being tortured by a mannish female brute. The author seems keen to insist that he is not homosexual. Early in the book, Bloom is made to feel a suspicion about M'Coy, who has irritated him by friendly gossip just when he wanted to see the ankles of a lady stepping into a carriage.

You and me, don't you know? In the same boat. Softsoaping. Give you the needle that would. Can't he hear the difference? Think he's that way inclined a bit. Against my grain somehow.

'That way' without telling the way has now a very specific meaning, whether or not it already had in 1904 (Joyce of course wrote the passage a good deal later). M'Coy has been boasting about his wife, also a singer, and Bloom forms a new suspicion, in a separate paragraph: 'Wonder is he pimping after me?' They both seem gratuitous; probably the author foisted them in merely as a clearance for Bloom. No doubt some homosexual feeling is needed for any happy triangle, but the difference here might be decisive for Stephen: Bloom only needs to lurk, watching Stephen with Molly, not touching him. Joyce himself felt disgusted by homosexuality, though he was not proud of that feeling; and he wanted to invent an Offer that Stephen might be supposed to accept. There is one positive accusation that Bloom ogles Stephen: it comes from the alert but imperceptive Malachi, and we are given an indication of what Bloom really feels there. For a second time he sees Stephen being led out to drink with prominent characters. On the first occasion, the end of the newspaper office chapter, Bloom acts like a humble mouse, but he feels confident that they are rapidly drinking themselves to death. It is not unreasonable, as one of them says to J. J. O'Molloy in Bloom's presence that the editor has 'incipient jigs'; and when Bloom reflects about J. J. O'Molloy 'that hectic flush spells finis for a man' he probably ascribes it to drink, not TB. As they troop out to the pub he thinks, 'Wonder is that young Dedalus the moving spirit', an absurd idea, but he is anxious about Stephen. Joyce himself would presumably laugh at Bloom here. His brother and his wife felt that they had only just managed to keep him from too much drink, but to James himself Kenner's belief that Stephen cannot become a novelist because he has taken to drink would seem merely typical of Bloom. However, it is consistent that when Bloom sees Stephen being led away from the library by Malachi he fears they are going for a drink, and regards Stephen with grave pity (it is only two hours since he left the press office). The novel needs to establish that Bloom is inclined to help Stephen.

The mental condition of Stephen is presented very clearly, and he seems unlikely to accept a triangle. But he had an extra quirk which is seldom recognised. He needs a woman who will provide stiffening and backing for him. as well as absorbing his sexual desires, and he presumes that she will have to be an older woman. This is why he might accept Molly, who is probably thirty-five but perhaps thirty-three. He is not really interested in the domestic life of Shakespeare except that Shakespeare, at eighteen, married a woman eight or nine years older, already pregnant. Stephen is twenty two. Early in the book, when he is yearning for love on a beach, he expects the woman to take the initiative ('I am quiet here alone'). No doubt the girls at Mrs Cohen's take it, and he is not versed in any other procedure, but in the Library chapter he definitely envies Shakespeare:

She put the comether on him, sweet and twentysix. The greyeyed goddess who bends over the boy Adonis, as prologue to the swelling act, is a boldfaced Stratford wench who tumbles in a cornfield a lover younger than herself.
    And my turn? When?
    Come!

This positively labours to assure us that he would not mind accepting a famous beauty in her thirties. Indeed one might suspect that Stephen has already guessed what is coming when Bloom turns up yet again at the hospital party, that evening: there seems no other reason why he should remark that Beaumont and Fletcher had but the one doxy between them, and 'Greater love than this ... no man hath that a man lay down his wife for his friend'. To Bloom, sitting beside him, this must sound like an encouragement. But as Joyce believed in omens he could be very free with dramatic irony: it is better to make Stephen astonished, and much sobered up, when the various fantasies of the day all crystallise into a simple proposal. This comes after his fit of the horrors at Mrs Cohen's, which has made plain that he needs some other motherly figure to exorcise the haunting of his real mother.

The main argument of Kenner, to reject this ending for the book, is that Stephen just cannot endure Bloom; he insinuates it by little cries of pain and other signals of knowingness. But part of the charm of Bloom and Stephen when talking together, and we get quite a lot of it in their two final chapters, is that each of them talks his own brand of nonsense without bothering about the other's. Bloom has been adroit enough to tell Stephen that his friends are plotting against him or at least taking advantage of him, especially Malachi, and this is very soothing for Stephen. Joyce really did imagine that Gogarty had wronged him; there was a formal meeting long afterwards, attaining peace though hardly pardon, but so far as one can make out the young Gogarty had been very helpful to Joyce, and had done nothing worse than laugh him out of some of his follies. As for saying, 'Let's corrupt Joyce, shall we:' (and teach him to drink), I have heard that said among young friends with a merely educative intention. Stephen, like the young Joyce, cannot bear to be laughed at, and finds the admiring Bloom a great comfort because he is sure not to do it, whereas he himself is free to laugh pretty coarsely at Bloom. It will do Stephen no good to be among people who reverence his learning. Bloom assures him that his BA degree is 'a huge ad in its way'. But it will not cause him any suffering.

Molly is the doubtful member of the triangle. At present, she is much gratified by her lover and the prospect of a tour with him; and, though she even yet remembers Rudy with sorrow, she does not express any craving, such as Bloom has, for a son – she is aware of the wrongs of women, forced by men into pain, danger and trouble. Yet it is while thinking about Mrs Purefoy, the type case of such wrong, that her mind swings back to the idea of having another child herself:

if someone gave them a touch of it themselves theyd know what I went through with Milly nobody would believe cutting her teeth too and Mina Purefoys husband... the last time I was there a squad of them falling over one another and bawling you couldnt hear your ear supposed to be healthy not satisfied till they have us swollen out like elephants or I dont know what supposing I risked having another not off him though still if he was married Im sure hed have a fine strong child but I dont know Poldy has more spunk in him yes thatd be awfully jolly...

She jeers at herself because this thought is too generous, and it does not recur, but it lies near the surface. The scrupulous fairness to Boylan show that he has displeased her. His virility may become bullying; his organ is too large for her sense of propriety; and it turns out that in a careless moment he treated her as a plaything or chattel:

no thats no way for him has he no manners nor no refinement nor no nothing in his nature slapping us behind like that on my bottom because I didnt call him Hugh...

She feels sure the poet will be more respectful, and as for Bloom, 'as hes making the breakfast for 1 he can make it for 2' – or she would make it for the poet herself. Earlier, she thinks with pleasure of such a triangle, realising that Bloom would like it too:

I wish some man or other would take me sometime when hes there and kiss me in his arms theres nothing like a kiss long and hot down to your soul...

In fact, she is presented with decent care as ready to play her part in the Bloom Offer.

Last of the list, the textual evidence for the Bloom Offer should now be given. There is none to give, as Bloom feels that plain words would put Stephen off, or give him an excuse for a refusal; but I could not think that this upsets the theory. So far from that, I find it hard to imagine a reader ploughing through the chapter of the Cabman's shelter without any idea of what is going on. Indeed I had printed this essay, thinking my case complete, before I realised that some people need leading by the hand all through that chapter. Kenner in *Dublin's Joyce* (1955) delighted in the parodies of journalism, and approved of their being so dull – they show that Stephen has learned nothing from his fit of horror in Nighttown, since it has not made him pious. This is like the teacher who encouraged his class to study the *Agamemnon* by saying it was a veritable storehouse of grammatical irregularities; but this pedant admired the irregularities, while Kenner only took pleasure in contempt. In his later *Ulysses* (1980) he admits that Bloom makes some kind of offer, and approves of Stephen for being too gentlemanly or squeamish to accept; but the offer seems merely the launching of Stephen as a concert-singer. This explanation is definitely wrong; Joyce excludes it at the cost of an extra improbability in the narrative.

One may expect the chapter to be sordid and dismal, because it touches bottom. The previous chapter was Hell, but there is a worse thing even than that; it is being poor. Joyce, I think, intended this effect; but it is partly balanced by his patriotism. In Dublin the down-and-outs are still indomitable, and hug a secret about an old political murder, besides pumping the older sailor for details about all the world. It makes them a fit background for a lyrical scene. Bloom is in full flower here; he is so funny that he is sweet, which one could hardly call him elsewhere. He is confident that to offer Stephen his wife is a good action, a rescue for Stephen as well as being needed for his own problems, and somehow this makes the conventions no obstacle for him (a formula for the lyric, perhaps). So far from feeling flat and bored, he is snatching recklessly at a chance. It demands an affectation of careless ease, with up-to-date jargon, and this perhaps is what makes him sweet, though he is earnest and straightforward too. The chapter is an unusually short one; the *scherzo*, one might say.

To make friends with Stephen, Bloom rightly thinks, there must be an intelligent conversation with him; but Stephen is 'a good Catholic' and Bloom a scientifically-minded man, which, as he says, makes an obstacle.

Stephen answers as an ignorant bigot, and makes his answers increasingly absurd; the effect is to treat Bloom with contempt, as Hamlet treats Polonius (over their cocoa in the next chapter they achieve this conversation, and Kenner is no doubt right to find both sides contemptible). Bloom is impervious to insult, and knows when a joke is being made, even though he sees no point in it; and a reader may be content to share his uncertainty. Stephen has had a bad time; he saw a ghost and was knocked out by a soldier when already drunk and starving; one can believe that he 'had to make a superhuman effort of memory' before producing his scraps of the definition of a soul. On the other hand, he is spry enough at the start of the chapter, while Bloom is leading him to the shelter. An old acquaintance, now down and out, begs for money to sleep at a doss-house, and Stephen while handing it over gets the address out of him without letting Bloom know. He remembers this address, towards the end of the chapter, while agreeing to go home for cocoa with Bloom (and, having secured a line of retreat, he is unlikely to go out and drown himself instead). The detail does not imply any determination to refuse the Bloom Offer, which he might do at once; he does not yet know what it is, so he plays a waiting game, leaving the main role to Bloom all through the chapter.

Probably Bloom feels able to deduce from the philosophical remarks that Stephen is not too pious to consider the Offer. Having got him to a drink a little coffee, he takes a high aesthetic line about Mediterranean women; recently he has been reminded of their merits by a visit to the Museum, just before he met Stephen in the Library:

... those antique statues there. The splendid proportions of hips, bosom. You simply don't knock against those kind of women here. An exception here and there. Handsome, yes, pretty in a way you can find, but what I'm talking about is the female form.

(Malachi had told Stephen in the Library what he had seen Bloom looking for in the statues.) This wins no reaction from Stephen, and the others are talking about disasters at sea, marine insurance, the falling off of shipping, politics, the expected fall of the British Empire. It seems to affect the mind of Bloom, though he does not take part. He talks about his own plan for a socialist utopia, and this irritates Stephen; when told that he is important to Ireland (a thing that the young Joyce was very willing to say) he answers that he expects 'Ireland must be important because it belongs to me'.

Bloom recognises this as girlish petulance, and decides that he is a sexual invert, one of the well-known decadents of the period: a splendid though foggy paragraph recalls some recent troubles of royalty and aristocracy with the London police, and he suspects the sailor is in it too ('16', tatooed over his heart, was presumably a code term for a homosexual technique, or the author's substitute for a real one). He tells himself bluffly that any such agitation is nonsense, because the difference between men and women is 'largely a matter of dress and all the rest of it':

Ladies who like distinctive underclothing should, and every welltailored man must, trying to make the gap wider between them by innuendo and give more of a genuine fillip to acts of impropriety between the two, she unbuttoned his and then he untied her, mind the pin, whereas savages in the cannibal islands, say, ...

this of course is not said to Stephen, and is in a very different style from the jargon of permissiveness. But it is not more sincere; in ordinary life, hardly anyone could find more difference between men and women than Bloom. He is cheering himself up, after imagining this new obstacle to bedding Stephen with Molly. Still, it makes him look for a new reason why he is doing these things at all – he is already several shillings to the bad. He tells himself he has an 'interest, and duty even, to wait on and profit by the unlookedfor occasion', and intellectual stimulation is a first-rate tonic for the mind, and besides, he will write an article about this visit to the shelter. Rather nervously, as Stephen is so touchy, he finds points of interest to him in an evening paper which is lying about.

The others are warming up at their patriotism and look back to Parnell, whose political career had been ruined by a divorce twenty years before; they say he had a false funeral and will soon return. Bloom and Stephen, after listening to this in silence, begin muttering to each other, taking care not to be overheard, and they do achieve a mental contact; they are both pacifists, and want no more political killing. Bloom also reflects that it was nonsense to make so much fuss about adultery, and the printed page gives us a flood of clichés on that topic. Kenner finds them merely vulgar, but they had been developed for a purpose – to recommend an advanced or permissive attitude to sex, which (for that matter) was prominent among the aristocracy. Their function here is to tell Stephen that Bloom will readily hand over Molly. It may be objected that Stephen is not recorded as hearing them, but it is rare to get a positive indication that he doesn't.

Bloom certainly tells Stephen how he handed back to Parnell the silk hat which had just been knocked off him ('he saw him once' would not introduce a private reverie); but to have the whole passage spoken, or rather muttered, would be intolerable. Even without being spoken, the thoughts of Bloom excite strong feelings which are directly conveyed:

North or south however, it was just the wellknown case of hot passion, pure and simple, upsetting the applecart with a vengeance and just bore out the very thing he was saying, as she also was Spanish or half so, types that wouldn't do things by halves, passionate abandon of the south, casting every shred of decency to the winds.

– Just bears out what I was saying, he with glowing bosom said to Stephen. And, if I don't greatly mistake, she was Spanish too.

Clearly, the time has come to bring out the old photo of Molly, taken before she had got so fat.

– Do consider, by the by, he said, thoughtfully selecting a faded photo which he laid upon the table, that a Spanish type?

He feels himself that

it did not do justice to her figure, which came in for a lot of notice usually ... She could without difficulty, he said, have posed for the ensemble, not to dwell upon certain opulent curves of the ...

Bloom feels a need to go out and relieve his bladder, which would leave Stephen 'to drink in the beauty' of the picture, but that would 'scarcely be professional etiquette', so he just looks thoughtfully away. The author is rather clumsy here, because the reader wants to know whether Bloom has done this kind of thing before, and without knowing that can hardly interpret the phrase. I expect Bloom has not done it before, and feels that the process deserves a ritual, but has not yet invented one. Be that as it may, his feelings are warming up, and a later paragraph begins;

All kinds of Utopian plans were flashing through his (Bloom's) busy brain.

It is unlike Joyce to report in person, and unlike him to be vague, but the mind of Bloom does need special treatment here. He has no plan, except to take Stephen with a concert party on a tour of the south coast of England, singing if he *can* sing, but anyway spreading culture. This will give them prestige. On the page just before he was thinking:

Everything pointed to the fact that it behoved him to avail himself to the full of the opportunity, all things considered, ... what mostly worried him was he didnt know how to lead up to it or word it exactly, supposing he did entertain the proposal ...

This proposal turns out to be giving him money, but the whole conversation has become a strain for Bloom. Once they are out in the open, walking home, he realises that he had better talk about the music he likes, as that is his only point of contact with Stephen. Molly may still be praised, but only for her singing.

He also yielded to none in his admiration of Rossini's *Stabat Mater*, a work simply abounding in immortal numbers, in which his wife, Madam Marion Tweedy, made a hit ... the sacred edifice being thronged to the doors to hear her ... suffice it to say in a place of worship for music of a sacred character, there was generally voiced desire for an encore. On the whole, though favouring preferably light opera of the *Don Giovanni* description, ... he had a *penchant*, though with only a surface knowledge, for the severe classical school such as Mendelssohn.

He has heard a good deal, and his odd opinions are not received by Stephen with easy contempt. Stephen in fact praises Elizabethan songs, and says he is 'contemplating purchasing' a lute from Dolmetsch, at 65 guineas, so he is finding it hard to outshine Bloom. He goes on to praise German ballads of the period, and Bloom gives his attention to the poor old municipal horse, whom he describes with deep sympathy. This seems to be the only admission that Stephen too can become a bore. Bloom recovers himself with a jerk:

Stephen went on about the highly interesting old ...
— What's this I was saying? Ah, yes! My wife, he intimated plunging *in medias res*, would have the greatest of pleasure in making your acquaintance as she is passionately attached to music of any kind.
He looked sideways, in a friendly fashion at the sideface of Stephen, image of his mother, which was not quite the same as the usual blackguard type they unquestionably had an indubitable hankering after ...

If only he could sing! But just then he does sing, to give the opening bars of his old German ballad, and Bloom begs him to go on. The problem of what to do about Stephen is solved.

A phenomenally beautiful tenor voice like that, the rarest of boons, which Bloom appreciated at the very first note he got out, could easily, if properly handled by some recognised authority on voice production such as Barraclough and being able to read music into the bargain, command its own price ... It was in fact only a matter of months ...

– before he becomes a great social success, able to pay off his tuition fees. Stephen may wonder, as the flood of congratulation goes on, whether he is to spend all these months at school, getting more and more into Bloom's debt. However, he is not reported as making any reply, and Bloom, for the rest of the walk home and till the cocoa has been drunk, seems to treat the matter as settled. The next chapter, which runs straight on, has the chill of negotiation, and when Stephen leaves the house he has only committed himself to exchanging some harmless tuition with Molly. He does not yet know what Bloom really wants from him, and Bloom does not want to tell him yet.

Still, that he is offering Stephen the favours of Molly, and not merely offering to launch him as a singer – this is plain because he does not hear Stephen's voice till the chapter has only two more pages to go. Artifoni knew already that his voice was remarkable, in the Wandering Rocks chapter, and Bloom has heard a good deal about Stephen, also he has an interest in finding voices – surely it is very improbable that he could be so surprised? The dramatic effect is a calculated one.

On the other hand, one might argue that Stephen knows the answer already, and is merely taking advantage of Bloom, intending to refuse. He foreshadows the main ideas of the story in the Library chapter, where he recommends himself as an author by drawing upon his preoccupations. He really is 'in search of a father' because his father refuses to help him; he needs a backer; but this can be put in terms of his theological studies. On the accepted view of Athanasius, the Father begot the Son, and then created all other beings by the agency of the Son. But, as he does not use a goddess, we cannot envisage, from our limited experience, any difference between begetting and creating. There is only one sensible meaning for the words: 'Thou art my son; this day I have begotten thee': it is a legal formula for use when adopting a son. It has long been so interpreted, especially among Arians (the second Psalm is then viewed as a relic of a coronation ritual). If Bloom is to use his adopted son as an agent in creating a real son, that will be a splendid application of the doctrine, working crosswise as Joyce likes to do with the story of Ulysses. Stephen seems chiefly concerned to make a mystery of the relation of father to son, which is also claimed by the priest:

They are sundered by a bodily shame so steadfast that the criminal annals of the world, stained with all other incests and bestialities, hardly record its breach.

Stephen is insinuating more experience and more reading than he has really had. The other main theme of the harangue in the library is the private life of Shakespeare, and it needs to be because the *Sonnets* report the only happy triangle in all literature (though perhaps only fairly happy and only for a short time): but the resentments of Stephen cripple his understanding here, and 'Take all my loves, my love' evokes a scene he can only enjoy as a scandal. He imagines that Shakespeare's brothers had seduced his wife, and that Shakespeare grizzled over this by giving their names to the villains of his plays; surely, whether there was any scandal or not, he was thankful when he escaped from Stratford into a larger air. All this is what Malachi meant by Stephen's lousy Jesuit jeering, but Joyce manages to get a bit of poetry out of it, which echoes into many of the references to horses. Shakespeare has urged his Earl to produce a legitimate heir, and Stephen, mixing this up with lending him the Dark Lady, titters at the result as 'the holy office the ostler does for the stallion'. Surely there is no reason to deduce that he is foreseeing anything; he is not in a fit frame of mind. The reader is to appreciate the dramatic irony by which the tormented theorizing boils down to something homely and practical,and perhaps Stephen may come to do the same, but not till a few days after the novel is over.

One has next to consider how the primal scene will be operated, bearing in mind that Stephen is probably more squeamish than he pretends. The author allows a useful pointer when Bloom leads Stephen from the cabmen's shelter, taking his arm: 'Yes, Stephen said uncertainly, because he thought he felt a strange kind of flesh of a different man approach him, sinewless and wobbly and all that.' Stephen is drunk and exhausted, but his reaction is clear-cut: he is not physically attracted by Bloom, the readers are assured, but also he does not feel a physical loathing, which would make the plan impossible. No contact will be needed: that is the point of making Bloom a voyeur. Still, Bloom has to be gazing while Stephen and Molly perform the the act, and when Stephen has reached crisis the thoughtful husband will need to see that the condom is still in place and unbroken. Stephen will then retire to the spare bedroom, no doubt making one of his jokes, and Molly is pretty sure to be still unsatisfied: thus the married couple are in an ideal condition to overcome their obstacle. It does not much matter whether Joyce was medically correct concerning this treatment for the phobia: the point is that he labours throughout the book to offer it as a plausible one. Admittedly, many questions are left unanswered by stopping the book at this point: what happened about the tour, and suchlike. But Joyce had a metaphysical or even theological answer: a man may describe himself when young, but only up to the point where the young man turns into somebody different. Nor is it a point only: the increasing fog, after the madness of Nighttown, marks an increasing difficulty for Joyce in knowing what Stephen would say. He has always had great scrupulosity as a truthful reporter, and here the language becomes contorted by the need to isolate what he can be sure of. And of course the reason for his difficulty is that the Bloom Offer was never actually made: it would have been, or something very like it, but a miracle happened instead. He saw Nora passing in the street – otherwise he would have lost his real self. I have never seen any other explanation for the shape of the book.

V

Why then does the book make a secret of it? Because the procedure which it regards as an innocent act of charity is heavily penalised by the law. A sexual act performed by two people in the presence of a third one, whatever their sexes, counts as 'gross indecency'. Prosecutions are seldom mounted, as any eye-witness confesses to the offence automatically: but there would be no such problem in one of the trials for indecency of Joyce's book. A proof that it recommended such an act would be decisive. The book was banned for many years in both England and America because of quite minor indecencies, but this, for the law, was a major one: and the lawyers never discovered it, or not before legal permission had been granted – 1933 in America, and a year or two later in England. The biography quotes a letter from Joyce saying he had to rewrite a good deal of 'Ithaca', the chapter at home with Bloom, 'on account of its scheme': this is an apology for being so slow. Several chapters of the novel had appeared separately by that time in magazines, with much fuss about decency in response, and Joyce, though happy at being lionised in Paris, realised that his book was running into great trouble. My friends have sometimes told me that, if Joyce had intended

Bloom to present a definite offer, he would have made it plain. If it had been made plain in the book, as at first in the draft it probably was, customs men would still be searching luggage for *Ulysses* at the ports of England and America.

Another question rises behind this. Why should he want to tell a story so remote from his experience that it had to be left unfinished? How could this be supposed to round off an account of his own early life? Nobody supposes that it really happened and yet he would be scrupulous about making it relevant to himself, to his own case, even if Bloom became the more interesting character. There is an unexplained detail of the biography which is at least consistent with this argument. Soon after finding Nora, on 27 August 1904, he shared the concert platform with the two leading singers of Dublin; it was Horse Show week, and he got fairly good notices, and might seem on the verge of success. But he did not appear again, and two days later he wrote to Nora that he had been trying to join a troupe of travelling actors. During 1917, long after, a friend in Zurich offered to find him work at the opera house, and he said at once: 'No, I don't want to sing professionally. I tried it once and did not care for it.' This was before he was given a pension by Mrs McCormick, so it was a lordly way to talk. He was prone to form unreasonable suspicions, and may have decided that singers can only prosper if they gratify the wives of their managers or promoters. Or perhaps he was made to feel that his voice was untrained to a humiliating degree. There is no need to suppose that the plot of the novel was put so directly into his hands. It did not require a great effort of invention.

The novel describes, or begins to describe, the louche world he would have fallen into, if Nora had not saved him. This gives her the praise she had earned without the indecency of putting her into a novel. In one way, it is a sad story, because it entails wasting the powers of Stephen, but in another, as he is doomed not to meet his Nora, it is the best thing that could happen to him. The author cannot be accused of writing propaganda for the happy triangle, since he presents it as a doom, though it is likely to succeed in its immediate aims. His chief need, as he plans the ultimate novel, it is to be fully abreast of progress; what he presents is a current problem, and that is inherently a high-minded thing to do, a blow for freedom. 'Lots of advanced people are doing it nowadays, didn't you know?' His intention was thus the opposite one to that ascribed to him in the earlier books by Kenner, which supposed him to bemoan the entire European development of thought since the Middle Ages.

Ellmann provides ample evidence that, around the time of finishing and launching *Ulysses*, when he was being lionised in Paris, he not only boasted that the book held a secret but found great difficulty in not telling it. Two letters to Miss Weaver in 1921 apologised for his slowness in finishing the book. In June he wrote; 'The nature of the legend chosen would be enough to upset anyone's mental balance.' This does not tell much, but would hardly fit the cheery view of Kenner that the end doesn't matter. In August he wrote that 'Ithaca' was having to be revised; he would not do that lightly. The troubles about earlier chapters, I submit, had made him realise that the last three chapters needed to hide their secret more deeply. But he evidently enjoyed hinting at it in Paris.

In November 1922 he reported getting an angry letter from Sylvia Beach, refusing to encourage further publicity about him. She had said: 'the rumours that were current in Paris about *Ulysses* and its author were such that it was more advisable that nothing more about me or the other be printed in any paper here for some time to come.' She would only talk in this way about something illegal. Joyce is being jolly when he writes in 1923 to a French translator of the final chapter, who has asked to be shown the secret scheme for the book, already shown to others. He is writing about formal matters, such as that each chapter of the book corresponds to a part of the body. 'If I gave it all up immediately, I'd lose my immortality. I've put in so many enigmas and puzzles that it will keep the professors arguing for centuries over what I meant ...' He then sent the young man the whole document. Unless this is empty fun, it means that some further secret is withheld.

The strongest piece of evidence was very ably recovered by Ellmann from the sculptor Suter, who had received a confidence from Joyce's old friend Budgen. (Budgen had worked for Suter, and would feel he had to tell someone.) While being lionised in Paris, Joyce had written to Budgen telling him a secret, afraid that Budgen might feel neglected perhaps, and then decided he must get it back. He induced Budgen to come and show him the letter again, made him drunk and took it off him, then 'deposited him at a bus-stop' from which he got home with difficulty (Joyce would not think much of this last atrocity, as he himself was good at getting home). Budgen was deeply hurt by the suspicion that he could not be trusted, and surely Joyce had only to ask for the letter back. But Joyce would be thinking about his immortal fame: what would best convince Budgen that he really must not tell this secret, let alone leave the letter among his papers? Budgen did not tell Suter what the secret was about, but these things happened in late 1922, when the secret of *Ulysses* was what Joyce could hardly contain.

It may seem that Budgen's book about the making of *Ulysses*, all shining with plain honesty, is enough to refute the suggestion. One needs to consider the circumstances. Budgen was estranged from Joyce for three years after the atrocity; then Joyce heard he was in Paris and invited him to call. As he left, after a pleasant evening, Joyce said: 'I hope you'll always believe that I'm a good friend, Budgen.' Just when Budgen started on his book is not clear, but Joyce supervised it throughout and was going over the galley proofs with Budgen in September 1933. One might think it just missed the bus, as the American judge cleared *Ulysses* in December, but its publication in 1934 may have helped the clearance in Britain soon after, and anyhow gave a soothing reassurance to help the sales of the new editions. Joyce said, when reading proofs of the English edition of *Ulysses* in 1936, 'I have been fighting for this for twenty years', and one must expect some warlike activity as the crisis approached. The book is as mild as milk, anticipating some of the views of Kenner (so he ought not to be blamed for them). Of the final talk between Bloom and Stephen, he says (Budgen, p. 281): 'What is revealed is the element of fatherhood in all social devotion ... When they take leave of one another we feel certain that they will never meet again.' There is a strong smell of tact here. If Bloom merely expresses fatherly feelings towards Stephen, why does that make certain that they will never meet again? Fathers are not always such pariahs, and it will actually be hard for this pair to avoid meeting, unless Stephen leaves Dublin. We can be sure of one thing that Budgen was sure about: he knew what his master wanted him to say.

The second edition of Ellmann's great biography reports an attempt to clear this up, by a further interview with Budgen in June 1964. The letter sent to him by Joyce, he explained, had been about Harriet Weaver's letter of June 1921, expressing anxiety about his health because she had heard he was drinking too much (Ellmann II. p. 542). 'Joyce asked what he ought to do, and referred slightingly to her aid', but soon afterward felt that this letter must be destroyed. At the time, he sent a splendid answer to Miss

Weaver, explaining that Paris was full of slanderous legends about him which he never tried to rebut. He was considered 'a jejune Jesuit, crafty and dissimulating', and did not deny even that, because 'it has been my habit to apply this alleged quality to safeguard my poor creations' (here is another hint that the novel held a secret). If it is true that he never drank before seven, and then only white wine at fashionable restaurants, he was doing his best to get the name of a drinker without damage to his health or his working hours and the genuine bouts with old friends might happen quite seldom. But the bout during which he stole back a letter from Budgen happened in late 1923, two and a half years after this very successful handling of his patron; surely he could not have gone on worrying about it for all that time? His wife and brother thought him tiresomely shameless about the matter. Of course it is just possible that Budgen confused two such occasions, but the 1923 one was a severe shock to him. It is far more likely that, forty years later, he was still acting as a loyal friend, who had sworn to tell any lie necessary to protect this secret. That is entirely to his credit, and he need not be blamed for being unpractised in deceit, so that he could only invent a very implausible lie. Nor need Ellmann be blamed for believing him; it is one of his charms that, having achieved an interview, he believes anything he is told at it, and indeed, this is probably why they all talked to him so freely. The effect is merely that the reader is given the evidence, and may decide for himself.

There is a long letter sent by Joyce to Budgen, written while he was re-writing the Hospital chapter, and describing his work enthusiastically; Kenner quotes this part in *Dublin's Joyce* with approving comments, and I confess that I had not realised when first reading his book how much support he has from the author. Joyce says:

Am working hard at Oxen of the Sun, the idea being the crime committed against fertility by sterilizing the act of coition.

There is no suggestion that it might sometimes not be a crime. The remarks of Kenner include:

The unfertilized ovum is pre-Christian Roman and Teutonic culture; the lightning-flash the Incarnation.... The waters, too, flood the Waste Land ... but Stephen and company go out and drown themselves in drink.

Very likely, but one should remember that this was written in March

1920, during the hurried rewriting of the last chapters for fear of prosecution; Budgen must be encouraged to say the right things.

One need not doubt that some good bits were added at this time. A brash young man comes in for the Hospital party and boasts that he would have seduced a nice young girl in Mullingar if he had had a condom with him at the time; it is Bloom's daughter, and Bloom thinks her too young to be forced to start. In the previous chapter, with Gerty MacDowell, he has had an apparently irrelevant reflection, after remembering the condom in his pocketbook, 'Cause of half the trouble'. Maybe both these bits were added to show that the author was tolerably right-thinking; and they do fill the story out; but how very cautiously they were added.

It was from the lawyers that Joyce needed to keep the secret, until the book had been cleared: once that had been done, one might expect him to tell it, or at any rate bring out a definitive edition. But he was deeply absorbed in *Finnegans Wake*, and keen to say that that book was much the better one, and still much upset by the illness of his daughter, as well as hampered by increasing blindness. Also it seems possible that he had got tired of being shocking, and had come to prefer the bowdlerised interpretation. It is at least equally possible that he felt *Ulysses* had been rather a damp squib; as nobody had guessed what it was all about. He would not realise that, moving with his immense patience upon the feet of elephants, he had been overtaken by a social change. In 1904, the secret would have been pretty obvious. A man who is confronted by a need to produce a son, in later life, having neglected it before – what sort of man is that? He has inherited an entailed estate, possibly with a title, and has married on the strength of it. He would thus be one of the Protestant Ascendency in the Ireland of that time, and Bloom would not be on calling terms: but he is particularly fascinated by the Ascendency ladies, especially when they ride astride, flourishing whips. We hear of him as a spectator at polo matches and two kinds of horse-race, and presumably he would only go there to peep at these viragos. During his Nighttown visions, such ladies plan at considerable length to horsewhip Bloom. Sydney Smith had remarked, a good deal earlier, that nothing astonished the country clergy more than the difficulty found by squires in producing heirs, and with the march of time such comment would have become more widespread. Bloom would have heard a good deal of salacious pub gossip about the breeding of such people, and their horses, of course, were also highly-bred. To call God an 'ostler' does not now seem a telling insult, a natural parallel to 'butcher', but ostlers were understood to tie the hind legs of mares, who would otherwise lash out at the expensive stallions. Bloom had no taste for atrocity, but he is a practical and resourceful man, ready to pick up an idea from anyone.

Some while ago I published an article about *Ulysses*, and one of the reviewers said he did not understand how Stephen could possibly help Bloom to become a father. I can bear witness to the familiarity of this idea, around the time when the plot was invented. As a little pitcher with long ears, I was keen to overhear the smoking-room talk of the gentlemen, and did hear talk about some elderly man who had produced the son he wanted – using a spare wheel, presumably? – oh yes, *he* was much in evidence – still, the old boy managed it himself; it has the typical squint of the family. Only the innocent child, hoping to remain invisible, felt flabbergasted by this, though others may have remained doubtful. Surely the scene ought not to feel too remote. But even a very remote and yet notorious scene has been found impotent to crack the shell of the modern literary critic. It does seem wildly absurd, a theme for a short story by Borges, to have had hundreds of Joyce experts flown to a world conference at Kathmandu, where the domestic habits of the neighbours should have given them a few tips about their subject, but they split hairs as usual, and came away still not knowing the story.

Index